Religion, Medicine and the Law

Is the legal protection that is given to the expression of Abrahamic religious belief adequate or appropriate in the context of English medical law? This is the central question that is explored in this book, which develops a framework to support judges in the resolution of contentious cases that involve dissension between religious belief and medical law, developed from Alan Gewirth's Principle of Generic Consistency (PGC).

This framework is applied to a number of medical law case studies: the principle of double effect, ritual male circumcision, female genital mutilation, Jehovah's Witnesses (adults and children) who refuse blood transfusions, and conscientious objection of healthcare professionals to abortion. The book also examines the legal and religious contexts in which these contentious cases are arbitrated. It demonstrates how human rights law and the proposed framework can provide a gauge to measure competing rights and apply legitimate limits to the expression of religious belief, where appropriate. The book concludes with a stance of principled pragmatism, which finds that some aspects of current legal protections in English medical law require amendment.

Clayton Ó Néill is a Lecturer in Law at Nottingham Law School, Nottingham Trent University, UK. He has recently co-edited a book, entitled *Global Patient Safety Law Policy and Practice* (Routledge).

Biomedical Law and Ethics Library

Scientific and clinical advances, social and political developments and the impact of healthcare on our lives raise profound ethical and legal questions. Medical law and ethics have become central to our understanding of these problems, and are important tools for the analysis and resolution of problems – real or imagined.

In this series, scholars at the forefront of biomedical law and ethics contribute to the debates in this area, with accessible, thought-provoking, and sometimes controversial, ideas. Each book in the series develops an independent hypothesis and argues cogently for a particular position. One of the major contributions of this series is the extent to which both law and ethics are utilised in the content of the books, and the shape of the series itself.

The books in this series are analytical, with a key target audience of lawyers, doctors, nurses, and the intelligent lay public.

Series Editor: Sheila A. M. McLean

Professor Sheila A. M. McLean is Professor Emerita of Law and Ethics in Medicine, School of Law, University of Glasgow, UK.

The Fetus as a Patient
A Contested Concept and its Normative Implications
Dagmar Schmitz, Angus Clarke and Wybo Dondorp

Health Research Governance in Africa
Law, Ethics, and Regulation
Cheluchi Onyemelukwe-Onuobia

Revisiting Landmark Cases in Medical Law
Shaun D. Pattinson

Healthcare Ethics, Law and Professionalism
Essays on the Works of Alastair V. Campbell
Edited by Voo Teck Chuan, Richard Huxtable and Nicola Peart

Religion, Medicine and the Law
Clayton Ó Néill

For more information about this series, please visit: www.routledge.com/Biomedical-Law-and-Ethics-Library/book-series/CAV5

Religion, Medicine and the Law

Clayton Ó Néill

Routledge
Taylor & Francis Group
LONDON AND NEW YORK

First published 2019
by Routledge
2 Park Square, Milton Park, Abingdon, Oxon OX14 4RN

and by Routledge
52 Vanderbilt Avenue, New York, NY 10017

First issued in paperback 2020

Routledge is an imprint of the Taylor & Francis Group, an informa business

British Library Cataloguing-in-Publication Data
A catalogue record for this book is available from the British Library

Library of Congress Cataloging-in-Publication Data
A catalog record has been requested for this book

ISBN 13: 978-0-367-58279-1 (pbk)
ISBN 13: 978-0-8153-5947-0 (hbk)

Typeset in Galliard
by Taylor & Francis Books

I wish to dedicate this book to my parents, Marina and Jim, who have always encouraged me to live out my dream and have been a constant support throughout my life. Táim iontach buíoch daofa as gach a rinne siad ar mo shon san aistear go dtí seo.

Contents

Acknowledgements

I wish to acknowledge the outstanding and dedicated contribution of Shaun Pattinson. This book would not have been completed without the expertise and knowledge that he so generously shared with me along the pathway of this investigative process. The most sincere and heartfelt thanks are due to him. I am also grateful to Ian Leigh whose support and earnest counsel are acknowledged with thanks. I am indebted to my PhD examiners, David Townend and Emma Cave, for their encouragement and advice.

My thanks to Jonathan Herring, former tutor, for his initial help in encouraging my studying of this area. That early encouragement started it all! I would like to thank my colleagues at Nottingham Law School for their support and belief in me, especially Tom Lewis, Helen Hall, John Tingle, Morgan Shimwell, Austen Garwood-Gowers, Jonathan Doak, and Janine Griffiths-Baker. I also wish to thank the staff at Routledge, especially Alison Kirk and Alexandra Buckley for their professionalism and helpful assistance. I am grateful to *Medical Law International* who have given me permission to reproduce some material from my case commentary entitled 'Conscientious Objection in *Greater Glasgow Health Board v Doogan and others* [2014] UKSC 68' in chapter 8. I wish to thank my family for the constant love and support they have given me throughout this journey.

1 Introduction

Aim and overview of the book

The aim of the book is to determine the adequacy of the legal protection that is afforded to Abrahamic religious belief in English medical law. This aim will be achieved through the application of a new framework to a number of specific case studies. The core research question that will be answered is as follows: is there adequate protection afforded to the Abrahamic religious beliefs of patients and healthcare professionals in English medical law? The book will show why and where the analysis of the law currently used by the courts, including the European Court of Human Rights (ECtHR), fails to answer questions which are fundamental for resolving the tensions presented by conflicts between doctors and patients in the context of Abrahamic religious belief.

This book proposes acceptance of Alan Gewirth's Principle of Generic Consistency (PGC) as the supreme principle of both morality and legality.[1] It follows that the substance and process of creating legal instruments and the substance and process of judicial reasoning must be compliant with the PGC. A provisional examination suggests that the legal protection that is afforded to the manifestation of religious belief is not fully aligned with the PGC. The importance of protecting the right to manifest religious belief is highlighted. The book proposes that an approach of *principled pragmatism* be adopted in respect of contentious medical law cases, so as to bring about a good faith attempt at applying the PGC.

Aim of the chapter

In cases involving disputes judges currently make deliberations that are fundamentally consistent with domestic precedent. They are also mindful of precedent in other jurisdictions. Discrete differences in each case are also allowed for and academic commentary is sometimes considered. The judges must be consistent with the principles laid down in common law. They retain their impartiality by merging their own legal expertise and experience with an ability to weigh alternative arguments in an open-minded manner in order to reach a judgment that is

1 Alan Gewirth, *Reason and Morality*, (The University of Chicago Press, 1978).

aligned to best practice in applying the legal principles at issue. Judges are, therefore, guided by precedent as it applies to case law, academic reasoning and practice in other jurisdictions. They must carefully consider the ECtHR and the implementation of its Convention under the Human Rights Act 1998 (HRA). Judges are, however, sometimes, faced with balancing rights where these rights can be situated from the standpoint of an individual interpretation of what constitutes a moral action. How can the judge weigh up different stances, some based upon religious belief and others based upon a different interpretation of the same belief or another belief altogether? This book will put forward a framework to help to find appropriate solutions.

This chapter explains the relevance of Rawls' concept of *Public Reason* as a preliminary issue in relation to legislative (parliamentary/collective) decision-making in the context of the manifestation of religious belief.[2] Differences in legislative and judicial decision-making are set out and analysed. The chapter sets out the limits of public reason and, as a consequence, elucidates why public reason is insufficient in answering questions before judges in their role as judicial decision-makers in more specific contexts and proposes that the PGC become the primary weight mechanism whereby legal procedures reflect the tenets and values of the PGC and make a good faith attempt at applying it.

The chapter also highlights and assumes the acceptance of legal idealism over legal positivism as a mechanism in interrogating the adequacy of legal protection concerning the manifestation of religious belief in medical law contexts. This discussion will lead into chapter 2's adoption of Gewirth's PGC as a principled tool for resolving disputes.

Rationale for focus on Abrahamic religions in the case studies

It is very difficult to define 'religion'. This is evident in the fact that judges have consistently avoided prescriptively defining 'religion' or 'religious belief'. Adhar and Leigh also point to defining religion as being a 'notoriously difficult task'.[3] They refer to, *inter alia*, a substantive content approach that has been used in English legal cases.[4] This perspective defines religion by identifying its 'essence' or 'core characteristics',[5] which could include, for example, the fact that a religion addresses fundamental and ultimate questions,[6] or religion is perceived to be a particular and comprehensive system of faith and worship.[7] Section 10(1) of the

2 John Rawls, 'The Idea of Public Reason Revisited', (1997) 64(3) *The University of Chicago Law Review*, 765–807.
3 Rex Adhar and Ian Leigh, *Religious Freedom in the Liberal State* (2nd ed, OUP, 2013) p 139.
4 ibid. p 148.
5 Roy Clouser, *The Myth of Religious Neutrality*, (Ind, 1991) p 10, as cited in Adhar and Leigh (n 3) p 144.
6 Judge Adams, *Africa v Commonwealth of Pennsylvania* (1981) 662 F 2d 1052 as cited in Adhar and Leigh (n 3).
7 See Adhar and Leigh (n 3) p 151.

Equality Act 2011 gives some breadth to the definition by stating that 'religion means any religion and a reference to religion includes a reference to lack of religion.' It provides a wide definition that is not specific to any one religion.

Audi considers that a religion possesses a number of important features, including, but not confined to the following: (1) belief in one or more supernatural beings; (2) a moral code believed to be sanctioned by the god(s); (3) a world view according adherents a significant place in the universe; (4) a more or less comprehensive organisation of one's life based on the world view; (5) a social organisation bound together by these features and others. According to Audi, Abrahamic religions exhibit all these features. Because they consider God to be 'omniscient, omnipotent and omnibenevolent,' these religions have considerable authority in the lives of their believers.[8] This research accepts this broad interpretation of 'religion'.

This monograph addresses its commentary on religious belief to Abrahamic religions, which include Christianity, Judaism, and Islam. The difficulty in defining 'religion' provides part of the rationale for restricting the book to Abrahamic religious belief. It was logical to confine the focus of this book to religions that were part of a similar theological 'root'. There are particular reasons why Abrahamic religions go together in a fairly logical way, given that they are monotheistic, founded in documented sources, and have historically been considered as important conduits of thought and belief within society. Islam, Judaism, and Christianity are organised religions, ecclesiastically and hierarchically structured to some degree. Abrahamic religious believers are all connected as they all trace a common origin to Abraham. Placing a focus on Abrahamic religions excludes from consideration other forms of religious belief, provides for a broad spectrum of legal and religious perspectives and also ensures that there are manageable research parameters in place. The specific focus on Abrahamic religions arose also from the fact that the case studies examined focus on situations when Abrahamic beliefs have come into conflict with other values protected by English medical law. While the book seeks to analyse the defensibility of the approach of English law to Abrahamic religious belief specifically, it is likely that many of the conclusions drawn from the analysis of that context would, however, be generalisable to non-Abrahamic religions.

Not all religious belief is, of course, encapsulated within the specific focus of Abrahamic religious belief. English law has historically often focused on issues arising from Abrahamic faith and this book continues with that specific focus. It is not within the remit of this book to definitively calculate the degree to which the focus on Abrahamic religions has evolved because the issues of other faiths are not explicitly articulated, or if English law has given preference to Abrahamic religions over non-Abrahamic religions, or because English law has failed to dynamically engage with the relationship between medicine and faith. It may be worth considering, however, how, in particular, the Judaea-Christian parameter of Abrahamic religions has reflected, in many ways, the established viewpoint, the

8 Robert Audi, *Religious Commitment and Secular Reason*, (CUP, 2000) p 35.

viewpoint of the majority, the viewpoint that has, to a degree, been tried and tested over centuries. That is not to say, however, that other religions should not in the past have been given equal meritorious consideration or could not in the future be considered with gravitas.

Religious adherents are not a homogenous group, with the same consequences affecting an individual if one of their religious beliefs is restrained in any way. For some people and some religious beliefs, interference with that religious belief undermines their very identity. In other contexts, for other people with different religious beliefs, interference with that belief might result only in momentary frustration. The consequences for the individual will depend on the belief and will depend on the context of the individual. The level of the belief and its relevance to the religious adherent in question in specific contexts needs to be measured. This is not an easy task for any regulatory structure, including the judiciary, charged with weighing and measuring the relevant harm caused by interference with the right to manifest religious belief. For the most part, this book is dealing with cases where the religious belief of some of those bringing cases in medical contexts is an intrinsic part of their self-identity, but this assumption cannot be simply made on a general level when dealing with these cases.

Rationale for consideration of legal idealism as an approach to evaluating the adequacy of the legal protection afforded to the manifestation of religious belief

Both law and religion interconnect within the society from which they evolve.[9] There are two main thoughts about law as a social institution. One is legal idealism, which sees the foundations of law's authority as based upon natural rights. As a consequence, rights and their principles define legal order. The second is legal positivism, where law is seen as the instrument of deliberate social engineering and where political stability and social order are brought about as a consequence of rules. The rules that underpin social order are conceived to be something valuable in their own right.[10] Both these viewpoints are attempts to theorise conceptions about the law, to make them intelligible and justifiable to the audience. Both, in some way, deal with legal order and a body of rules.

In the end, legal positivism and legal idealism differ in their conception of the rule of law, but they both come from a perception of social order. What matters in terms of these rules is that they are not imposed, but reflect the underpinning of social life.[11] However, the two perspectives are not as apart as might be thought. Idealists see the law as: don't interfere with people's freedoms. Positivists see law as the pursuit of goals.[12] All of this changes with the society of the time and the

9 John Witte, 'Law, religion, and Human Rights', (1996) 28 *Columbia Human Rights Law Review*, 1–31, p 8.
10 Sean Coyle, *From Positivism to Idealism* (Ashgate, 2007) p 3.
11 ibid. p 13.
12 ibid. p *x* (preface).

political nature of that society. Dworkin wants society to consider principles and law as involving interpretative practices.[13] He says that beliefs in society are a product of its shared history, tradition and culture, and the content of beliefs is arbitrary because we have all different shared experiences of community. For example, in a society characterised by *laissez-faire* economic liberalism, the law leaves a lot to the freedom of people.[14] If, alternatively, the main political concern is with social justice, then the law is perceived as being made up of rules that are concerned with the protection of individual and group rights and interests. Usually, society moves between the two in light of prevailing political conditions: thus, there is a link between what constitutes social order and the law.

In order to evaluate the adequacy of legal protection in the context considered by this book, it is not sufficient to look simply at how legal rules are followed. What is required is an examination of the 'idealism' behind the concepts that underpin the rules.[15] For that reason, a purely positivist approach to this research is rejected in favour of an analysis of the reasoning, moral or otherwise, in which legal rules are subliminally or overtly embedded. The law has to reflect the complexities within society and the shifting sands of political thought.

Context of the book

The idea that religious belief and affiliation to it could result in patient death or cause significant harm was brought home to this writer by the shocking facts of the Savita Halappanavar case where it was reported in an Irish hospital that a miscarrying woman was refused life-saving treatment because 'this is a Catholic country, we don't have abortion here'.[16] The case serves to outline the fact that, in some instances, adherence to religious belief can be seen to outweigh the autonomous decisions of patients, with, as in this case, tragic consequences. The fact that the case may have had more to do with medical negligence than religious affiliation is not immaterial, but it still remains that a woman reportedly died unnecessarily and that the religious belief of the hospital personnel, enshrined within the societal culture of a specific Irish hospital, may have been a factor in that death. This case served as a catalyst to question whether religious belief can or should impact upon autonomous decisions made by patients and arbitrated on by judges. The recent repealing of the Eighth Amendment of the Irish Constitution (*Bunreacht na hÉireann*)[17] has implications for how future societies in that jurisdiction will arbitrate on the

13 Ronald Dworkin, *Law's Empire* (Fontana, 1986).
14 Coyle (n 10) p 126.
15 ibid. p 65.
16 See Olivia O'Leary, 'A Remarkable Account of Savita's Death' (The Irish Times, 26 October 2013) available at: http://www.irishtimes.com/culture/books/a-remarkable-account-of-savita-s-death-1.1570398 (accessed 27 January 2017).
17 Namely: '[t]he State acknowledges the right to life of the unborn and, with due regard to the equal right to life of the mother, guarantees in its laws to respect, and, as far as practicable, by its laws to defend and vindicate that right'.

degree to which manifesting religious belief can have, should have, or should not have an impact on healthcare practices and medical law and ethics.

History proves that society needs to stem the worst excesses of religious practice. The evils inflicted by even young children at the time of the Crusades needed to be curtailed by the inept society of the time. Nazism's capacity to inflict the most grievous of harm is an indicator that society, including religious-imbued society, can be wrong and humanity cannot always draw its values from society or from a fundamentalist approach to the interpretation of religious texts. When society makes decisions that are based upon one form of faith, there can be no universal acceptance of those decisions just because they are based upon one version of life and one interpretation of human value. It is always legitimate for the state and/or democracy to constrain the expression of religious belief if that expression conflicts with widely held, fundamental values that respect human dignity, human life and human rights.

Dworkin seeks to argue for a tolerant secular state over a tolerant religious state.[18] He defines a tolerant secular state as encompassing a wider view of religious freedom and rejecting state monotheism.[19] The concept of a secular state implies a type of neutrality of perspective, which is not, in fact, a reality; secularism has, at its root, a principled stance that isn't necessarily neutral. Therefore, it could be argued that it is not fully possible for a tolerant secular state to be neutral, because a state that is secular is one that is grounded on a principled stance of its own and is, as a consequence never really neutral. Therefore, neutrality would not exist between faiths and/or between faith and non-faith. A non-religious state that tolerates faith would ensure better neutrality.

A person with religious views often lives in a liberal democratic society that is predominately secular. Most societies can be seen to adopt particular stances in respect of religion as follows: anti-religious, non-religious, and religious. The non-religious state adopts a middle position: it is neutral between pro-religious and anti-religious stances, but this does not mean that it is neutral in itself. The non-religious or secular state does not deny religion and the rights, responsibilities and beliefs attached to it. If a spirit of tolerance is to exist, a balance must be in place between what can just about be tolerated and what cannot. It must have reasons where all involved learn to take the perspectives of the others.[20]

Two things are happening to religions at the one time: there is, firstly, a growing surge of fundamentalism and a burgeoning of a religious form of traditionalism. At the same time, there has been a parallel secularisation of almost all European countries since the end of World War II. The movements for religious renewal in the West are strengthening political division. The significance of the use of religion as a political end has grown all over the world. Religious traditions are going forward in some ways and, it can be argued, backwards in others. The

18 Ronald Dworkin, *Is Democracy Possible Here Principles of a New Political Debate* (Princeton University Press, 2006) p 64.
19 ibid.
20 ibid.

separation of church and state is fragmented, but there is general disquiet in the society of today about the political role of religion and the change in religious consciousness. Religion has had a strong basis in forming the principles upon which democracies of the present are based. Weithmann, for example, describes churches and religious communities as factors that fulfil functional imperatives for the reproduction of democracy.[21] They provide arguments for public debates on crucially morally loaded issues. They inform their members. They encourage members to take part in political process. He contends that there are also obvious historical examples to the contrary: the oppressive role of churches has seen the crushing of people, but he says churches and religious communities generally perform functions that are not unimportant in stabilising and advancing liberal political culture. It is clear also, however, from history that secular ideologies such as communism and fascism have just as much 'evil' as religion.[22]

Paradoxically, increased secularisation in some contexts suggests that, for many people, religion doesn't exist, therefore religion has no voice. Adhar and Leigh demonstrate how, at one level, 'respect for people's beliefs is one of the hallmarks of civilised society' and how, at the same time, this religious belief is constantly under question.[23] People of belief must, in some way, prove the validity or, at the very least, the harmlessness of their beliefs.[24] They cite a greater number of religions, rapid growth of Islam, growth of the role of the state,[25] the blurring of the domains of public and private,[26] and the changing nature of liberalism itself[27] as reasons for this change. The limits that are placed on religious practice and religious freedom are not explicitly and easily quantifiable. The case studies that form the cornerstone of this book are embedded within complex medical, social and religious contexts.

Human rights, religious belief and medical law

Human rights reasons exist to safeguard the manifestation of religious belief in the context of medical law. The protection that is afforded to religious belief, from a human rights perspective, is not boundless: the right to express one's beliefs must be balanced with the requirement to protect harm being caused to people. Harris, O'Boyle and Warbrick argue that '[c]ompared to most other international human rights treaties, the Convention has very strong enforcement mechanisms. It provides for both state and individual applications'.[28] Thus, a discretion is allocated to

21 JP Weithmann, *Religion and the Obligations of Citizenship* (CUP, 2002).
22 Jonathan Chaplin, 'Beyond Liberal Restraint: Defending Religiously-Based Arguments in Law and Public Policy', (2000) 33 *UBC L Rev*, 617, p 641.
23 Adhar and Leigh (n 3) p 1.
24 ibid. p 12.
25 ibid. p 14.
26 ibid. p 15.
27 ibid. p 16.
28 Harris and others, *Harris, O'Boyle & Warbrick Law of the European Convention on Human Rights* (2nd ed, OUP, 2009) p 4.

states.[29] Convention rights are incorporated into UK law as a result of the Human Rights Act.[30] The implementation of the Act means that ECHR rights are indirectly applied in UK law as Convention rights. Article 9 ECHR provides for freedom of religion, thought, and conscience. However, this right is limited by Article 9 (2) which limits the right to manifest religious belief based on health, public order, public safety and 'for the protection of the rights and freedoms of others'.

What does Article 9 ECHR, as incorporated in the HRA, mean for UK citizens? Essentially, it allows citizens the opportunity to have their religious beliefs protected. It allows people to change their beliefs and to worship, teach, or observe these religious beliefs either individually or in a group.[31] This is not Article 9's only function. It also safeguards the freedom of conscience of people. No definition is given to 'religion' in the Convention. The State has no role in assessing whether or not the religious beliefs and opinions of people are legitimate or the manner in which they are manifested.[32] Article 9 ECHR includes a positive obligation on the State to ensure that everyone can enjoy their rights under the Article by protecting them by law and by implementing sanctions if the rights are breached by the State or other institutions.[33] The State also has a negative obligation not to impede on people's rights to have either religious or non-religious beliefs.

According to the *Travaux préparatories*, religion is a central right that deserves to be included in the Convention.[34] It was recognised by the drafters that such a right is important. It is worth noting that Article 9 protects both religious adherents and non-believers. In *Kokkinakis v Greece*,[35] it was stressed that the values enshrined within the Convention were foundational aspects of a democratic society. In their discussion of the general principles of this Article, the ECtHR said the following:

> As enshrined in Article 9 (art. 9), freedom of thought, conscience and religion is one of the foundations of a 'democratic society' within the meaning of the Convention. It is, in its religious dimension, one of the most vital elements that go to make up the identity of believers and their conception of life, but it is also a precious asset for atheists, agnostics, sceptics and the unconcerned. While religious freedom is primarily a matter of individual conscience, it also implies, inter alia, freedom to 'manifest [one's] religion'. Bearing witness in words and deeds is bound up with the existence of religious convictions.

29 ibid. p 11.
30 ibid. p 24.
31 Equality and Human Rights Commission, 'Article 9: Freedom of thought, conscience and religion', (2012) *Human Rights Review* 313–329, 314 available at: https://www.equalityhumanrights.com/en/human-rights-act/article-9-freedom-thought-belief-and-religion (accessed 27 January 2017).
32 For example, see *Hasan and Chaush v. Bulgaria* [2002] 34 EHRR 55 at [78].
33 Equality and Human Rights Commission, 'Article 9: Freedom of thought, conscience and religion' (n 31).
34 Carolyn Evans, *Freedom of Religion under the European Convention on Human Rights* (OUP, 2001) p 39.
35 *Kokkinakis v Greece* A 260-A (1993); 17 EHRR 397.

> According to Article 9 (art. 9), freedom to manifest one's religion is not only exercisable in community with others, 'in public' and within the circle of those whose faith one shares, but can also be asserted 'alone' and 'in private'; furthermore, it includes in principle the right to try to convince one's neighbour, for example through 'teaching', failing which, moreover, 'freedom to change [one's] religion or belief', enshrined in Article 9 (art. 9), would be likely to remain a dead letter.[36]

Abrahamic religious belief, thus, fits into the protection afforded by Article 9. The court uses a broad definition and has avoided defining 'religion'. The inclusion of the term 'belief' allows the ECtHR to avoid the problems associated with 'religion'. This, however, can lead to uncertainty.[37] Malcolm Evans says that 'it is best to reserve the term "manifestation" to describe a particular form of expression which is only relevant to religion or belief [and that] there can be no question of manifestation or "actualizing" thought or conscience under Article 9'.[38] It is very hard to see how this perspective aligns with Article 9's protection of both religious manifestation and thought and conscience. The latter of which must surely involve acting upon the thought and conscience that are fuelled by religious conviction.

There are two aspects of Article 9: the internal aspect (*forum internum*) and the external aspect (*forum externum*).[39] According to the external element, it is recognised that everyone has the right to manifest 'religion or belief' in 'worship, teaching, practice and observance'. *Buscarini v San Marino* confirmed the stance of the European Court in respect of the manifestation of religious belief: 'the believer's right to freedom of religion encompasses the expectation that the community will be allowed to function peacefully free from arbitrary State intervention'.[40]

Other Articles also protect the manifestation of religious belief. For example, Article 10 (freedom of expression), allows people the freedom to express themselves and to communicate or receive information without being subjected to interference by public authority.[41] Manifestation of religious belief is also supported by Article 8 ECHR—the right to respect for private and family life.[42] This protection is afforded due to the obvious connection between private life and religious beliefs.

The oft-times contentious intersection between the practices associated with religious belief and the law has entered the human rights legal arena in recent years. The judgment of the European Court of Human Rights in the case of *S.A. S. v France*[43] that France's ban of the burka is compatible with the Convention

36 ibid. p 31.
37 See Harris and others (n 28) p 427.
38 Malcolm Evans, *Religious Liberty and International Law in Europe* (CUP, 1997) p 285.
39 See Harris and others (n 28) p 428.
40 *Buscarini v San Marino* 1999-I; 30 EHRR 208 at [34].
41 Art 10 (1) ECHR.
42 Art 8 (1) ECHR.
43 *S.A.S. v France* [2014] ECHR (application no. 43835/11).

due to the wide margin of appreciation highlights the fact that there is a clear rise in secularisation. Baroness Hale has said that, following the rejection of a case where Christian Bed & Breakfast owners did not allow gay guests to stay (*Bull v Hall*[44]), the issue of religion and gay rights need to be revaluated.[45] According to Baroness Hale, the law has not done enough to safeguard the beliefs of Christians. She appears to recognise that the Supreme Court and indeed, she, were wrong in the above judgment. At her speech to the Law Society of Ireland, entitled 'Freedom of Religion and Belief', she said that a 'conscience clause' ought to exist for Christians.[46] She stated that 'I am not sure our law has found a reasonable accommodation of all these different strands'[47] and that '[a]n example of treatment which Christians may feel to be unfair is the recent case of *Bull v Hall.* Should we be developing an explicit requirement upon providers of employment, goods and services to make reasonable accommodation for the manifestation of religious belief?'[48] These two cases seem to be paradoxical. At one level, more rights are being ascribed to the anti-religion camp and, on another level, fewer rights. The cases reflect a reality that the priority that has been given to religious belief has always shifted with the political landscape of the time. Attitudes to religious beliefs are not static, stagnant entities. Religious belief, while theologically founded, is contextually operated. Testimony to this is the recent Northern Irish *Asher* case where a bakery firm, acting in accordance with their religious beliefs, refused to bake a cake that was to be decorated with a pro-gay rights slogan.[49]

Occasionally, domestic courts are involved in scenarios where cases dealing with the manifestation of religious belief present arguments in the context of Article 8. The autonomy and self-determination of individuals is evident in Article 8 jurisprudence. In *Pretty v United Kingdom*, the ECtHR stated that '[i]In the sphere of medical treatment, the refusal to accept a particular treatment might, inevitably, lead to a fatal outcome, yet the imposition of medical treatment, without the consent of a mentally competent adult patient, would interfere with a person's physical integrity in a manner capable of engaging the rights protected under Article 8 (1) of the Convention'.[50] Thus, there seems to be a link between manifesting one's beliefs and Article 8 in the context of medical practice. Article 8 incorporates the use of parental responsibilities, which includes the right to make decisions on behalf of children.[51] These decisions include decisions involving medical treatment. In *Nielsen v. Denmark*, the Court held that:

44 *Bull v Hall* [2013] UKSC 73.
45 Lady Hale, 'Freedom of religion and Belief' Annual Human Rights Lecture for the Law of Ireland, 13 June 2014 available at: http://supremecourt.uk/docs/speech-140613.pdf (accessed 27 January 2017).
46 ibid.
47 ibid. p 20.
48 ibid. p 5.
49 See Fran Cranmer, 'The "gay cake" case: Ashers Baking loses its appeal' in *Law and Religion UK*, 24 October 2016, available at: http://www.lawandreligionuk.com/2016/10/24/the-gay-cake-case-ashers-baking-loses-its-appeal/ (27 January 2017).
50 *Pretty v UK* [2002] ECHR 423 at [63].
51 Also see *Glass v UK* (Application No 61827/00).

> Family life in this sense, and especially the rights of parents to exercise parental authority over their children, having due regard to their corresponding parental responsibilities, is recognised and protected by the Convention, in particular by Article 8. Indeed the exercise of parental rights constitutes a fundamental element of family life.[52]

An important right in the context of beginning and end-of-life scenarios is the right to life – Article 2 ECHR. The European Court has stated that Article 2 'enshrines one of the basic values of the democratic societies making up the Council of Europe'.[53] According to Article 2 (1), there is an 'obligation to protect the right to life by law'. In *LCB v UK*[54] the positive obligation on the part of states to take 'appropriate steps to safeguard the lives of those within their jurisdiction' was endorsed, thus requiring states to take appropriate steps to safeguard life and, in particular instances, to take preventative steps.

Article 3 concerns the prohibition of torture, inhuman, or degrading treatment. It is connected to the notion of 'harm'. It is of particular interest when one considers the 'harm' that is caused to a child when he is circumcised. The book, and particularly the chapter on circumcision, will explore the relationship between Article 3 and the manifestation of religious belief/liberty.

Much of the case law involving religious belief, medical law, and ethics concerns children. Parents have many responsibilities in the rearing of their children. These responsibilities include for some the need to 'hand on the faith' to future generations, to hand on the religious belief and practice that they value. Is this a limitless responsibly and do parents have an automatic right to do anything in order to protect their religious values? Their rights are to some degree protected under Article 8 ECHR. Religious freedom is recognised in international human rights law.[55] But there are limits to parental autonomy and the courts, to a large degree, have imposed limits on the degree to which the religious beliefs of parents can impact upon the health of the child.[56] It has been cautioned that 'the scope of parental right to manifest religion excludes doing or omitting anything likely to place at risk the life, health or welfare of the children'.[57] Fundamentally, in most cases, parental religious convictions are overridden when the life of the child is at stake. Their interests need to be protected. This book will argue that human rights law can and ought to be supported by a supreme moral principle to ensure that such protections exist.[58]

Convention jurisprudence is a source of English law. Both the relevant Article 9 principles and case law coming from other countries as well as England and Article

52 *Nielson v Denmark* (1988) ECHR 23 at [61].
53 *McCann v UK* A 324 (1995); 21 EHRR 97 at [147] GC.
54 *LBC v UK* 1998-III; 27 EHRR 212 at [36].
55 Adhar and Leigh (n 3) p 135.
56 ibid. p 205.
57 *Re J (An Infant)* [1996] 2 NZLR 134, 146. Also see Adhar and Leigh (n 3) p 205.
58 This is Alan Gewirth's Principle of Generic Consistency (PGC). See chapter 2.

8 case law are sources of law under the HRA. An analysis of Convention jurisprudence is, therefore, required throughout the book.

Public reason and the formation of legislation: theory around legislative decision-making

The rationale that has been given to date about recognising religious belief as an important facet in English society finds support in one of the main theories governing public political discourse, namely Rawls' concept of *Public Reason*. This section will set out how public reason provides a further vindication of the role of religion and the validity of religious tolerance in democratic society.

Dworkin provides a very clear synopsis of Rawls' theory of public reason, as follows:

> [R]easonable people in political community will wish to live together on terms of mutual respect and accommodation and will therefore accept the constraints of... public reason. They will accept that they must justify collective political decisions to one another in terms that each can understand and whose force each can appreciate given his own comprehensive religious, moral, and ethical beliefs. That constraint would rule out appeals to even an ecumenical religious faith in a community some of whose members reject all religion. It would command a tolerant secular state.[59]

In other words, Rawls holds that we must ground our political discourse in principles that we can all initially accept. Rawls argues that public reason is about political relation and that it is not about one person's truth.[60] It concerns democracy and relational pluralism. Public reason is distinct but related to the background culture and the culture of civil society. It is central to the concept of political liberalism. In liberal society, according to Rawls, public appeals to 'comprehensive views' should not be permitted. He contends that public debate should be acceptable to all reasonable citizens and that this should be concluded by arguments and justifications that are accessible.[61] According to Rawls, '[p]ublic reason is a way of reasoning about political values shared by free and equal citizens that does not trespass on citizens' comprehensive doctrines so long as those doctrines are consistent with a democratic policy'.[62]

Does Rawls' theory of public reason concur with a religiously-inspired world view? Rawls says that religious belief (comprehensive doctrine) can be used in public political discussion provided that proper political reasons are presented to support whatever the religious belief was said to support.[63] This is Rawls' proviso.

59 Dworkin, *Is Democracy Possible Here Principles of a New Political Debate* (n 18) p 64.
60 ibid.
61 Adhar and Leigh (n 3) p 61.
62 John Rawls, *The Law of Peoples: With, The Idea of Public Reason Revisited* (4th printing, HUP, 2002) pp 179–180.
63 Rawls, 'The Idea of Public Reason Revisited' (n 2) p 784.

Even though the proviso is added in, the justification must still be made on public reason. Public reason is always linked to public justification. That justification involves valid reasoning, an argument that suggests 'we think this, you think that, we can conclude that we all think such and such'.

Rawls concedes that no absolute bar exists in relation to 'non-public reasons' and that there is no total exclusion of religion.[64] This is a modified position which says that where a comprehensive view (e.g. religious reason) is offered it corresponds to sufficient 'secular' or 'public' reason.[65] Public reason, thus, can be accepted within a pluralist, religious or non-religious, society. What is needed by society is what Habermas calls the epistemic ability to consider one's faith from the outside and relate it to secular views. The answer to the public/private conflict is not to deny your own views, but to consider them from the outside and then relate them to secular view.[66] This results in the need for a process of what Habermas calls 'translation'. There is no need to split identity between public and private. It is just necessary to translate the private religious conviction into a public discourse in a format that is acceptable to those who hold what could be called public reason values, in effect, to those who hold almost common sense values, values that are reasonable to the reasonable person.[67] The private religious conviction has to be translated into a public discourse.

The criterion of reciprocity applies: citizens must come to the most reasonable conception of political justice.[68] The process towards some form of reciprocal consensus could be defined as a deliberative democracy, where there is explicit deliberation about democratic viewpoints. Another essential in the deliberative democracy process is deliberating in accordance with a framework of constitutional institutions. For example, some of the precepts of the conscience clause in the Abortion Act 1967 (s 4) were founded upon a religious base. The Parliamentary debates that happened in parallel to the issuing of the various Bills associated with the eventual Act involved the translation of religious arguments to a more neutral format, which potentially rendered these arguments palatable to people of all religions and none.[69] This Parliamentary process is an exemplar of reciprocity in action, where the viewpoints of politicians were shared, debated, and, perhaps, reformulated in light of reciprocal arguments. This process of deliberative democracy, engaged at legislative level, serves to highlight the way in which public reason has come to shape legislative thought and action.

If such a deliberative democracy were in place when decisions around religiously-inspired autonomous reasoning are being arbitrated, then it is argued here that this deliberative process could surely be a helpful adjunct. The purpose of

64 Adhar and Leigh (n 3) p 63.
65 ibid.
66 ibid. p 10.
67 ibid.
68 Rawls (n 2) p 767.
69 See HC Dec 27 July 1989, vol 157, cc 1271–90, available at: http://hansard.millbanksystems.com/commons/1989/jul/27/abortion-act-1967 (accessed 27 January 2017).

public reason is not to make determinations about specific instances. Instead, it is concerned with decisions that are formulated within the public political sphere. The common perception of public reason might be that it debars consideration of religious belief, but that is not the case. Fundamentally public reason is not an objection to the inclusion arguments in litigation. It does not debar consideration of the manifestation of religious belief in any way. However, there are considerable limits to the power of public reason to provide a watertight explanation.

Public reason is beset by objection and controversy. The first problem is that of the potential exclusion of multiple voices in political discourse. Weithmann argues that citizens have the right to justify in the context of a comprehensive world view or of a religious doctrine[70] if two conditions are met: the Government is (1) justified in carrying out the laws and (2) willing to declare why they believe what they believe. Another reason for concern is that public reason can, itself, hold entrenched views that are couched in politically acceptable formats. Smith argues that public or secular reason has smuggled in comprehensive and partisan world views into the neutral democratic process.[71] There is an implicit danger that public reason can have hidden views that can dictate a hidden agenda of a hidden body politic and that the political stance of public reason holds within it an implicit partisan ideology.

Public reason is a reason-based perspective of the world and takes as valid what is reasonable. One of public reason's perceived weaknesses is the lack of determination of what constitutes a reasonable person in a reasonable society: it is difficult to define what is meant by reasonable people and reasonable society because what is reasonable to one may not be reasonable to another. It may be difficult to apply an objective barometer to the concept of reasonable people that could be acceptable to all.

Although public reason is useful in providing a rationale for collective political/legislative viewpoints, it cannot resolve specific issues. It cannot resolve the conflicts addressed in the case studies. It is only a preliminary perspective of how Parliament deals with the manifestation of religious belief from the point of political and legislative dialogue. In the case studies, the fact that religious arguments in these cases rest on specific legal provisions means that further justification, including justification on the basis of public reason, is not required. But public reason does not debar the manifestation of religious belief as a component in decision-making. Public reason and what happens in the legislature are linked and, as a consequence, legislative law making is reflective of public reason. If public reason does not debar the manifestation of religious belief, it follows that legislative law-making needs to consider religious belief or, at the very least, needs not to ignore it, where relevant. By the same token, these laws are interpreted by judges

70 JP Weithmann, *Religion and the Obligations of Citizenship* (CUP, 2002), as cited in Jurgen Habermas, 'Religion in the Public Sphere' (2006) 14(1) *European Journal of Philosophy*, pp 1–15, p 11.

71 Steven Smith, *The Disenchantment of Secular Discourse* (Mass, 2010) ch 1, pp 27–28, pp 33–38.

in judicial decisions and, so, public reason in the formation of that legislation influences judicial decision-making. The manifestation of religious belief and its acceptance by the processes of public reason is, therefore, relevant as a preliminary way of understanding how religion is dealt with in democratic society.

The primary focus of the book is on judicial decision-making and how judges interpret legislation. However, the role of the legislature is also of relevance. Consideration is required of how the legislature forms legislation that governs, in this particular case, the manifestation of religious belief. The legislature comes to a decision through Parliament and its elected representatives, acting collectively. A process of discussion, involving different stages of parliamentary/governmental discourse, results eventually in the formation of legislation. To deal, for example, with issues pertaining to religion, the parliamentary process can use public reason and its procedures of translation, reciprocity and deliberation to deal with issues requiring legislation in this area. While that discursive process is procedurally important, the process of public reason will not provide answers to moral questions. To bridge that gap, the book will apply a particular moral framework to answer different questions pertaining to the intersection between law, medicine and Abrahamic religious manifestation.

Chapter roadmap

This monograph involves an examination of a number of different cases studies, from the perspective of the application of the framework adopted:

1 The principle of Double Effect in English medical law
2 The refusal of blood transfusions by adult Jehovah's Witnesses
3 The refusal of blood transfusions by children who espouse Jehovah's Witness beliefs
4 Ritual male circumcision, medical law and Abrahamic religious belief
5 Female genital mutilation in English medical law
6 Conscientious objection to abortion by healthcare professionals

The cases under consideration are chosen because they involve judicial comment, statute, interpretation of statute, legal principles, and tests that relate specifically to the manifestation of Abrahamic religious belief in English medical law. They cast a very definite eye on the way English law and the European Court of Human Rights have dealt with these cases, they analyse the sufficiency of the approach in the context of the PGC and they propose alternative PGC-compliant approaches. The reader is taken on a journey *from* religious and moral principles *to* medical practice in the context of both patients and healthcare professionals. This journey arrives at an informed destination where the medical, legal and religious landscapes are drawn in detail, leading to specific, and potentially generalisable, conclusions. This theoretical voyage is situated within a context where tensions can exist between religious traditions and the broader field of medical ethics. In turn, tension can also appear when the emphasis on defending freedom of religion is juxta-positioned against other rights.

The following is a brief summary of the chapters discussed in this book.

Chapter 2 Mode of inquiry: an indirect application of the PGC

This chapter describes the core components of the PGC and it delineates the potential of its use. The chapter outlines a framework that can be used in the resolution of contentious medical law cases. Beyleveld's recent dialectically contingent argument for the PGC is accepted as a justification for the use of the PGC as the supreme moral principle.[72] In order to assess the appropriateness of current law in the studies and to suggest alternative PGC-compliant approaches, the chapter proposes three methodological questions that are subsequently applied in each of the case studies.

Chapter 3 The use of a religious-based principle (double effect) in decision-making, including issues surrounding end-of-life and palliative care

This chapter addresses what double effect means in principle and demonstrates how it is applied in practice. The chapter also measures its usefulness or otherwise in medical law and ethics and cites and analyses case law in respect of palliative care. The chapter further addresses how judges approach the doctrine and its religious undertones. The indirect application of the PGC in respect of double effect is scrutinised. It is found that this principle is at variance with the indirect application of the PGC due, *inter alia*, to its direct association with the principle of sanctity of life (which is not supported by the PGC). A new Act of Parliament dealing with palliative care in English law is proposed that is founded upon human rights/PGC-compliant principles. In the event that this principled approach is not accepted, then the chapter proposes more pragmatic approaches that will, nonetheless, suffice as good faith attempts at applying the PGC.

Chapter 4 Refusal of blood transfusions by Jehovah's Witnesses adults and medical law

The chapter examines the current approach in law to the autonomy of adult patients to refuse blood transfusions based upon religious belief. The sufficiency of the current approach to Jehovah's Witnesses who refuse blood transfusions in the context of the PGC is assessed. The current legal position pertaining to adults is endorsed by the application of this methodological framework, notwithstanding some reservations in relation to the issues of borderline legal capacity, undue influence and the best interests test.

72 Deryck Beyleveld, 'The Principle of Generic Consistency as the Supreme Principle of Human Rights' (2011) 13(1) *Human Rights Review*, 1–18.

Chapter 5 Refusal of blood transfusions by Jehovah's Witnesses children and medical law

This chapter focuses on the refusal of blood transfusions by Jehovah's Witness children and adolescents. Following examination of case law and statute, it proposes that the current legal approach is incompatible with the PGC and is overly paternalistic and negates the rights of many children/adolescents to exercise their will-rights. The approaches suggested put a direct focus on legal capacity, meaning, *inter alia*, that judges should not simply overrule the decisions of children without giving sufficient weight to their mental competence to accept or refuse the treatment. These decisions need to support the attainment of Gewirth's concept of capacity-fulfilment of the child,[73] in a context where societal competencies are relevant to the determination of the legal capacity of a child.

Chapter 6 Ritual male circumcision, medical law and Abrahamic religious belief

This chapter assesses the current legal approach to ritual male circumcision and considers the place of circumcision within Abrahamic religious belief. It provides a description and analysis of differing beliefs and practices in respect of circumcision that are held by some Abrahamic religions. The legal framework underpinning circumcision is outlined and the particular effectiveness of the Children Act 1989 and related medical guidelines is assessed. The approach taken by English law and the courts to circumcision, including the best interests test, is analysed and assessed. It is contended that ritual male circumcision constitutes basic harm and should not be permitted until the child has legal capacity and can make his own decision. Amendments in the current law and legal instruments are, consequently, required, including a new Act of Parliament on ritual male circumcision that puts a focus on legal capacity rather than best interests.

Chapter 7 Female Genital Mutilation in English medical law

The chapter assesses the practice of female genital mutilation as a manifestation of religious belief and considers the connection between the two as well as its link to embedded cultural ethnicity and practice. The paucity of case law is considered testimony to cultural relativism. The recent *Re B and G*[74] case is assessed and, drawing upon Gewirth's idea that cultural pluralism should accord to the values of the PGC, the illegal status afforded to female genital mutilation is endorsed.

73 See Alan Gewirth, *Self-Fulfillment* (Princeton University Press, 1998).
74 *Re B and G (Children) (No 2)* [2015] EWFC 27.

Chapter 8 Conscientious objection to abortion by healthcare professionals

This chapter focuses on healthcare professionals who refuse to carry out particular procedures due to their own deeply held religious beliefs. In particular, this chapter focuses on conscientious objection in the context of abortion because a specific conscientious objection provision exists in the legislation pertaining to this area. The current legal approach in English law and under European Convention jurisprudence is analysed, including the particular context of the recent *Doogan*[75] Supreme Court judgment. The degree to which this approach is compliant with the PGC is assessed.

Chapter 9 Conclusion

The book concludes that the right to the manifestation of religious belief is protected under human rights law and has certain validity under the methodological framework. The alternative approaches considered in some of the case studies are brought together and explored further in the context of the need for English medical law to work within a framework that represents an indirect application of the PGC. The final chapter also examines general issues concerning medical care from the broader context of non-Abrahamic religions and the current and future possible challenges that can exist or might exist into the future, given the expansion of reproductive technologies and the related potential to challenge existing physiological, medical, moral and legal parameters. Contributing factors to these parameters need to include the protection of cultural pluralism, recognition of the importance of societal competencies, and the overarching aim to promote the self-fulfilment of agents. It will be necessary to ensure that these future challenges are met in a PGC-compliant manner that embraces principled pragmatism.

Potential impact of the book

The research adds to the body of knowledge that exists in the dialogue around the adequacy of protection that is given to the manifestation of religious belief in English medical law. The research is unique in using the PGC and its indirect application in the context of assessing medical law and religious belief. A PGC-compliant method is devised that could be used by judges in the resolution of cases. It connects the indirect application of the PGC to the interpretation and use of the ECHR/HRA, legal instruments and principles in English law. This book allows for a more detailed and apparently objective assessment of the right to manifest Abrahamic religious belief, particularly in the context of differing case studies. A number of alternative approaches to existing law that represent indirect applications of the PGC are articulated. Such approaches have potential to give more appropriate protection to the manifestation of religious belief in English law, from the perspective of the PGC.

75 *Greater Glasgow Health Board v Doogan and Another* [2014] UKSC 68.

In the proposed alternative approaches to English law, the manner in which a judge might rule in the future is contrasted with how such ruling might be made in Gewirthia (a fictional world where everyone accepts the PGC). Such an approach adds to a deeper understanding of the relationship between society and the PGC. It is recommended that any alternative approach be based upon a stance of ***principled pragmatism*** that allows for both an ideal and a pragmatic way of bringing about a good faith attempt at applying the PGC in English law. Specifically, for example, Gewirth's concept of 'self-fulfillment' is uniquely linked to procedures around the determination of the legal capacity of a child under 16, in a context where societal competencies are relevant. Additionally, cultural pluralism, as a related factor in the indirect application of the PGC, is also explored with a new eye, particularly in the context of supporting the retention of the current legal prohibition of FGM.

Conclusion

To date, judges have had difficulty in coming to decisions when challenging medical law cases. Their judgments have had to rely upon very valid factors such as precedent and context and individual circumstance and these have all formed legitimate pathways towards decisions. All of this is subject, however, to intuitive argument, a certain amount of subjectivity, the potential for bias in favour of or in opposition to religious-based argument. This book will set out a framework to support judges in the decision-making process. The framework will then be applied to a number of case studies, where the reasonable accommodation that can be afforded to the manifestation of religious belief will be discussed. The framework evolves from, and is situated within, a wide range of literature and text that forms the basis of an approach that is primarily doctrinal in nature.[76]

References

Adhar, Rex and Leigh, Ian, *Religious Freedom in the Liberal State* (2nd ed, OUP, 2013).

Audi, Robert, *Religious Commitment and Secular Reason* (CUP, 2000).

Beyleveld, Deryck, 'The Principle of Generic Consistency as the Supreme Principle of Human Rights (2011) 13(1) *Human Rights Review*, 1–18.

Clouser, Roy, *The Myth of Religious Neutrality* (Ind, 1991) p 10, as cited in Adhar, Rex and Leigh, Ian, *Religious Freedom in the Liberal State* (2nd ed, OUP, 2013).

Coyle, Sean, *From Positivism to Idealism* (Ashgate, 2007).

Chaplin, Jonathan, 'Beyond Liberal Restraint: Defending Religiously-Based Arguments in Law and Public Policy' (2000) 33 *UBC L Rev*, 617.

Cranmer, Fran, 'The "gay cake" case: Ashers Baking loses its appeal' *Law and Religion UK*, 24 October 2016, available at: http://www.lawandreligionuk.com/2016/10/24/the-gay-cake-case-ashers-baking-loses-its-appeal/ (accessed 27 January 2017).

76 Some of the main texts include the following: Alan Gewirth, *Reason and Morality* (n 1); Beyleveld (n 72); Shaun D Pattinson, *Medical Law and Ethics* (5th ed, Sweet & Maxwell, 2017).

Dworkin, Ronald, *Law's Empire* (Fontana, 1986).

Dworkin, Ronald, *Is Democracy Possible Here Principles of a New Political Debate* (Princeton University Press, 2006).

Equality and Human Rights Commission, 'Article 9: Freedom of thought, conscience and religion' (2012) *Human Rights Review*, 313–329, 314, available at: https://www.equalityhumanrights.com/en/human-rights-act/article-9-freedom-thought-belief-and-religion (accessed 27 January 2017).

Evans, Carolyn, *Freedom of Religion under the European Convention on Human Rights* (OUP, 2001).

Evans, Malcolm, *Religious Liberty and International Law in Europe* (CUP, 1997).

Gewirth, Alan, *Reason and Morality* (The University of Chicago Press, 1978).

Gewirth, Alan, *Self-Fulfillment* (Princeton University Press, 1998).

Hale, Lady, 'Freedom of religion and Belief', Annual Human Rights Lecture for the Law of Ireland, 13 June 2014, available at: http://supremecourt.uk/docs/speech-140613.pdf (accessed 27 January 2017).

Harris and others, *Harris, O'Boyle & Warbrick Law of the European Convention on Human Rights* (2nd ed, OUP, 2009).

HC Dec 27 July 1989, vol 157, cc 1271–1290, available at: http://hansard.millbanksystems.com/commons/1989/jul/27/abortion-act-1967 (accessed 27 January 2017).

O'Leary, Olivia, 'A Remarkable Account of Savita's Death' (*The Irish Times*, 26 October 2013) http://www.irishtimes.com/culture/books/a-remarkable-account-of-savita-s-death-1.1570398 (accessed 27 January 2017).

Pattinson, Shaun D, 'The Human Rights Act and the Doctrine of Precedent' (2015) 35 *Legal Studies*, 142.

Pattinson, Shaun D, *Medical Law and Ethics* (5th ed, Sweet & Maxwell, 2017).

Rawls, John, 'The Idea of Public Reason Revisited' (1997) 64(3) *The University of Chicago Law Review*, 765–807.

Rawls, John, *The Law of Peoples: With, The Idea of Public Reason Revisited* (4th printing, HUP, 2002).

Smith, Steven, *The Disenchantment of Secular Discourse* (Mass, 2010).

Witte, John, 'Law, religion, and Human Rights' (1996) 28 *Columbia Human Rights Law Review*, 1–31.

Weithmann, JP, *Religion and the Obligations of Citizenship* (CUP, 2002).

Weithmann, JP, *Religion and the Obligations of Citizenship* (CUP, 2002), as cited in Jurgen Habermas, 'Religion in the Public Sphere', (2006) 14(1) *European Journal of Philosophy*, 1–15.

2 Mode of inquiry: an indirect application of the principle of generic consistency

Introduction

The chapter seeks to establish a workable framework in order to gauge the appropriateness of protection given to the manifestation of religious belief. In the first instance, it is necessary to outline the main precepts that are generally understood to be contained within this supreme principle, which is now identified as being Alan Gewirth's Principle of Generic Consistency (PGC).[1] There are many counter arguments that cast scepticism on this principle, which have been dealt with in great detail by Deryck Beyleveld, a latter day proponent of the PGC, along with Brownsword and Pattinson.[2] For example, objections have been made in respect of number of key areas: just what constitutes a moral principle, the role of human rights within the PGC, allegations that the voluntary nature described in the PGC is false, suppositions that the whole idea of agency is, itself, indefensible, lack of belief that an agent must regard purpose as a necessary good.[3] Rather than engaging in full defence of the PGC and addressing all these counter arguments, this chapter will explain why the PGC is being applied in this book and what is contained within the principle at its most relevant level.

The chapter explains and supports Beyleveld's 2011 dialectically contingent argument for the PGC, which has particular force in this context because step two of the dialectically contingent argument (the contingent premise of the argument—the assumption of impartiality) is one that is presupposed by English law, particularly the Human Rights Act 1998 (HRA)/European Convention on Human Rights (ECHR), and is presupposed by Abrahamic belief. This chapter then considers the meta-principles by which the PGC is to be applied (including its hierarchy of rights, will-rights vs. interest rights and precautionary reasoning) and the need to address some matters procedurally and, thereby, apply the PGC indirectly. This chapter develops an understanding of the indirect application of the PGC in recognition that England is not 'Gewirthia' and contends that this

1 See Alan Gewirth, *Reason and Morality* (The University of Chicago Press, 1978).
2 See, for example, Deryck Beyleveld, *The Dialectical Necessity of Morality: An Analysis and Defence of Alan Gewirth's Argument to the Principle of Generic Consistency* (The University of Chicago Press, 1991).
3 ibid.

indirect application can be used to provide appropriate procedures that allow for the balancing of rights, based on religious belief.

The case study chapters

The book proposes that this moral principle can be indirectly applied to reason-based arguments that happen within society. For that reason, a number of medical law cases that have proven difficult to resolve will be analysed through an evaluative framework. The PGC is defended as a principle that has the potential to provide resolution to such difficult medical law cases.

The book then examines the approach of English law and the European Court of Human Rights (ECtHR) to a number of issues of importance to the resolution of conflicts between doctors and patients in the context of Abrahamic religious belief. Each chapter assesses the current approach (legal mechanisms/instruments/judgments) and then determines whether or not they are compatible with the PGC or whether something more suitable can be provided, that acts as an indirect application of the PGC.

Three questions provide the framework for each of the case studies.

1 How have English law and the ECtHR dealt with the issue?
2 Why is this sufficient or insufficient in the context of the PGC?
3 Is there an alternative approach that will provide greater compliance with the framework?

Definitions of key terminology concerning the PGC

An understanding of the PGC encompasses engagement with concepts whose definitions require specification. For that reason, a number of key terms used in the discussion of the PGC need to be defined and explained.

Agent/agency: an agent is a being who voluntarily pursues chosen purposes and is, according to the dialectically necessary argument, required to act in accordance with the PGC. An agent who acts inconsistently with the PGC thereby acts immorally, but does not cease to be an agent.

Generic Conditions of Agency: according to Beyleveld and Brownsword, generic conditions of agency 'consist of what…agents need, *irrespective of what their purpose might be*, in order to be able to act at all or in order to be able to act with general chances of success'.[4] They can be divided into 'freedom' and generic 'well-being'. They can also be referred to as 'voluntariness' and 'purposiveness'. These terms will be used interchangeably in the book.

Generic Rights: these are rights to the generic conditions of agency.[5]

4 Deryck Beyleveld and Roger Brownsword, *Consent in the Law* (Hart, 2007) p 39.
5 Gewirth (n 1) pp 25–26.

Dialectical: the reasoning that is proposed here includes a hypothetical dialogue from the viewpoint of the claims of an individual agent, made within a first-person perspective, and that is consequently dialectical.

Dialectically necessary: Pattinson explains that Gewirth's 'dialectically necessary method' is 'dialectical' because it takes the form of an internal dialogue and 'necessary' because all the steps of the argument follow logically (hence necessarily) from premises that cannot be coherently rejected within this perspective (hence necessary premises).[6]

Dialectically contingent: the dialectical arguments are contingent in the sense that they start from moral premises that can be coherently denied.[7] A dialectically contingent argument uses logical necessity, but its starting point is contingent.

Moral: the understanding of morality that underpins this book is crucial to the development of argument presented in the chapters. There are many other definitions of morality: in some way, they all deal with what is conceived to be right and wrong. Pattinson provides a definition that is accepted here, as follows: moral is defined as prescriptive requirements that are other regarding and categorical.[8] This definition can be sub-divided into a number of correlating and co-dependent elements. Morality, according to this definition, refers to prescriptive imperatives, which are action guiding and address others, they are categorical, in the sense of being categorically binding (something is binding irrespective of inclination, and has precedence over other 'imperatives'), and other-regarding, in the sense that the agent is required to be concerned about the interests of others.[9]

The above definitions have provided clarity about many of the concepts that underpin the Principle of Generic Consistency and that shall be used throughout this discussion. There are two different ways of looking at the PGC. The first, and original conception of the PGC, is based upon Gewirth's dialectically necessary argument. The second is the dialectically contingent argument. This chapter will begin by exploring the original argument, before considering the merits of the dialectically contingent argument as a justification for the PGC.

Three stages of the dialectically necessary argument for the PGC

The seminal form of the dialectically necessary argument of the PGC was presented by Gewirth. Gewirth's position has been defended by Beyleveld and extended and adapted by others, such as Brownsword and Pattinson. Below is a summary, based on Beyleveld's reconstruction of that argument. Three stages are identified.

6 Shaun D Pattinson, *Medical Law and Ethics,* (5th ed, Sweet & Maxwell, 2017) p 579.
7 ibid. p 581.
8 ibid. p 579.
9 ibid. p 567.

First stage

The object of the first stage, which is dialectically necessary, is to move from the position of recognition of own agency ('I am an agent') to a recognition that 'I am (categorically instrumentally) required to act to defend my possession of the generic conditions of agency'. The first stage of this argument starts off with the idea that an agent has purposiveness and voluntariness, henceforth freedom and wellbeing. An agent must accept that he acts (or intends to act) for a purpose that he has freely chosen. This choice comes from the reasoning he goes through, according to the principle of instrumental reason.[10] According to Beyleveld and Bos, '[i]f doing or having C is necessary for me to pursue or achieve E then I ought to attach the same proactive value to C as to E or give up my pursuit of E'. This is the principle of instrumental reason.[11] Beyleveld provides the following clarification:

> If Albert thinks that doing *X* is necessary for him to achieve *E* then he ought to value *X* as much as he values *E*, or give up pursuit of *E*. This expresses the principle of instrumental reason. If Albert does not accept this principle, then it is clear that he does not understand what it is to be an agent. The point of acting is to achieve one's purposes. This point is utterly negated if the agent does not appreciate the need to do what is necessary to achieve the agent's purposes. So, on pain of contradicting that he is an agent (i.e., on pain of failing to act consistently with a proper understanding of what it is to be an agent), Albert must recognise that he ought to be motivated to pursue whatever he views as necessary to achieve his purposes or abandon these purposes.[12]

That means he has to understand what it means to be an agent. In stage one, the agent doesn't have to value agency in itself.[13] His purpose must be good, in the sense of worth pursuing and constituting a motivating factor. Any purpose freely chosen has positive value for the agent. Thus, he must pursue a purpose, but not a particular purpose. No matter what the purpose is, the fact that the agent has the generic conditions is categorically instrumentally good. No moral judgements or claims are made about the purpose. The generic conditions are categorically needed, the purpose cannot be achieved without them; thus, the agent must be willing to defend them and be committed to their defence. The agent commits to categorically pursuing and defending his having the generic conditions of agency. If he does not do so he has to accept generic damage to his capacity to act.

10 Shaun D Pattinson, *Revisiting Landmark Cases in Medical Law* (Routledge, 2018) p 15.

11 Deryck Beyleveld and Gerhard Bos, 'The Foundational Role of the Principle of Instrumental Reason in Gewirth's Argument for the Principle of Generic Consistency: A Response to Andrew Chitty' (2009) 20(1) *King's Law Journal*, 1–20, p 5.

12 Deryck Beyleveld, 'The Principle of Generic Consistency as the Supreme Principle of Human Rights' (2011) 13(1) *Human Rights Review*, 1–18, p 4.

13 ibid. pp 4–5.

Second stage

The second stage of the dialectically necessary argument is that the agent must recognise that he has generic rights. The agent is not required to think that his own agency is good. But, as he necessarily needs to use his agency, he has to think that his freedom or well-being, is categorically instrumentally good.[14] This requires him to claim that other agents must not interfere with his generic conditions and should help him if he can't do it on his own, if he wants that help.[15] Others should not interfere with their generic goods. This is basically the same as saying that they have rights to the generic goods upon which others should not infringe. This can be summarised, as follows:

> Other agents categorically ought not to interfere against my will with my having the generic conditions of agency, and ought to help me to secure them when I cannot do so by my own unaided efforts if this is my will. I only want *to* pursue and defend the conditions if others don't prevent me or help me if I can't attain the conditions of agency in any other way. This state is a categorically unconditional and instrument one. If I deny this, then I deny the first stage of the PGC.

Freedom and well-being are the interests that are in question when the overall question of morality is considered. As Pattinson points out, the agent has negative and positive rights to the generic conditions if a rights claim is used—collectively these rights are known as generic rights.[16] This means that, in short, 'I have the generic rights. Others can ignore me (at this stage in the argument). They do not have to accept my demands, but I must accept that I have these rights and that others have obligations'.[17]

Third stage

This brings us to the third, and most controversial, stage of the dialectally necessary argument. This stage tells us about the moral status of the generic rights. In stage 2, it was established that the agent must claim that he has these generic rights. What follows from that is, then, the formal 'logical principle of universability'.[18] Gewirth's use of the principle of universability allows for the move from 'I have rights as an agent' to 'you have rights as an agent' and then to 'all agents have generic rights'.[19]

Before the principle of universability comes into effect, it must be shown that an agent recognises that he is an agent as the sufficient reason for the assertion that

14 Gewirth (n 1) pp 48–52.
15 Pattinson, *Medical Law and Ethics* (n 6) p 580.
16 ibid.
17 See Shaun D Pattinson, *Influencing Traits Before Births* (2002, Ashgate) p 5.
18 Gewirth (n 1) p 105.
19 Pattinson, *Medical Law and Ethics* (n 6) pp 580–581.

he possesses generic rights. This means that the agent must demonstrate that his claim to possess the generic rights arises from the fact that he is an agent. This is done by what Gewirth calls the 'Argument from the Sufficiency of Agency' (ASA).[20]

The argument for the sufficiency of agency shows that the assertion 'I have the generic rights *because* I am an agent' is a dialectically necessary claim. When the logical principle of universalisability is applied, acceptance of the premise that every agent has the generic rights because it is an agent is now demanded. This represents a shift from the internal principle of universability (what I must accept) to an external operating of this principle (what others must accept). Therefore, all agents possess the generic rights. Thus, by the application of the logical principle of universability, it is dialectically necessary for every agent to accept that *all* agents have the generic rights (i.e. the Principle of Generic Consistency, the PGC).

The summative consequence of the three stages is a dialectically necessary claim that all agents have generic rights. Pattinson explains that if you apply, then, the principle of universability to this, you deny that you are an agent if you don't accept that all agents have these generic rights.[21] As such, it is dialectically necessary for every agent to accept that all agents have these generic rights.[22] Under the dialectically necessary argument, the PGC requires moral agents to act in line with their own and others' generic rights.

Beyleveld's dialectically contingent argument for the PGC

As highlighted above, the PGC is presented in two forms, the first comprising the more controversial one: the dialectically necessary method. The fact that a logical philosophical sequence for the development of the PGC has been outlined here does not mean that it has been met with universal acceptance. It has been a source of contentious debate amongst and between philosophers. At the root of the philosophical debate is the difficulty of moving from an individual sense of agency, with related conditions of agency, to an acceptance that all agents have generic rights. There is disquiet about the implications of assigning generic rights to all agents and the related implications that this might have for human rights, for example. It is controversial due also to the fact that not all people, including those of religious persuasion, can accept the content and the logical outcomes of the direct application of the principle of universability that comprises stage 3 of the dialectically necessary argument.

Working on the assumption that the dialectically necessary argument of the PGC would not be palatable to all, Beyleveld produced alternative ways of perceiving the PGC, including a number of iterations of the dialectically contingent argument. This book relies upon Beyleveld's (2011) dialectically contingent argument. It uses this version only for the sake of clarity. This dialectically

20 See Gewirth (n 1) p 110. Also see Pattinson, *Medical Law and Ethics* (n 6) p 580.
21 Pattinson, *Medical Law and Ethics* (n 6) pp 580–581.
22 ibid. p 573.

contingent argument, in a way, puts a limiting brake on the substance of stages 2 and 3 above. It modifies the philosophical leap that is made in respect of agency and generic rights. One of Beyleveld's modifications, accepted within this book, conceptualises the PGC as comprising stage 1 of the dialectically necessary argument above plus the idea that all agents basically count for the same: they are equal in dignity and rights (the impartiality assumption).

This dialectically contingent argument can justify the PGC as a supreme principle. Recognising the PGC as the supreme principle in a mediation process involving the weighting of competing rights would be ethically rational. In practical terms, according to this contingent argument, the first stage of the dialectically necessary argument is accepted. Stage 1 of the dialectically necessary argument involves accept that 'I am an agent' and that 'I (categorically instrumentally) ought to defend and pursue my having the generic conditions of agency'.

Stage 2 in this dialectically contingent argument differs from the dialectically necessary argument as human rights are now given validity. This means that if an agent claims that all agents should be treated with equal concern and respect, no agent should be privileged over another in relation of their possession of their generic conditions.[23] The impartiality assumption makes the assumption that all human beings are equal in dignity and rights: for any claim that I make, I must recognise that others have the same entitlements and I must give equal weight to the interests of others. It can be inferred that 'I and all agents have generic rights'. Thus, acceptance of stage 1 of the dialectically necessary argument and the impartiality assumption leads to the PGC.

This impartiality assumption is compatible with the moral theories of utilitarianism and the duty-based theories of an Abrahamic religious believer. It is compatible with both, but they reach very different conclusions. Conflicts within the impartiality assumption are dealt with by stage 1 of the dialectically necessary argument which forces you to adopt a non-aggregate moral theory, one that doesn't try to weigh up and add people together.

Who can Beyleveld's dialectically contingent argument convince? The impartiality assumption is compatible with the audience this book is trying to persuade. It can be accepted by adherents of Abrahamic religions. They also accept one of the conclusions of stage 1 of the dialectically contingent argument which is that individuals can't be aggregated.

In human rights law, there is debate over whether rights are will-rights or interests-rights. Stage 1 of the dialectically necessary argument commits agents to those rights being will-rights at conception. Following the application of the precautionary thesis, they become interest rights as well in application. This contrasts with the Catholic perspective that accepts that human rights have only interest rights by conception. Stage 2 assumes an acceptance of impartiality, but it doesn't establish this impartiality. This assumption of impartiality should not be overly problematic in the legal or societal arena. Those whose moral frame of reference is

23 Beyleveld 'Supreme Principle of Human Rights' (n 12) p 2.

informed mainly by human rights, will only find this assumption of impartiality problematic if they choose to interpret those human rights from a purely positivist perspective. Doing so, however, would rob the human in human rights. The rights-based part of the PGC does not come from the impartiality assumption: it derives from stage 1 of the dialectically necessary argument. The generic conditions of agency provide the content of rights and these evolve from stage one of the dialectically necessary argument and not from the impartiality assumption. All of this means that the methodology involves applying the PGC, not the impartiality assumption because what is done by bringing together stage 1 of the dialectically necessary argument and the impartiality assumption is getting to the PGC. This involves a combination of Gewirth's not very controversial stage 1 and an ethical view of the world that is accepted by most people.

If the first stage of the dialectically necessary argument is sound, it, therefore, follows that agents should interpret and act upon human rights in a manner that is consistent with the PGC.[24] If they fail to do that, then they consequentially deny two very basic precepts: they deny something that determines the essence of human rights, that is the concept that human beings are equal in dignity and rights, and they also deny that they are agents. If they deny this agency, then this equates to saying that people are not really subject to any rules at all.[25]

Beyleveld claims that the dialectically contingent argument joins up the premise that agents need to categorically defend their own categorical rights with the dialectically contingent premise that all human beings need to be treated as equal in human rights.[26] It does not mean that all human rights are equal. This means that a hierarchy of such rights can apply. Even if the dialectically necessary argument is not perceived to be valid in its totality, people within a wide spectrum of cultures and societies accept the concept that all human beings deserve to be treated with the equal respect and concern for their agency.[27] All who accept this premise must, if it is accepted that stage one of the dialectically necessary argument is valid, also accept the PGC as the supreme principle of morality and of practical reason.[28]

The PGC, therefore, provides a plausible theory as to how to address the balancing of religious and non-religious arguments. The dialectically necessary argument is not used as a justifying basis for the PGC because fewer people are willing to accept stages 2 and 3. The dialectically contingent argument is accepted as the basis for justifying the PGC because this version involves everyone: it can be accepted by those who argue from a human rights perspective, it can be accepted by religious adherents and non-religious adherents and can be acceptable to judges/the legal system. It is, ultimately, more palatable to a wider section of society.

24 ibid. p 3.
25 ibid.
26 ibid. p 6.
27 ibid. p 17
28 ibid. p 17.

It is, thus, argued that the status of the PGC as the supreme principle of morality can be demonstrated by either the dialectically necessary argument or a dialectically contingent argument and the latter 2011 argument is relied upon in this book. The theoretical justification for the PGC has now been set out. What are the principles that underpin the application of the PGC and what is the framework that can be constructed to allow for the PGC be indirectly applied?

Direct versus indirect application of the PGC

Applying the PGC is not just a matter of making existing value arguments accessible to the world. It is about making them compatible with an attempt to give effect to the generic rights.

Direct application of the PGC

Direct application of the PGC is used in straightforward situations. If the case is made to say that all red-headed children should not be educated, then the PGC can be applied directly to reject this claim. It is not always possible, however, to directly apply the PGC in practice. The cases considered in this book are ones that evoke reasonable disagreement and, maybe, unreasonable contention. The only controversy that would count is controversy within the tenets of the PGC. Unreasonable disagreement could not support violation of the PGC by failure to directly apply it.

Indirect application of the PGC

There are situations where the PGC cannot be applied directly. In these circumstances, the PGC is indirectly applied. The determination of this indirect application is situationally contingent. Let us think about how and why the indirect application might apply in practice. Beyleveld and Brownsword use the analogy of the rules of the road to illustrate how the PGC needs to support order in society.[29] In order to provide a resolution, a mechanism is needed to determine the side of the road to be used by vehicle drivers. A specific rule for this is required because if such a rule did not exist, life would be endangered, which is a direct violation of the PGC. The PGC cannot answer this conundrum directly because the PGC can accept the idea that drivers must drive on one side of the road, but it will not prescribe upon which side of the road these drivers should drive. The PGC is, therefore, morally neutral about the side of the road on which a driver should drive. There needs to be a rational way, an agreed procedure, to choose the 'accepted' side of the road on which to drive. A procedure is needed to determine which side of the road the drivers can drive on because, if this were not the case, the drivers and, potentially, pedestrians would be in danger and this

29 Deryck Beyleveld and Roger Brownsword, *Law as a Moral Judgment* (Sheffield Academic Press, 1994) pp 331–332.

would constitute generic harm. There is no need to apply this side of the road procedure to footpaths because there are no major consequences to the absence of a specific rule. It doesn't matter whether a person walks up or down the side of a footpath because, although variety in practice might be inconvenient, and you might bump into people along the way, there are no compelling consequences in connection to which side of the footpath one walks upon. It would not constitute generic harm. In effect, it doesn't really matter. The issue in the context of the side of the road has importance because of the potential for grave consequence, as measured by the PGC. The PGC is indirectly applied, in the context of the vehicle drives, by a specific rule that says that drivers must drive on a particular side of the road. Thus, for the indirect application of the PGC to apply, legitimate disagreement and conflict in relation to the generic rights needs to exist and it only applies when failure to resolve these conflicts directly would contradict the PGC. In the same way that a rule (procedure) is needed to determine the side of the road, each of the case studies here requires a procedure by which to indirectly apply the PGC and so lead to a PGC-compliant resolution in English law.

Brownsword and Beyleveld, in the context of the indirect application, say that its role is to determine what's right, what's wrong, and what's permissible.[30] They present the PGC within two worlds: (1) where a community accepts the PGC, but queries its application (Gewirthia) and where (2) the community is not committed to the PGC. This fictional world of Gewirthia will be addressed and described in further detail in a later section of this chapter. Each of the chapters will outline PGC-compliant proposals acceptable both within this Gewirthia and exterior to it. The PGC, therefore, is used to resolve conflict and the authority to resolve that conflict lies in different spheres, internal and external. The PGC can directly and specifically authorise action by saying that any actions must comply with its precepts.[31]

Brownsword and Beyleveld in *Law as a Moral Judgment* didn't answer the questions posed in this book relating to the conflict between doctors and patients in the context of Abrahamic religious belief in the English legal system. They didn't address the question of dealing with deficient parliamentary processes which are, in fact, different to the democratic process in Gewirthia. The question not directly addressed by them is 'How has English law got to this specific point in terms of each of the case studies and what is needed to apply the PGC in these contexts, especially for legislators or judges who act in a context where the PGC is not actually a constitutional principle?' It is this key question that is addressed and answered throughout in the case studies.

30 Deryck Beyleveld and Roger Brownsword, 'Proceduralism and Precaution in a Community of Rights', (2006) 19(2) *Ratio Juris*, 141–168, p 142.

31 Gewith (n 1) pp 272–365. Also see Beyleveld and Brownsword, *Law as a Moral Judgment* (n 29) p 148.

Meta-principles of the PGC

The PGC has been justified by using the dialectically contingent argument. A number of precepts form the core of application of this moral principle. Many of these points are only of tangential relevance and some will provide the key throttle of the case studies. The following sections will describe the aspects of the PGC that will be applied in the context of the case studies. In each of the case studies, the current law will be assessed in terms of its compliance with PGC and, indeed, its meta-principles. These principles provide substance in terms of assessing compliance with the PGC.

What has been outlined here to date is a fairly simple argument that, perhaps, belies the complexity of aspects of the PGC. The complexities surround providing clarification to the need to balance rights by considering issues such as proportionally and the hierarchy of rights. Given that this book involves constructing a weighting scales to balance rights, then consideration of these complex concepts, that nonetheless provide an important function, is necessary.[32]

Rights: a colourful tapestry (generic rights/will-rights and interest-rights/ positive and negative rights)

Gewirth outlines a supreme principle of rights that considers the conditions of agency that relate to and are generic to all people, namely the PGC. The PGC is a rights-based theory in principle. However, in application, it is both rights-based (will-rights) and duty-based (interest-rights). (The language of will-rights and interest-rights will be used). Both will-rights and interests-rights are conceptions of claim rights. Beyleveld explains that an agent's own rights are will-rights, the generic rights of agents. This means that agents have no duty to safeguard or not harm their own generic interests if this is not their wish. This holds unless allowing agents to harm or not protect themselves puts equally important generic rights or interests of others in danger.[33] Therefore, you can kill yourself, but you can't fly a plane that kills everybody. We have no duty to protect ourselves. We only have a duty to do so if, by not doing it, somebody else is harmed. Using the PGC terminology, we have no duty to protect our own generic interests. We cannot prevent people from doing something that is against their generic interest, because to do so could be contrary to the retention of their dignity. Dignity is related to agents' capacity to direct their actions by their own choice.

Arising from the fact that the generic rights are rights under the will conception, there is a consequent implication that there are no 'imperfect duties' to an agent under the PGC.[34] This means that the PGC cannot argue for imperfect duties of which there is no perfect duty to try to achieve its object. According to Beyleveld and Brownsword, '[p]erfect duties are duties that are only discharged if

32 See Gewirth (n 1) pp 95–96.
33 Beyleveld 'Supreme Principle of Human Rights' (n 12) p 13.
34 ibid. p 41.

the outcomes they demand are fully achieved'.[35] So, therefore, the PGC cannot create any imperfect duties to the agent himself or to other agents that do not come from, in a direct or indirect way, the duties that are ascribed to others.[36]

The duties that we owe to apparent non-agents are interest-rights (under precautionary reasoning, to be discussed below). It is impossible to discriminate between the strength of the generic interest protected in an interest-right or a will-right.[37] Beyleveld provides additional clarification: '[t]he weight that is given to the will right of an apparent agent must be greater than the interest right of an apparent non-agent when the same interest defines the right'.[38]

In broad terms, the main difference between will-rights and the interest-rights is that the former gives the person the capacity to waive the protection that his rights give him. According to the will-conception, an agent can theoretically waive the protection of any right following an act which might breach his right. This capacity to waive the benefit of rights is not implied by interest-rights. The different approaches to waiving the benefits derives from diverse views of the general characteristics or norms of rights.[39]

Hierarchy of rights

A hierarchy of rights exists when applying the PGC. Gewirth shows how all agents have generic rights. This is known as the criterion of degrees of needfulness for action. Agents possess the rights to the generic features of action. Not all of these rights can be allocated the same value and Gewirth subdivides these rights into a hierarchy of capacities.[40] This hierarchy includes the capacities that must be in place for an agent to act at all and those that are necessary to act successfully. The capacities that are necessary to act at all are defined by Gewirth as 'basic' capacities. The next capacity that is necessary for action to be successful has two types. The first of these is the 'nonsubtractive' capacity and that is the capacity to maintain the existing level of purpose fulfilment. The second of these latter capacities is the 'additive' capacity where capacities exist that increase the current

35 Beyleveld and Brownsword, *Consent in the Law* (n 4) p 40.
36 ibid.
37 Beyleveld 'Supreme Principle of Human Rights' (n 12) p 16.
38 ibid.
39 Neil MacCormick, 'Rights in Legislation' in P. Hacker and J. Raz (eds), *Law, Morality and Society* (Clarendon, 1977) p 192. Note that there is an explicit distinction between negative and positive rights that is directly related to aspects of the human condition, to perhaps an interpretation of Natural law. See Beyleveld and Brownsword, *Consent in the Law* (n 4) p 41. The generic rights under the will conception that are levied on others by positive rights are predicated on the person who has the rights wanting help. By the same token, duties that come from negative rights 'are subject to interference being imposed by the right-holder's will'. See Beyleveld 'Supreme Principle of Human Rights' (n 12) p 5. According to negative rights, agents cannot deprive others of the conditions of agency. In parallel to that, an agent's positive rights compels him to help other agents to get the generic conditions if he is able to do so.
40 Gewirth (n 1) p 110.

level of purpose fulfilment. The existence of these hierarchically conditioned capacities creates a hierarchy of possible harm to the generic conditions. This harm is aligned to the degree to which the generic capacity in question is required by the agent to fulfil his purpose. The hierarchy relates, therefore, to the degree of harm that could be put as a barrier to the fulfilment of purpose. Arising from this hierarchy, Gewirth concludes that a measure can be put in place to estimate the degree of generic harm. This measuring tool is called the 'criterion of degrees of needfulness for action'.[41] In situations involving conflict, the generic rights can be ranked in descending order. According to this order, basic rights trump nonsubstractive rights and nonsubstractive rights trump additive rights.[42] Thus, to interfere with a basic right involves interference with someone's life in the sense that there is interference with someone's capacity to act at all. A non-substractive right is infringed upon when there is an interference with the agent's current level of purpose-fulfilment. An additive right is breached when an individual is deprived of the means to further themselves and achieve their purpose.[43]

There is no distinction made between a will-right and an interest-right under this criterion.[44] There is a distinction, however, between the weight given to a being who possesses very evident and displayed characteristics of agency and to the weight that is afforded to a being who does not exhibit these characteristics in as obvious a fashion.[45] This is known as precautionary reasoning and can be explained as follows:

Precautionary reasoning

There is a knowledge gap between ourselves and others. It involves the application of the concept of agency in the empirical world. I can know directly that I am an agent, but I do not have direct access to the mind of another, so cannot know directly whether any other being is or is not an agent. The precautionary thesis applies the PGC to that knowledge gap. Beyleveld and Pattinson's argument centres around the idea that it is empirically impossible for any agent to be a hundred per cent certain that another being is or is not an agent. Jim, for example, cannot be certain as to the agency status of Tony, another being, and Jim does not know whether Tony is an agent.[46] Beyleveld and Pattinson argue that, due to the fact that the PGC is categorically binding and the fact that it is impossible to know what another being is thinking, the PGC enacts a precautionary duty against carrying out actions that are contrary to the other being's generic rights if they were agents and whom it is impossible to know if they are not agents.[47] One

41 ibid.
42 ibid. pp 53–58.
43 For further discussion, see Pattinson, *Medical Law and Ethics* (n 6) pp 588–589.
44 Beyleveld 'Supreme Principle of Human Rights' (n 12) p 58.
45 ibid.
46 Deryck Beyleveld and Shaun D Pattinson, 'Defending Moral Precaution as a Solution to the Problem of Other Minds: A Reply to Holm and Coggon' (2010) 23(2) *Ratio Juris,* 253–273, p 260.
47 ibid. p 258. Also see Deryck Beyleveld and Shaun D Pattinson, 'Precautionary Reasoning as a Link to Moral Action' in M Boylan (ed), *Medical Ethics* (Prentice-Hall 2000) p 51.

conclusion of the precautionary thesis is that we must treat those who behave like agents (apparent agents) as agents with will-rights and those who behave as if they are partial agents (apparent partial agents) as having interests-rights.

In situations where there is a conflict, all parties should be treated as agents using the criterion of avoiding protective harm where we have a more defined duty to those who are more likely to be agents than to those who are less likely to be agents.[48] The degree of moral protection, therefore, that is given to a being is proportionate to the degree to which they behave like agents. The PGC allows for the treatment of infants as having the moral status that is proportionate to the behaviours that they show. Pattinson says that there is no real evidence that exists to suggest that babies are agents.[49] He suggests that they do not *appear* to make voluntary choices. If they are not agents, then they are owed no duties of protection. It is only because we cannot know that they are not agents that we must grant them duties of protection. This leaves us acting as if infants are agents and affording them the moral status proportionate to the probability that they are agents. This is the essence of Beyleveld and Pattinson's precautionary reasoning. They explain what happens when duties of protection come into conflict:

> All other things being equal, such conflicts are to be handled by a criterion of avoidance of more probable harm, according to which, If my doing y to Z is more likely to cause harm h to Z than my doing y to X (and I cannot avoid doing y to one of Z or X) then I ought to do y to X rather than to Z. Since I am more likely to mistakenly deny that a being is an agent the more probable it is that the being is an agent, it follows that my duties of protection to those who are more probably agents take precedence over my duties of protection to those who are less probably agents.[50]

Beyleveld and Pattinson put forward a mathematical index to define the notion of probability in agency, as follows:

> … where X is an ostensible agent, the probability that X is an agent must be taken to be 1, and where X is apparently only a partial agent, the probability that X is an agent must be taken to be >0 but <1 in proportion to the capacities of agency that X displays.
>
> Thus, we establish that apparent partial agents are owed duties of protection by agents in proportion to the degree to which they approach being ostensible agents—not qua their being partial agents—but qua their possibly being agents.[51]

48 ibid.
49 Pattinson, *Medical Law and Ethics* (n 6) p 591.
50 Beyleveld and Pattinson, 'Precautionary Reasoning as a Link to Moral Action' (n 47).
51 ibid.

Under this theory, there are, therefore, no differing levels of agency. Instead, the precautionary theory concerns different levels of characteristics that are portrayed by different beings. A newborn baby displays some of the characteristics of agency that lead him to having only interest and not will-rights. In effect, the precautionary theory does not recognise Gewirth's ideas around partial agency or full agency.[52] As the child grows older, the characteristics of agency become more mature and, so, by this reasoning, a two-year-old child shows the characteristics that determine that he is sometimes apparently an agent and sometimes not apparently an agent. There is inconsistency in the characteristics of agency and so there is inconsistency in the apparent existence of the agency of this young child. A ten-year-old child can display the characteristics of agency. There are some simple situations and decisions that a child can make between two variables, where the child is clearly mentally competent to make those decisions. For example, if a dispute exists between the need to play rugby or football, the child is clearly mentally competent to make this type of decision. For grave medical decisions, however, where potential life-shortening consequences can apply to decisions made, a higher standard in the determination of characteristics of agency exists.

An agent must, therefore, regard a being who apparently seems, by their characteristics and behaviours to be agents, as agents,[53] even though they cannot be certain that they are agents. This obligation arises under the PGC because it is better to treat a non-agent as an agent than to fail to treat an agent as an agent and, consequently, deny him or her the generic conditions of agency.[54]

What is the relevance of issues such as hierarchy of rights, proportionality, and precautionary reasoning to this book? Some of the cases outlined in this monograph involve the need to give weight to arguments that seem to have the same strength and validity and come from strong religious-based reasoning. This is where the will conception and the hierarchy of rights will support judges in indirectly applying the PGC in order to balance these competing rights.

Resolution: adoption of three questions

In order to bridge this gap and resolve the issues pertaining to this book, three questions are posed. These questions are interrogated in the case studies, leading to potential PGC-compliant resolutions. As indicated, these questions are as follows:

1. How have English law and the ECtHR dealt with the issue?
2. Why is this sufficient or insufficient in the context of the PGC?
3. Is there an alternative approach that will provide greater compliance with the framework?

52 See Gewirth (n 1) p 344 in relation to his principle of proportionality.

53 Beyleveld and Pattinson, 'Precautionary Reasoning as a Link to Moral Action' (n 47) pp 113 & 120.

54 Beyleveld and Pattinson, 'Defending Moral Precaution as a Solution to the Problem of Other Minds: A Reply to Holm and Coggon' (n 46) p 260.

Question 1: How have English law and the ECtHR dealt with the issue?

This question involves a review of current English law and practices, as they pertain to the manifestation of religious belief in the case studies. This review will also extend beyond English law and consider, in particular, the ECHR and the ECtHR jurisprudence on a number of relevant Articles, due to the fact that English law is connected to Convention jurisprudence. As noted by Harris, O'Boyle, and Warbrick, '[t]he Convention has had a considerable effect upon the national law' and has 'served as a catalyst for legal change that has furthered the protection of human rights at the national level and has, in so doing, assisted indirectly in the process of harmonizing laws in Europe'.[55] The law governed by the Convention directly impacts upon English (medical) law through the application of the HRA 1998. This means that the methodological framework acts within a legal context that explicitly, overtly and proactively seeks to promote in its instruments and applications the expression of individual and societal human rights. This review will show how far the existing law has gone and if its provisions are adequate in terms of addressing the right to manifest religious belief in English medical law, in the context of the ECHR/HRA. For example, the issue of the degree to which English law has given effect to Article 9 ECHR will be explored in particular contexts. Following this doctrinal review, the current stance of the law and any gaps/ambiguities within it will be clear.

Question 2: Why is this sufficient or insufficient in the context of the PGC?

Arising from the conclusions of the review of existing legal practice, this aspect of the mode of inquiry assesses, from the point of view of the PGC, whether or not this law is sufficient. It is determined if a particular approach represents an indirect application of the PGC. If such a determination is made, then this approach is sufficient in the context of the framework. If it is determined that the approach adopted in the case study is not compliant with the PGC and so cannot represent an indirect application of the PGC, then this legal approach is deemed to be insufficient in respect of how it deals with the manifestation of religious belief.

This sufficiency is gauged within the context of a society (England) that is governed by legal instruments that protect human rights (ECHR). The PGC cannot be seen as something that exists outside or beyond the existing human rights laws and mechanisms. Rather, the principles which underpin the PGC are closely aligned to and complement the European Convention. For the most part, the Convention is PGC-compliant and is consequentially relied upon by this framework. Rights under the Convention can be, thus, considered to involve either will- or interest-rights. Therefore, will-rights and interest-rights under the PGC are a sub-division of the broad world of human rights.[56] The concept of 'equal in dignity and rights' is, therefore, compatible

55 Harris et al, *Harris, O'Boyle and Warbrick Law of the European Convention of Human Rights* (2nd ed, OUP, 2009) p 31.

56 See Benedict Douglas, 'The Necessity and Possibility of the use of the Principle of Generic Consistency by the UK Courts in Order to Answer the Fundamental

with the international human rights instruments. Thus, this framework is rights-focused and works in parallel with the ECHR.

Douglas' call for the courts to be guided by the PGC in the way that they interpret fundamental questions about human rights is legitimate.[57] He shows how the open nature and semantic looseness of the Convention principles lead to uncertainty in the interpretation of these principles. Such principles include dignity, autonomy and equality. The courts are not always fully consistent in their interpretation of Convention rights. Douglas demonstrates how the courts already use the will-conception and interest-rights in some of their judgements.[58] An acceptance by the courts of the PGC as an underpinning principle that is aligned with the current principled approach of the Convention would allow for greater certainty in the application and interpretation of Convention rights.[59]

Amongst the Convention rights given particular attention is freedom of religion, thought and conscience under Article 9 ECHR. Article 9 can encompass both interest and will-rights. For example, in the context of the will-conception, Nadiya is a Muslim and wears a hajib. Under the will-conception she can waive the benefit of the right to wear a hajib, insofar as she has such a right. The freedoms to both wear the hajib or to waive this benefit are both protected by Article 9. The question is, therefore, relatively simple when it comes to apparent agents who are apparently mentally competent. Article 9's protections are more open to more scrutiny when it comes to apparent partial agents (e.g. babies) and the interest-conception. The chapter dealing with ritual male circumcision will show that infants, as apparent partial agents, should not be circumcised until they are mentally competent to make such a grave decision.[60] The protection given to infants under Article 9 in applying the interest-conception under the PGC, in this particular instance, is inappropriate. Therefore, while Article 9 provides an important safeguard for the manifestation of religious belief and is also straightjacketed by a range of legitimate limitations, nonetheless, the current judicial interpretation of Article 9 is not without its flaws. Chief of this is a difficulty in judicial interpretation of assigning rights to partial apparent agents under the interest-conception. In individual cases, a particular interpretation is necessitated by the text and context of Article 9 itself.

Question 3: Is there an alternative approach that will provide greater compliance with the framework?

Engaging with question 2 provides an initial conclusion that aspects of the current law are insufficient in respect of the PGC. This third question invites different types of response. Alternative legal approaches/procedures that represent

Questions of Convention Rights Interpretation' (Unpublished PhD, Durham University, 2012).

57 ibid. p 17 and pp 91–98.

58 ibid. p 57.

59 ibid. p 234.

60 Decision making abilities can vary by degree but reaching the threshold for making a particular decision cannot.

indirect applications of the PGC are, thus, proposed in respect of some of the case studies. A distinction is made between the application of the PGC indirectly through a parliamentary democratic process and its indirect application through a judicial process and a theory is now developed to exemplify this distinction. The focus of the method is on the options available (a) in Gewirthia and (b) in future (non-Gewirthian) English law/society. This includes, in the context of (b), suggesting both principled and pragmatic alternative positions which represent good faith attempts at applying the PGC.

Gewirthia

Beyleveld and Brownsword once provided an illustration of an imaginary country called Gewirthia. In this country, they conceived of citizens as being 'universally committed to the PGC as both the supreme principle of morality and the constitutional first principle of dispute resolution'.[61] Everybody agrees with the PGC in Gewirthia and the legal system is such that all the laws that are enacted there must conform with the PGC.[62] We now, once again, enter that land of Gewirthia. Here, the citizens are joined by deep moral consensus, a commitment to conscientious objection as a principle that allows agents to respect each other's rights. In Gewirthia, notwithstanding this consensus, there is no definitive answer to moral questions such as those posed in the case studies. However, Gewirth suggests that the PGC will help to find such resolution by directing that procedures that the PGC authorises are applied or obeyed.[63]

Citizens in Gewirthia are required by the PGC to resolve challenges posed in contentious cases by making a decision that is relative to the values that are protected by the PGC.[64] Sometimes, more than one answer is compatible with the PGC, but we must determine which is the more correct answer. A procedural justification could be enacted whereby all concerned agreed to refer the matter to an expert panel and all would be bound by the findings of this panel. If, however, they fail to agree to this choice, then another layer of proceduralism is called for. If they are all in agreement, then they are then bound by what Beyleveld and Brownsword call 'procedural justification'. However, the procedural aspect is also limited by the PGC because it only permits decisions to be reached that are not contrary to the PGC. The degree to which the procedures are accepted will rely upon the criteria that are set in place to determine whether one is better or worse off by proposed action: in Gewirthia these criteria must comprise of values that are supported by the PGC.[65] These values constitute the basic generic conditions of action, life and its means (e.g. food and shelter), mental equilibrium sufficient for voluntary action to be possible, and freedom to make choices.[66] Within this

61 Beyleveld and Brownsword, 'Principle, Proceduralism, and Precaution in a Community of Rights' (n 30) p 143.
62 ibid. p 147
63 Gewirth (n 1) pp 272–365.
64 Beyleveld and Brownsword, 'Principle, Proceduralism, and Precaution in a Community of Rights' (n 30) p 149.
65 ibid. p 153.
66 Gewirth (n 1) pp 53–54.

process, the generic rights will always trump the procedures. The method of consent is the procedural turn. Procedural turn or method of consent provides, therefore, the basis for binding Gewirthians to defending or promoting the values of the PGC.[67]

Gewirthia, according to Beyleveld and Brownsword, is not 'the finished article', and Gewirthia is not just a debating society but, rather, it is a political community and debate should be fostered within this interpretative community.[68] Beyleveld and Brownsword call Gewirthia 'a community that is committed to a moral form of life that flows through and infuses its regulatory activities' in order to 'set the standard for public debate'. Gewirthians place a huge emphasis on consent as being an 'enforced and informed source'.[69] Citizens must debate and come to a decision as to who has rights in the context of conscientious objection and must be clear as to those whose rights are to be excluded. Beyleveld and Brownsword also suggest that different forms and types of community of rights could exist in different Gewirthias, but, where disagreement exists between different Gewirthian communities, they should be guided by the principle of mutual respect and learn from one another. Gewirthia has PGC-compatible procedures and people/governing bodies who are committed to the PGC.

While there are different communities in different Gewirthias, there is a homogenous acceptance of the PGC throughout. In the England of today and in the future, where it is unlikely that Gewirthian principles will prevail in a universally uncontested manner, this is not the case. Communities are not joined by any one principled moral stance and comprise of people with differing, diverse and often conflicting ways of viewing the world. Such a community includes those who hold religious beliefs. In Gewirthia, decisions will derive from consideration of the degree to which actions adhere to the values of the PGC. In non-Gewirthia, there is no such moral constraint or freedom and the decisions made will derive from particular legal rules, such as legislation and precedent and will be unique to individual contexts/jurisdictions. In Gewirthia, the process of discourse will always recognise the rights of other Gewirthians to have dissenting viewpoints, but all will accept, without necessarily consenting to, the primacy of the PGC in determining the peaceful outcome of the case.

Non-Gewirthia (English law/society)

Due to the existence of differing and often conflicting views in society, the process of discourse in England will be more contentious and is liable to be fraught with dissension.

Ultimately, where the law is shown not to be sufficient, there is emerging evidence that procedures used in a PGC-compliant manner can fill the gap. The

67 Beyleveld and Brownsword, 'Principle, Proceduralism, and Precaution in a Community of Rights' (n 30) p 154.
68 ibid. p 155.
69 ibid. p 158.

alternative approaches adopted in terms of the case studies offer the potential for resolution. Obviously, there are other approaches that could have parallel validity, but these approaches are proposed as one arguably valid response to the resolution of difficult case studies.

In some case studies new legislation is called for in non-Gewirthian England. It will be accepted into the future that the current law that exists is too ambiguous and that the current legal approaches are insufficient. New Acts of Parliament may be needed instead of simply developing the law through the jurisprudence of the courts. An Act of Parliament is strengthened by the existence of parliamentary sovereignty.[70] Legislation is the highest form of law within the UK (particularly in the light of a impending post-Brexit era) and this would provide definitive guidance in relation to what is allowable in particular medical law contexts. A clear Act setting out the parameters of what is and is not permissible would be welcomed in some cases. There will always be difficulties in relation to interpretation, but this is the true role of the courts. The courts should be involved in interpreting the provisions of the proposed Act instead of jumping from one principle or another or potentially introducing or wiping out existing legal practice through the common law. However, in other cases, as in some of the case studies, an Act is not always needed, due to the developmental nature of the common law.

Ultimately, where the law is shown not to be sufficient, there is emerging evidence that procedures used in a PGC-compliant manner can fill the gap. The alternative approaches adopted in terms of the case studies offer the potential for resolution. Obviously, there are other approaches that could have parallel validity, but these approaches are one, arguably, valid response to the resolution of difficult case studies.

This will involve setting out, in a number of case studies, a possible statute that could comply with the PGC and be used by the future judiciary. The proposed legislation will be adopted to represent indirect applications of the PGC. The relevant chapters will explain why an Act of Parliament is a suitable approach. Every effort will be made to explain how the Act would apply in practice and why this would serve as a useful PGC-compliant mechanism.

Conclusion

This book deals with decisions made in the public legal arena and, in the end, these decisions reflect personal viewpoints and provide a personal response to a given situation. Contention can exist between individuals who have different rights, different ideas, and different interpretations of the same situation. They can have different moral perspectives and different religious perspectives on a situation. What is required to meet these diverse perspectives is a principle or a stance or a governing thought that overrides and supersedes principles that they might have. The PGC, as a moral barometer, will now be used as a specific mechanism to

70 See Albert V Dicey, *Introduction to the Study of the Law of the Constitution* (8th ed, Liberty Fund Inc, 1982).

gauge the appropriateness of the pervading legal instruments and approaches in the context of morally challenging scenarios where religious belief intersects contentiously with medicine and law.

References

Beyleveld, Deryck, 'The Principle of Generic Consistency as the Supreme Principle of Human Rights' (2011) 13(1) *Human Rights Review*, 1–18.
Beyleveld, Deryck, *The Dialectical Necessity of Morality: An Analysis and Defence of Alan Gewirth's Argument to the Principle of Generic Consistency* (The University of Chicago Press, 1991).
Beyleveld, Deryck and Bos, Gerhard, 'The Foundational Role of the Principle of Instrumental Reason in Gewirth's Argument for the Principle of Generic Consistency: A Response to Andrew Chitty' (2009) 20(1) *King's Law Journal*, 1–20.
Beyleveld, Deryck and Brownsword, Roger, *Consent in the Law* (Hart, 2007).
Beyleveld, Deryck and Brownsword, Roger, 'Proceduralism and Precaution in a Community of Rights' (2006) 19(2) *Ratio Juris*, 141–168.
Beyleveld, Deryck and Brownsword, Roger, *Law as a Moral Judgment* (Sheffield Academic Press, 1994).
Beyleveld, Deryck and Pattinson, Shaun D, 'Defending Moral Precaution as a Solution to the Problem of Other Minds: A Reply to Holm and Coggon' (2010) 23(2) *Ratio Juris*, 258–273.
Beyleveld, Deryck and Pattinson, Shaun D, 'Precautionary Reasoning as a Link to Moral Action' in M Boylan (ed) *Medical Ethics* (Prentice-Hall, 2000).
Douglas, Benedict, 'The Necessity and Possibility of the use of the Principle of Generic Consistency by the UK Courts in Order to Answer the Fundamental Questions of Convention Rights Interpretation' (Unpublished PhD, Durham University, 2012).
Dicey, Albert V, *Introduction to the Study of the Law of the Constitution* (8th ed, Liberty Fund Inc, 1982).
Gewirth, Alan, *Reason and Morality* (The University of Chicago Press, 1978).
Harris et al, *Harris, O'Boyle and Warbrick Law of the European Convention of Human Rights* (2nd ed, OUP, 2009).
MacCormick, Neil, 'Rights in Legislation' in P Hacker and J Raz (eds), *Law, Morality and Society* (Clarendon, 1977).
Pattinson, Shaun D, *Revisiting Landmark Cases in Medical Law* (Routledge, 2018).
Pattinson, Shaun D, *Influencing Traits Before Births* (Ashgate, 2002).
Pattinson, Shaun D, *Medical Law and Ethics* (5th ed, Sweet & Maxwell, 2017).

3 The religiously inspired principle of double effect in English medical law

Introduction

This book attempts to get to the very core of determining what action is permissible or not permissible in terms of the manifestation of religious belief from the vista of an ethical framework. Drilling into that core entails looking at the question of life itself, what constitutes that life, and what drives the permissibility of action. To do this means interrogating the essence of life and its potential sacredness, inviolability, and the actions or non-actions that potentially compromise that sacred space. Whether life, however, holds within it that sanctity, or should hold within it, is central to this exploration of the intersection between law, medicine, and religion. Thus, there is a need to explicitly focus attention on a religiously inspired principle that has been used in the courts and that holds within it a very explicit vindication of a sanctity of life perspective.

This chapter on the principle of double effect frontloads the subsequent case studies, which deal with very specific instances of PGC-compliant or non-compliant actions. That frontloading is very deliberate because the issue of sanctity of life and the related perspectives that inform moral, legal, and medical action pertaining to beginning of life and end of life permeate the entrails of the debate in the next chapters. In effect, this means that this chapter provides a principled starting point for the journey into the chosen case studies, a journey that veers into how religiously inspired action can have an impact upon practical medical realities that subsequently promote legal debate.

The explication of sanctity of life through the enaction of the principle of double effect and from evidence in related case law will go some way to providing for an understanding of the importance of this concept within some religious traditions. It has, for example, held a relatively uncontested position with Catholicism, but contemporary social change, such as the recent repealing of the Eighth Amendment of the Irish Constitution in Ireland, suggests that its place in the heart of religious adherents, if not in the hierarchical structures that guide ethical thought in religious traditions, is changing apace. A very real challenge exists for Catholic religious leaders to bridge the gap between what can be perceived to be intransigent religious dogma in this area and the practices of the adherents that can, equally, be considered to be at variance with Church teaching.

In the field of medical law and ethics, the doctrine or principle of double effect is sometimes used, explicitly or implicitly, when medical decisions find themselves at question at the bedside of a patient or in courts of law. The principle of double effect is a dogma, rooted certainly in the religious, but practised within the secular/neutral context of the medical arena.

This chapter addresses what double effect means in principle and demonstrates how it is applied in practice. The chapter will also measure its usefulness or otherwise in medical law and ethics and cites and analyse case law in respect of palliative care. According to the World Health Organisation (WHO), palliative care is defined as:

> ...an approach that improves the quality of life of patients and their families facing the problem associated with life-threatening illness, through the prevention and relief of suffering by means of early identification and impeccable assessment and treatment of pain and other problems, physical, psychosocial and spiritual.[1]

They further state that palliative care 'provides relief from pain and other distressing symptoms', 'affirms life and regards dying as a normal process', 'intends neither to hasten or postpone death', and 'will enhance quality of life, and may also positively influence the course of illness'.[2]

The chapter further addresses how judges approach the doctrine and its religious undertones. It also seeks to explore whether giving credence to religious beliefs compromises the secular neutrality of the court. This chapter differs from the other case studies in so far that it does not so much deal with the rights of patients/healthcare professionals to manifest their religious beliefs as it does interrogate the use of a religious principle in the courts and its use in questions concerning palliative care/cases concerning sanctity of life. The case study was chosen as a means of teasing out the degree to which a religious principle has a place in resolving, in particular, palliative care situations, which apply to both religious and non-religious adherents. In measuring the adequacy of the law, as it pertains to the manifestation of religious belief, it is necessary to look at a practice that involves a specific religiously based principle, including its relationship to the religious principle of sanctity of life. The framework addresses, initially, current/previous practices involving double effect. Secondly, it scrutinises whether this approach is tenable within the context of the framework and, thirdly, in light of the conclusions that current English law, with its ambiguities and covert reliance on the principle of double effect, which is implausible in the context of the PGC, some new approaches are proposed to give a more PGC-compliant solution/path that world promote greater certainty in the resolution of the issue concerning palliative care. These approaches include the courts' interpreting Article 9 in a

1 World Health Organisation, 'WHO Definition of Palliative Care' available at: http://www.who.int/cancer/palliative/definition/en/ (accessed 27 January 2017).
2 ibid.

PGC-compliant manner and the adoption of new legislation, drawing upon some ideas of the doctrine of necessity and human rights. The chapter considers the way the courts have used double effect and interpreted its precepts. The purpose of analysing this interpretation in case law is to determine whether the way in which double effect has been used could constitute an indirect application of the PGC and whether there are alternative PGC-compliant approaches that do not use double effect to which the courts could refer when dealing with difficult decisions.

Double effect and its roots in Catholicism

The principle of double effect is a tool that can be used in order to help vindicate or condemn a medical action or decision. Its primary purpose is to differentiate between actions whose devastating consequences are foreseen and those whose actions have devastating consequences that are specifically intended.

The principle of double effect is relevant to this book as a whole for a number of reasons. Double effect has a strong theological root and it is an essential principle within one of the Abrahamic religions. It is a religious principle whose use in medical law and ethics moves it from the theological domain to the practical context of law and medicine. It intersects religious belief, law, and medicine. Examining the application of the principle of double effect in law and medicine will give an insight into the weight afforded to a religious-inspired principle in this context.

The deliberate intention of an individual to carry out an action that has death-threatening consequences is often considered morally repugnant in society unless it is undertaken consensually. Foresight is a less questionable moral reality. We can foresee that actions may have tragic consequences in a somewhat nebulous, ephemeral, out-of-sight way. But if we do not intend those actions, then foresight only is permissible. This is the fairly simple dogma of the principle of double effect.

The principle of double effect, therefore, deals with the consequences of actions and whether they are foreseen or intended.[3] They have their origins in Catholic theology but are in daily use in medical/secular contexts. The Catholic theologian St Thomas Aquinas is seen to be the father of this principle. In his *Summa Theologica* the question is posed as to whether it is lawful to kill a man in self-defence and the idea of *praetor intentionem* (outside the intention) is introduced.[4] Aquinas believes that moral acts 'take their species according to what is intended and not according to what is beside the intention, since this is accidental'.[5] This is the basic essence of the principle of double effect. To explain this further, Aquinas refers to Aristotle who distinguishes between the accidental and the unintentional. The accidental action is based upon involuntary chance over which a person has no control.[6] The unintentional involves some degree of personal responsibility. The action may have derived from undue care.

3 Foster and others, 'The Double Effect Effect' (2011) 20(1) *Cambridge Quarterly of Healthcare Ethics*, 56–72, p 57.
4 Fathers of the English Dominican Province (translators), Summa *Theologica of Saint Thomas Aquinas* (Benziger Bros, 1947), Section 2 of part 2, question 64, article 7.
5 ibid. 2a2ae, q 64, a 7.
6 ibid. 2a2ae, q 64, a 8.

Aquinas' principles around double effect are summarised as the following:

1 The end or intention of the act must not be evil;[7]
2 The object of the action must not be evil;[8]
3 The circumstance of the action must be fitting.

Aquinas may have been the father of this principle, but there have been many iterations, interpretations, and variations that vary according to the emphasis that is given to criteria that are almost universally shared. Gury, for example, added a fourth dimension to Aquinas' principles. He stated that 'there must be a *proportionately serious reason* for actuating the cause, so that the author of the action would not be obliged by any virtue, e.g. from justice or charity, to omit to the action'.[9] Joseph Mangen also expands upon the criteria. His third criterion is that 'the good effect shall not be produced by means of the evil effect'.[10] This harks back to ideas of the apostle, St Paul, who condemned the notion that one could 'do evil that good may result'.[11] This stance is relevant in medical ethics because accepting this premise forbids a person from giving life-shortening medication if there is an explicit knowledge and intention that this treatment will result in the death of the patient. Mangan's fourth criterion 'that there be a proportionately grave reason for permitting the evil effect' brings a very real acknowledgement of the balancing act that is required in making moral decisions that govern good acts that have bad consequences.[12] This is a movement away from seeing things in black and white to weighting positive and negatives.

In practical terms, the principle of double effect often involves end of life contexts. Biggs explains how terminal pain is usually controlled by giving narcotic drugs but the effectiveness of the drugs decreases as the body becomes acclimatised to them.[13]According to her, controlling pain in terminal care cases presents a clinical situation where double effect can become a frequent reality.

The principle of double effect is generally accepted today as:

1 The nature of the act must be morally good.
2 The bad effect must not be a means of achieving the good effect.
3 The good effect is directly intended; the bad effect is merely foreseen and tolerated.
4 Proportionality, the reasons for performing the good action must outweigh the unintended bad consequence.[14]

7 ibid. la 2ae, q 18, a 4, ad 3.
8 Ibid. la2ae, q 18, a 2.
9 JP Gury, *Comtempendium Theologicae Moralis*, 2 vols, F Pustete 1874: 1.8 as cited from Foster and others (n 3) p 57.
10 ibid.
11 See *The Holy Bible* (OUP, 1991) Romans 3:8.
12 Foster and Others (n 3) p 58.
13 Hazel Biggs, *Euthanasia, Death with Dignity and the law* (2001, Hart) p 55.
14 Glenys Williams, 'The Principle of Double Effect and Terminal Sedation' (2001) 9(1) *Medical Law Review*, 41–53, p 45.

Double effect is based on components of both *choice* and *proportionality*.[15] Where it is subject to challenge, scrutiny, query, or attack, this challenge is normally focused on two key elements of the principle: the notion of foresight and intentionality and it is to these two concepts that attention now turns.

Foresight versus intentionality

The governing principle of double effect involves the determination of whether bad consequences are intended or merely foreseen. This might suggest that the principle of double effect is relatively simple: just don't intend to do harm, it is okay to foresee bad consequences as long as they are not intended. The reality is somewhat less simple; argument and counter-argument as to the validity and applicability of the principle of double effect abound. The main source of this disquiet lies in differing interpretations and definitions and distinctions between the key concepts of intention and foresight.[16] Those who criticise the principle of double effect say that the distinction between intention and foresight cannot be maintained.

Proportionality also has to come into play when measuring foresight versus intention. The principle only applies to situations to where there has been a bad effect, usually where somebody dies. If the doctor gives a person the lethal injection in the full knowledge that a person will die then the principle does not apply; there is no weighing up of good versus bad; no weighting of positives versus negatives; there is just an action and a consequence. Can it be argued that the principle of double effect gives an easy way out for medical practitioners? Does it give them an unacknowledged, unvoiced permission to kill? Should the doctor who intends to kill out of concern for a suffering patient and doesn't prevaricate about it be condemned ahead of the doctor whose actions produce the same result but whose motivations—acknowledged and stated and described—are more pearly white and not subject to chastisement and punishment?

The sanctity of life and its connection to double effect

Sanctity of life has often been recognised in the common law. Pattinson points to the fact that sanctity of life has a different meaning to different people and that it must be used with caution.[17] Our understanding of sanctity of life may differ somewhat from the actual intent of sanctity of life.

Sanctity of life is connected to the view that human life has intrinsic and special value and that life is sacred. This fundamental worth is something that should be enjoyed by everyone, regardless of ability or disability. Keown describes it as 'a fundamental constituent of human flourishing'[18] and contends that under the

15 ibid.
16 Shaun D Pattinson, *Medical Law and Ethics* (5th ed, Sweet and Maxwell, 2017) p 19.
17 ibid. p 18.
18 John Keown, *The Law of Ethics and Medicine: Essays on the Inviolability of Human Life* (OUP, 2012) p 6.

sanctity of life principle 'there can be no moral obligation to administer or undergo a treatment which is not worthwhile'.[19] Adopting a sanctity of life position means that it is never permissible to intentionally kill an innocent person. However, life does not need to be protected at all costs.[20] Sanctity of life is a view held and shared, albeit in differing ways, by the main Abrahamic religions. Islam holds that human life starts from conception and will only end in natural death.[21] Judaism holds a sanctity of life perspective and affirms the need to protect life, although it does not recognise a foetus as being human.[22] Catholicism holds a strict sanctity of life view. The Church of England and Protestant denominations of Christianity adopt slightly less rigid views of sanctity of life. While respecting the sanctity of life position, these denominations believe that this position needs to be balanced by the commandment to 'love thy neighbour'. For example, abortion may sometimes be seen as the lesser of two evils.

It is the opinion of Keown that the principle should be referred to as 'inviolability of life' instead of 'sanctity of life' because the original term 'may have distracting theological connotations'.[23] However, the word 'inviolability' has, itself, a strong theological root. The specific Catholic basis for this concept of inviolability is to be found in *Evangelium Vitae*.[24] Pope John Paul II, using the story of Cain and Abel, as a parable to outline the impermissibility of killing, stresses '[t]'he sacredness of life gives rise to its inviolability, written from the beginning in man's heart, in his conscience.[25] The commandment 'You shall not kill'[26] is seen to reflect this inviolability.[27] The importance of the sacredness of life/inviolability is further delineated in *Donum Vitae*:

> Human life is sacred because from its beginning it involves from the creative action of God, and it remains forever in a special relationship with the Creator, who is its sole end. God alone is the Lord of life from its beginning until its end: no one can, in any circumstance, claim for himself the right to destroy directly an innocent human being.[28]

19 John Keown, 'Restoring Moral and Intellectual Shape to the Law after Bland' (1997) 113 *Law Quarterly Review*, 282–503, p 482.
20 ibid. p 485.
21 Majid Katme, 'The Sanctity of Human Life is a Basic Concept in Islam' (Society for the Protection of the Unborn Child), available at: https://www.spuc.org.uk/about/muslim-division/euthanasia (accessed 27 January 2017).
22 Fred Rosner, 'The Beginning of Life in Judaism', available at: http://www.myjewishlearning.com/beliefs/Issues/Bioethics/Abortion/Fetus_in_Jewish_Law/Beginning_of_Life.shtml?BFIS (accessed 27 January 2017).
23 Keown, *The Law of Ethics and Medicine: Essays on the Inviolability of Human Life* (n 18) p 3.
24 Pope John Paul II, *Evangelium Vite*, 25 March 1997, available at: http://www.vatican.va/holy_father/john_paul_ii/encyclicals/documents/hf_jp-ii_enc_25031995_evangelium-vitae_en.html (accessed 27 January 2017).
25 ibid. para 40.
26 Ex 20:13.
27 *Evangelium Vite,* para 1.
28 Congregation for the Doctrine of the Faith, Instruction on Respect for Human Life in its Origin and on the Dignity of Procreation *Donum Vitae* (22 February 1987), Introduction, No. 5: *AAS* 80 (1988), 76–77; cf. *Catechism of the Catholic Church,* No. 2258.

The application of sanctity of life is evident in the European Convention on Human Rights (ECHR) and is allied to the concept of human dignity in English law. It was recognised in *Airedale NHS Trust v Bland*[29] where Sir Thomas Bingham said that '[a] profound respect for the sanctity of human life is embedded in our law and our moral philosophy, as it is in that of most civilised societies in the East and the West. That is why murder (next only to treason) has always been treated here as the most grave and heinous of crimes'.[30] This opinion was repeated by Lord Goff who recognised the importance of the principle in both society and in Article 2 ECHR.[31]

Sanctity of life relies upon the principle of double effect and its distinction between foresight and intention.[32] According to Keown, the sanctity of life view adopts the principle of double effect in order to deal with the distinction between foresight and intention. Keown regards sanctity of life as a 'right to life' and it is a principle that he believes concerns believers and non-believers in God.[33] He does not adopt a vitalistic perspective. This is, according to Keown, the principle that '[h]uman life is the supreme good and one should do everything possible to preserve it'.[34] He sees sanctity of life as rooted in the dignity that is afforded to all humanity by virtue of their existence.[35] He calls into question subjective arguments that can be made to determine 'best interests' of people.[36] Keown's discussion of sacredness of life and its link to double effect reflects some of this Catholic-inspired reasoning. He claims that '[t]he doctrine or principle of IOL [inviolability of life] were originally formulated by theologians, but can stand on purely philosophical grounds'. Double effect is related to sanctity of life because the position that preserves the sacredness of life gives a theological basis to the duty not to intentionally kill. There is always going to be some sort of value judgement in this process because people will come to these decisions with differing perspectives on life, ranging from giving some value, limited value, or no value to life in different stages of genesis as in the case of, for example, the foetus.[37]

The practical application of sanctity of life can be seen in hospital contexts where decisions about the quality of treatment given to patients at varying stages of sometimes debilitating illness have to be made. Keown suggests that 'the sanctity principle holds that there can be no moral obligation to administer or undergo a treatment which is not worthwhile'.[38] In other words, there is no moral obligation to provide treatment when 'the benefit is outweighed by its burdens'.[39]

29 *Airedale NHS Trust v Bland* [1993] AC 789.
30 ibid. p 14.
31 *Bland* (n 29) 863–864.
32 See Pattinson, *Medical Law and Ethics* (n 16) pp 18–19.
33 Keown, The Law of Ethics and Medicine: Essays on the Inviolability of Human Life (n 18) p 4.
34 ibid.
35 ibid. p 18.
36 ibid.
37 ibid. chapter 3. Keown states that dignity is a 'core value of English law', in a similar way to sanctity/inviolability of life chapter 3.
38 Keown, 'Restoring Moral and Intellectual Shape to the Law after Bland' (n 19) p 482.
39 Pattinson, *Medical Law and Ethics* (n 16) p 19.

Pattinson suggests, however, that different judgements can be made as to whether the benefits of treatment are proportionate to the related burdens. Such different judgements could potentially produce dissention between those who favour treatment and those who reject it.[40]

Question 1: How have English law and the ECtHR dealt with the issue?

The position of double effect in the current law is uncertain. However, Lord Goff, in *obiter*, has stated in the House of Lords case of *Bland*:

> The established rule that a doctor may, when caring for a patient who is, for example, dying of cancer, lawfully administer painkilling drugs despite the fact that he knows that an incidental effect of that application will be to abbreviate the patient's life.[41]

This statement shows judicial recognition of double effect, albeit in *obiter*, at the highest court of the land. This chapter considers whether this recognition is outdated and is not fully in line with the relevant case of *R v Woollin*[42] or with the suggested framework.

The current legal approach is unclear, but evidence exists that the courts have relied upon the religiously inspired principle of double effect. In order to answer question 1, the chapter will now examine how this double effect principle and the related sanctity of life rationale underpinning this precept has (or has not) been adopted in English law in situations concerning palliative care. This section of the application will then consider the position under human rights law (including an analysis of the ECHR/ECtHR) to palliative care and how this impacts upon the current legal stance in English law.

Due to the historical presence of religion in England and the fact that the Sovereign was/is Defender of the Faith, there is no doubt that religion has always had, and to a lesser degree continues to have a part to play in legal positioning in this context. Evidence of this is to be found in the statement made by Brook LJ in *Re A (Conjoned Twins)*[43] where he said the following in relation to the Archbishop of Westminster's submission in the case:

> There can, of course, be no doubt that our common law judges were steeped in the Judaeo-Christian tradition and in the moral principles identified by the Archbishop when they were developing our criminal law over the centuries up to the time when Parliament took over the task. There can also be no doubt that it was these principles, shared as they were by the other founder members

40 ibid.
41 *Bland* (n 29) at [876]. Also see Lord Donaldson in *Re J* [1991] 1 Fam 33 at [46].
42 *R v Woollin* [1999] AC 821.
43 *Re A (Conjoined Twins)* [2001] 2 WLR 480.

> of the Council of Europe 50 years ago, which underlay the formulation of Article 2 of the European Convention on Human Rights.[44]

Article 2 ECHR is the 'right to life' where '[e]veryone's right to life shall be protected by law. No one shall be deprived of his life intentionally save in the execution of a sentence of a court following his conviction of a crime for which this penalty is provided by law'.[45] This Article of the Convention gives value to life, but does not adhere to a strict sanctity of life position: it is not a general right to life but one aimed at State. Following *Vo v France*[46] individual member states were allowed to adopt a margin of appreciation in respect of decisions around the legal status of the foetus.[47] The Article has been used to defend both the rights of the mother and the rights of the unborn. It is impossible to agree explicitly with the idea that the drafters of the Article were influenced by their religious perspectives. However, the prevailing principles of Abrahamic religions, in particular, are certainly implicit within this Article

It is necessary to briefly consider how case law has considered arguments that have presented themselves in relation to a potential right to die and how much of the responses made by the Court represent adherence to a sanctity of life position. In this context, the case of *Pretty v UK* is relevant. In this case, an applicant wanted to be assisted in committing suicide. However, under English law, the person assisting in suicide could be prosecuted. It was held by the ECtHR that Article 2 ECHR could not 'without distortion of language, be interpreted as conferring the diametrically opposite right, namely a right to die; nor can it create a right to self-determination in the sense of conferring on an individual the entitlement to choose death rather than life'.[48] Prior to reaching the ECtHR, the House of Lords rejected Mrs Pretty's arguments. In affirming a sanctity of life position, Lord Bingham said that:

> Whatever the benefits which, in the view of many, attach to voluntary euthanasia, suicide, physician-assisted suicide and suicide assisted without the intervention of a physician, these are not benefits which derive protection from an article framed to protect the sanctity of life.[49]

To expand further upon his reasoning, he referred to Hoffmann LJ's expression in *Bland* that '[s]ubject to exceptions like self-defence, human life is inviolate even if the person in question has consented to its violation'. In a similar manner, Lord Wilson at the Supreme Court in *Nicklinson* also adopted a firm sanctity of life position, stating that 'sanctity (or, for those for whom that word has no meaning, the supreme value) of life… lies at the heart of the common law and of international human rights and it

44 ibid. (Brook LJ).
45 European Convention on Human Rights, Article 2.
46 *Vo v France* (2005) 40 EHRR 12.
47 ibid. at [82].
48 *Pretty v United Kingdom* (2002) 35 EHRR 1 at [29].
49 *The Queen on the Application of Diane Pretty* v DPP [2001] UKHL 61 at [6].

is also an ethical principle of the first magnitude'.[50] In *Nicklinson*, Lord Sumption, however, deliberated upon the idea that adopting a sanctity of life perspective was not necessarily fully in keeping with the protection of the dignity and autonomy of individuals 'in a case where the individual, being of sound mind and full capacity, has taken a rational decision to kill himself'.[51] According to the ECtHR, these principles of human dignity and autonomy are core tenets of the Convention.[52]

However, the judgments in right to die cases, by and large, did not err on siding with autonomy or dignity approaches. In summary, these determinations confirm that a right to die does not exist in English law or, indeed, under the ECHR. While these judgments do not reflect overly an acceptance of double effect or recognise its authority, they, nonetheless, broadly take a perspective that mirrors aspects of sanctity of life. The lack of extensive exploration of Convention rights in palliative care cases in the particular contexts of Articles 2 and 9 is problematic.

Double effect in the courts

At times, decisions about medical treatment are not just made between doctor and patient and patient's family. At times they are played out in the courts. *How* has the principle of double effect been used in the courts and *should* this principle, founded in what is a partisan religious belief, not shared universally, be used in the judicial process?

R v Adams and double effect

R v Adams[53] is regarded as the case where the principle of double effect was introduced to the law of England in Devlin J's direction to the jury. In this case Dr Bodkin Adams had given a lethal dose of painkillers to a patient who was terminally ill but was acquitted of murder. Dr Bodkin Adams said about his actions: 'Easing the passing of a dying person is not all that wicked. She wanted to die. That can't be murder. It is impossible to accuse a doctor.'[54] Under section 1 (1) of the Murder (Abolition of the Death Penalty) Act 1965 someone who is convicted of murder must receive a life sentence. This is mandatory! Note that, however, the Law Commission has suggested the introduction of new degrees of intentional killing in a recent report.[55] Under the Law Commission's recommendations, it has been suggested that first degree murder would encompass

50 *R (on the application of Nicklinson and another) v Ministry of Justice* [2014] UKSC 38 at [199].
51 ibid. at [209].
52 See *Pretty* (n 48) at [65].
53 *R v Adams* [1957] Crim LR 365.
54 27 March 1957, *The Times.*
55 Law Commission, *Murder Manslaughter and Infanticide*, (Law Com No 304, 2006) available at: https://www.gov.uk/government/uploads/system/uploads/attachment_data/file/228782/0030.pdf (accessed 27 January 2017).

intentional killing or 'killing through an intention to do serious injury with an awareness of a serious risk of causing death'[56] and that second degree murder would include:

> (1) killing through an intention to do serious injury (even without an awareness of a serious risk of causing death); or (2) killing where there was an awareness of a serious risk of causing death, coupled with an intention to cause either: (a) some injury; (b) a fear of injury; or (c) a risk of injury.[57]

This new definition of second degree murder includes specific mention of 'intention' and, as a consequence, is somewhat reflective of some of the facets of double effect.

Reverting to the case, Devlin J brought the principle of double effect into play implicitly, rather than explicitly in his summing-up statement:

> If the first purpose of medicine, the restoration of health, can no longer be achieved there is still much for a doctor to do, and he is entitled to do all that is proper and necessary to relieve pain and suffering, even if the measures he takes may incidentally shorten human life.[58]

This statement by Devlin J supports double effect in allowing for a good consequence to override the bad consequence. In his statement Devlin J does not, however, make explicit reference to the principle itself. This principle is, nevertheless, present in the unwritten words. His direction provides evidence of its application. It is acceptable for Devlin J that doctors might foresee the incidental shortening of human life by the pain-relieving measures that they take, but these measures do not have the intention of causing death. Devlin J's failure, however, to explicitly refer to the principle of double effect brought about some unnecessary ambiguity that does not help overcome the legitimacy of about double effect. It is probable that if he had given more direct reference to double effect and to the underlying principle of foresight versus intention, his direction would have been clearer and less subject to query.

Patrick Devlin, unusually, wrote a book based on the *R v Adams*[59] case entitled *Easing the Passing the Trial of Dr Bodkin Adams.*[60] This gives an insight into Devlin J's approach to this fascinating case. According to Devlin's interpretation of the law, he argues that murder involves the cutting short of someone's life, whether this is by a long or short period. He says that 'it does not matter that Mrs Morrell's days were numbered'.[61] However, he also states:

56 ibid. 1.35.
57 ibid. 1.36.
58 *R v Adams* (n 53).
59 ibid.
60 Patrick Devlin, *Easing the Passing: The Trial of Dr John Bodkin Adams* (The Bodley Head, 1985).
61 ibid. p 171.

> [T]he proper medical treatment that is administered and that has an incidental effect on determining the exact moment of death is not the cause of death in any sensible use of them. But... no doctor, nor any man, no more in the case of the dying than of the healthy, has the right deliberately to cut the thread of life.[62]

This supports the principle of double effect. It shows that if a doctor intended to kill the patient, instead of merely foreseeing a possible death, he or she would be guilty of murder.

Devlin was a committed Catholic and believed that 'abortion and euthanasia are similar crimes'.[63] Following his Catholic reasoning, it is apparent that he places a great deal of value on the sanctity of life and implicitly agrees with the concept of double effect. From the moral perspective of double effect, the nature of Dr Adam's act was morally good, Dr Adams did not benefit to a discernible degree from the actions taken, the wish to save the suffering of the patient was intended but her eventual death may have been foreseen, but was not explicitly intended. The patient was suffering significantly, and his actions were proportionate to the need to alleviate this pain. Thus, the overt evidence points to specific use and reliance of each aspect of the principle of double effect. It must be noted also, however, some worrying aspects to this case exist which might point to less laudable intentions, but these are not sustained within the case. In essence, this case confirms that double effect was used: the specific principles, as originally outlined by Aquinas and as adapted subsequently, are to be seen.

R v Cox and double effect

Other cases demonstrate tangentially the applicability of double effect. *R v Cox*[64] is a case involving a doctor who administered two ampoules of potassium chloride to a patient who suffered from rheumatoid arthritis and was subsequently dying. This injection of potassium chloride led to the patient's death. Consequently, the doctor was indicted on a charge of attempted murder.[65] During the case, it was put forward by the prosecution that his administration of the drug was intended to cause of the death of the patient. However, defence counsel contended that the doctor's sole aim was to reduce the pain suffered by the patient and that his intention was not to kill her. The jury convicted Dr Cox of attempted murder. The jury had no alternative but to convict Dr Cox of attempted murder due to the fact that he satisfied both the *mens rea* and the *actus reus* of attempted murder. This is in spite of the fact that his actions were regarded by the patient's family as merciful due to the fact that he allowed an elderly woman to pain to die mercifully and with dignity.[66] Therefore, *R v Cox*[67] highlights that the deliberate

62 ibid. pp 191–192.
63 ibid. p 200.
64 *R v Cox* (1992) 12 BMLR 38.
65 ibid.
66 Biggs, *Euthanasia, Death with Dignity and the law* (n 13) p 27.
67 *R v Cox* (n 64).

killing of another is a crime in English law even if for a so-called greater good. Dr Cox was charged with and found guilty of attempted murder. However, he was only given a 12-month suspended sentence. As well as this, at the GMC disciplinary hearing he was allowed to continue to practise as a physician and only had to attend a number of training courses and supervision.[68] Does this mean that it is impossible to punish a medical professional in such circumstances?

Ognall J says that deliberately taking someone's life is the same for a doctor as for any other person under the law:

> Their [doctors] role is to improve or to sustain the quality of human life, and, in certain circumstances, by the alleviation of suffering, they may ease the passing from our mortal existence by making it as pain-free as practicable. But more than that, they may not, and the must not, do.[69]

Following Ognall J's remarks, it is not surprising that Dr Cox was found guilty. Wells has suggested that if the doctor had administered another drug that would merely relieve pain instead of certainly causing death, he would have been able to use double effect as a shield.[70] The principle of double effect can really only have relevance where certainty of death does not apply. Biggs notes that the use of a pain-relieving drug by Dr Cox would have supported Devlin J's claim. However, his main aim was to kill the patient, even though his reasons were commendable.[71] She argues that the cases of *R v Adams*[72] and *R v Cox*[73] provide evidence that purposefully shortening another's life, even by a medical professional, is a crime. She regards them as 'testimony to the hesitancy of juries to disregard the compelling motives of the individuals concerned, unless the evidence is incontrovertible'.[74]

R v Woollin and the Lord Steyn's ignoring of double effect

In the House of Lords case of *R v Woollin*[75] Lord Steyn, in the leading judgment, makes absolutely no reference to the principle of double effect. Therefore, it could be argued that double effect is no longer relevant in courts of law. In this case the appellant caused the death of his son by throwing the baby against a hard surface when he lost his temper. The judge made the direction to the jury that no

68 Hazel Biggs, 'Decisions and Responsibilities at the End of Life: Euthanasia and Clinically Assisted Death' (1996) 2(3) *Medical Law International*, 229–245, p 243.
69 ibid.
70 Celia Wells, 'Patients, Consent and Criminal Law' (1994) 1 *Journal of Social Welfare and Family Law*, 65–78, p 73.
71 Biggs, *Euthanasia, Death with Dignity and the law* (n 13) p 28.
72 *R v Adams* (n 53).
73 *R v Cox* (n 64).
74 Hazel Biggs, 'Euthanasia and death with dignity: still poised on the fulcrum of homicide' (1996) Dec *Criminal Law Review*, 878–888, p 881.
75 *R v Woollin* (n 42).

inference could be made that he had the intention of severely harming the child unless they were certain that the severe harm had been a practical certainty from his actions and that he knew this to be the case. At trial and at the Court of Appeal the appellant was convicted of murder. At the House of Lords, nevertheless, Mr Woolin's appeal was granted and his conviction of murder was quashed and changed to manslaughter. At this case the Court identified that '[t]he mental element of murder is concerned with the subjective question of what was in the mind of the man accused of murder'.[76]

In *Woollin*, Lord Steyn relied upon the judgment of Lord Lane in *R v Nedrick*.[77] Lord Steyn contended that Lord Lane's judgment in *Nedrick*[78] has given a great deal of assistance to trial judges. Lord Lane said that two questions should be asked by the trial judge when making a decision about the defendant's intention:

1 How probable was the consequence that resulted from the defendant's voluntary act?
2 Did he foresee that consequence?[79]

Lord Lane said that if the person did not foresee his actions causing grievous bodily harm or death, then no intention existed, and he felt that if there were a slight risk that the action could kill the person then he did not have intention. However, if the defendant were 'virtually certain' that the action would cause death, then intention exists.[80] Lord Steyn argues that the trial judge was incorrect not to have relied upon *Nedrick*.[81] Therefore, the murder conviction was quashed and replaced with manslaughter.

The manner in which Lord Steyn delineated the conditions of murder clashes with the principle of double effect.[82] He said, in relation to Lord Lane's statement in *R v Nedrick*, that members of the jury who are agreed that:

> ...the defendant recognised that death or serious harm would be virtually certain (barring some unforeseen intervention) to result from his voluntary act ... may find it easy to infer that he intended to kill or do serious bodily harm, even though he may not have had any desire to achieve that result.[83]

Arising from this view, if a voluntary act results in intended, but unwanted death, then juries may infer that this death was intended. There is no direction given by Lord Steyn as to the difference between foresight and intention. Intention and

76 ibid. at [101] (Lord Steyn).
77 *R v Nedrick* [1986] 1 WLR 1025.
78 ibid.
79 *R v Nedrick* (n 77) (Lord Lane) at 1028.
80 ibid. at 1028.
81 *R v Nedrick* (n 77). See p 96 C.
82 *R v Woollin* (n 42).
83 ibid. [96], citing *R v Nedrick* (n 77) (Lord Lane) at 1028.

resultant death are the only factors taken into consideration here. The fact that the principle was not invoked in this case is highly significant. It could sound somewhat of a death knell for the principle. This is in line with the general shift away from the use of the double effect in legal judgment making.

Keown, however, calls for the principle of double effect to be retained in the courts. He is very critical of Lord Steyn and *Woollin*[84] and claims that the case should be overruled. He regards it as a 'retrograde step' for a number of reasons.[85] Keown argues that the result in *Woollin*[86] makes the suggestion that medical professions who carry out proper palliative care have the intention of killing the patient. He says that this is a 'gross misrepresentation of their state of mind'.[87] He states that:

> Had their Lordships in *Woollin* turned their minds to the situation of life-shortening palliative care, and the cases of Adams, Cox and Moor, they would surely have been alerted to the damage of confusing intention with foresight of virtual certainty.[88]

Keown also argues that the case brought to light some doubts about whether or not proper palliative care was necessary. He feels that doctors ought to be able to carry out their jobs without fear of being prosecuted and shouldn't have to rely on defences such as necessity.[89] Another criticism of the case made by Keown is that it may have a 'chilling effect on the provisions of much-needed palliative care and leave patients dying in pain and distress.'[90] He contends that the argument concerning foresight and intention was not even addressed by Lord Steyn. Therefore, he argues that the case's authority is undermined. This may be an overreaction because that judgment does not reflect the totality of usage of the double effect principle in the courts. *Woollin*[91] has not been challenged even though the judgment was made as far back as 1999. Pattinson suggests that, arising from this, the likelihood of the case being overturned at the Supreme Court is minimal.[92]

The case of *Bland* provides an additional example of the surreptitious interpretation and use of double effect in so far as it found in this case that the removal of a gastro tube from a dying patient lacked foresight and intention.[93] *Bland* has been criticised by sanctity of life supporters due to the fact that Mr Bland was still a human being and that the House of Lords accepted that, by withdrawing the

84 *R v Woollin* (n 42).
85 John Keown, *Euthanasia, Ethics and Public Policy: An Argument Against Legislation*, (CUP, 2002) p 28.
86 *R v Woollin* (n 42).
87 Keown, *Euthanasia, Ethics and Public Policy: An Argument against Legislation* (n 85) p 28.
88 ibid.
89 ibid.
90 ibid. p 29.
91 ibid.
92 Pattinson, *Medical Law and Ethics* (n 16) p 491.
93 *Bland* (n 29).

treatment, the medical professionals intended to kill Mr Bland. As such, sanctity of life was breached.[94] Keown is critical of *Bland* on the basis that their Lordships held that 'it is lawful to withdraw tube-feeding from a patient in a "persistent vegetative state" (pvs), even with intent to kill him.'[95] The crucial aspect to this, according to Foster, was that the tube was removed by medical personnel rather than by a lay person and so there was no *mens rea* for murder.[96] Pattinson interprets *Bland* differently: the difference is that a lay person would perform an 'act', rather than the 'omission' of the doctor. This is *actus reus*, rather than *mens rea*.[97]

Foster also alleges that the judgment found in favour of medical policy rather than any agreed principle. *Bland* didn't provide any judgment of substance on the use of double effect and, indeed, the use of the Mental Capacity Act 2005 would have constituted a more intuitive and measured legal instrument had it been able to be invoked at the time of *Bland*.[98] The English courts have said in *Bland* that the approach in this case is compatible with Article 2 ECHR: essentially 'intentionally' is interpreted in a narrow way, giving rise to a need to consider aspects of double effect. Without a narrow interpretation of the word 'intentionally' in relation to the ECHR, then the scope of Article 2 is potentially very wide. Evidence to this effect is the fact that English law hasn't fully resolved the dispute between *Adams* and *Woollin* and the ECtHR doesn't appear to directly address this point. What the English courts have done with regard to *Bland* is they said that this is compatible with Article 2 ECHR, essentially because we need to interpret 'intentionally' in a narrow way. That narrow interpretation imports some aspects of double effect. If the word 'intentionally' is not interpreted narrowly in the ECHR, then Article 2's ambit is potentially very wide indeed.

The use of defence of necessity in the courts instead of reliance on the principle of double effect

In the context of palliative care, the law on murder states what is or is not permissible. The administration of pain relief by a doctor does not constitute murder. This would mean that the doctor is guilty of murder if a patient's life is shortened. Under the current law, it is possible for the principle of double effect to be relied upon to determine that the doctor has not committed murder. Pattinson argues that an alternative and better approach would be the doctrine of necessity.[99] The defence of necessity is a mechanism that can be used to defend action that is taken that is necessary to prevent another more serious harm taking place. This action is

94 ibid.
95 John Keown, 'Beyond *Bland:* A Critique of the BMA Guidance on withholding and withdrawing medical treatment' (2000) 20(1) *Legal Studies*, 66–84, p 66.
96 Charles Foster, 'Airedale NHS Trust v Bland' in Jonathan Herring and Jesse Wall (eds), *Landmark Cases in Medical Law* (2015, Hart) pp 96–97.
97 Shaun D Pattinson, *Revisiting Landmark Cases in Medical Law* (Routledge, 2018) p 109.
98 For a fuller discussion of the MCA, see chapter 4.
99 Pattinson, *Revisiting Landmark Cases in Medical Law* (n 97) pp 34–35.

necessary because the law is prohibiting something that should not be prohibited: defence of necessity provides a mechanism for preventing what would otherwise be a crime.

In the case of *Re A (Conjoined twins)*[100] the defence of necessity was used instead of relying on double effect. *Re A* concerned conjoined twins, Mary and Jodie. It was the opinion of the medical professionals that, unless they were separated before their first birthday, both babies would die. However, in carrying out the operation it meant that the weaker child, Mary, would definitely die. One of the reasons why this case was so contentious was because the issue arose whether carrying out the operation without the parents' permission could be regarded as murder. In order for someone to be guilty of murder he or she must have caused the victim's death and have intended to kill or injure the victim. The Court of Appeal was mainly concerned with whether the surgeon would be guilty of murder if he carried out the operation and, if he did carry out the operation, whether the defence of necessity would apply.[101] They considered if it should be extended to this type of situation where the doctor could be regarded as acting for the greater good. It was claimed by the doctors that the operation would be in the best interest of both Jodie and Mary.

The children's parents said that the operation was not in the best interests of Mary and that the High Court judge was incorrect in holding that the operation was in Jodie's best interest and was legal.[102] At the Court of Appeal an argument was submitted that the principle of double effect justified the doctors carrying out the operation and removed the essential *mens rea* element of murder. The argument was made that the 'primary purpose' of the doctors was to save the life of Jodie and that Mary's hastened death would not give good reason for a charge of murder. Nevertheless, the Court's majority did not agree that the principle would apply to the given facts because, even though the doctors would have the 'murderous intent' in carrying out the operation, they would not be guilty of murder under the doctrine of necessity. It was held that the operation could lawfully be undertaken and the appeal was dismissed because of the defence of necessity (and not double effect). However, the *Nickinson* (Court of Appeal) case has put a halt to the extension of the necessity defence.[103] It was argued by Nicklinson that the defence could be used 'to fashion means of permitting doctors to act in a way which accords with the demands of humanity'.[104] The Court of Appeal held that necessity should not be extended to *Nicklinson*-type situations. The Court said that an extension of the defence to include the necessity for patients to make clear and informed decisions at the end of their lives, when they are terminally ill, would not be allowed.[105] The Court also claimed that 'it is simply not appropriate for the

100 *Re A (Conjoined Twins)* (n 43).
101 Sally Sheldon and Stephen Wilkinson, '"On the Sharpest Horns of Dilemma" Re A (Conjoined Twins)' 9 (3) *Medical Law Review*, 201–207, p 203.
102 ibid.
103 *R (Nicklinson) v Ministry of Justice* [2012] EWHC 2381; [2013] EWCA Civ 961.
104 ibid. at [63].
105 ibid.

court to fashion a defence of necessity in such a complex and controversial field; this is a matter for Parliament'.[106] The findings from these cases suggest that there is ambiguity and lack of consistency in the way that the courts apply both double effect and the defence of necessity. While necessity is the better of the two options, the lack of principled basis for its use means that, in practice, it would be difficult to use in a consistent manner.

Summary of existing stance

Double effect is a principle whose use is both confined to palliative care and is covert rather than overt. This is problematic in so far as a legitimate legal principle ought to be generalisable to broader contexts. It cannot, consequently, have substantive justification. The courts need to use principles that can be apparently consistently and objectively applied in all contexts of medical law. That consistency of application does not apply to double effect and, so, the principle of double effect should not be used as a principle in English medical law.

This examination of current law has led to the following conclusions:

1 There is a lack of consistency and clarity in the law. This lack of certainty applies to whether double effect, the defence or necessity or the approach adopted by Lord Steyn in *R v Woollin* is the correct one.
2 The sanctity of life principle, that underpins double effect, is evident as a historical and prevalent working principle, albeit functioning in a covert manner.
3 The approach taken in relation to the ECHR, where there has only been a limited exploration of relevant Convention rights, in the context of Article 2, is problematic.

Question 2: Why is this sufficient or insufficient in the context of the PGC?

The chapter has set out what has happened in the courts to date in respect of cases where the principle of double effect was a visible or, indeed, invisible ingredient in the deliberations. It is now timely to consider the degree to which these judgments and the overall approach adopted towards double effect is compliant with the PGC.

It is proposed that double effect is not sufficient in the context of the PGC. As indicated in question 1, double effect adopts a sanctity of life position and it is now argued that the PGC does not accept this principle. According to the PGC, the doctor who acts to shorten life with the patient's consent does not act immorally because the patient has waived the benefits of his generic rights.[107] They can waive the benefits to the right to life. This is contrary to the principle of

106 ibid. at [56].
107 Pattinson, *Revisiting Landmark Cases in Medical Law* (n 97) p 42.

sanctity of life and, consequently, double effect. Pattinson elucidates how a doctor who shortens the life of a patient who properly consents is not acting immorally. An agent has freely chosen purposes. He has a choice between pursuing or not pursuing a particular purpose.[108] Will-rights concern patients who are still apparently agents while 'interest rights' involve patients who are not apparent agents. Under the PGC, a being who appears to be a partial agent has interest-rights.[109] The mentally incompetent patient has interest-rights and they are protected under the PGC.[110] Double effect doesn't really assign any rights to people who lack legal capacity or mental competence.[111] Even for a patient who lacks legal capacity, the PGC calls for the doctor to act consistently with the patient's rights—their will- or interest-rights. All patients, with legal capacity or otherwise, have a basic right to pain relief. Very serious pain can obstruct the ability of a mentally incompetent patient to act for any purpose at all. As a consequence, assistance will be needed by the patient to meet the basic generic need.[112] When the doctor acts to give the patient relief from pain, this is not inconsistent with acting in accordance with the patient's rights and accords with the PGC.[113] Double effect does not act demonstrably for the patient and it is not an advocate for patient rights, those with legal capacity or not, and is not, therefore, in keeping with the PGC.

More importance is given to the concept of agency under the PGC than under double effect. An agent is autonomous and, according to the PGC, can justifiably make a decision that contravenes the sanctity of life principle. For example, it is acceptable for an agent to commit suicide. Sanctity of life and double effect prohibit intentional killing. However, according to Pattinson '[c]ontrary to the SoL, intentionally taking one's own life only violates the PGC where it thereby violates the generic rights of others, such as where the suicidal person is piloting a passenger plane or wishes to jump in front of a train'.[114] The PGC accepts as legitimate the call of the terminally ill patient for the right to enact his suicidal purpose in circumstances where this desire has been clearly outlined to the treating doctor. In working for the patient and in line with the PGC, a doctor can make medical decisions that shorten life: if she considers that there is a choice between a longer, more painful life and a shorter less painful one, then the doctor can act for the patient. This arises from the fact that the benefits to life are waivable and that relief from pain is a basic right. Double effect does not allow for the doctor to knowingly administer treatment that will hasten death even if it is at the cost of the patient experiencing debilitating pain. Thus, the two are incompatible.[115] Allowing the patient to put limits on extreme suffering is wholly defensible under the PGC due to the fact that the doctor's conduct involves enabling action that may include life-shortening treatments that include intentional

108 ibid.
109 ibid. p 43.
110 ibid.
111 Refer to chapter 4 for definitions of these terms.
112 Pattinson, *Revisiting Landmark Cases in Medical Law* (n 97) p 43.
113 ibid.
114 ibid. p 42.
115 ibid.

lethal conduct. It falls within our understanding of the PGC that a doctor can, thus, participate in the patient's suicidal purpose.[116]

In a way, the application of the PGC takes away the comfort blanket of the double effect principle. The doctor cannot hide behind the linguistic nuances of whether the patient's death was foreseen or intended. Under the PGC, the doctor is cognisant of the suicidal purpose of the patient and arguably complicit in the enaction of that purpose, but there is no artifice here because, as Fenwick shows, the doctor has no legitimate role in providing medication for life-shortening treatment that really does not exist.[117] Perhaps, there is an honesty in the PGC. It does not allow the patient's autonomy or agency or rational decision to be diminished by the comfort of sanctity of life or by the application of the double effect principle. Beyleveld points out, however, that although agents have a PGC-supported right to be assisted to commit suicide under a generic right to freedom of action (autonomy), this right is subject to other conditions and related limits:

> ...because the exercise of this right is subject to it not conflicting with at least equally important rights of others, agents do not have a duty to assist those wishing to be assisted in committing suicide if they do not wish to do so under their own right to freedom of action. In practice, if not in concept, this entails that there is no positive right to such assistance in this case. Any effective positive right to be assisted to commit suicide needs to be rooted in a substantive right, such as the right not to be subjected to inhuman or degrading treatment or torture, which is recognised by Article 3 of the European Convention on Human Rights.[118]

How compliant with the PGC are the approaches that have been adopted in English law in cases dealing with palliative care? Initially, let us examine how sufficiently the direction given to the jury by Devlin J in *R v Adams* complies with the PGC. Devlin J's use of the principle of double effect cannot be supported by the PGC. The central reason for this relates to the reliance on the principle of sanctity of life, which is inconsistent with the PGC. Under the PGC, a mentally competent patient (agent) can waive the benefits to his generic rights. This may include his right to life. Therefore, it is clear that reliance on sanctity of life is contrary to the patient's will-rights and that reliance on this principle by Devlin J was inappropriate. *R v Cox* is not dissimilar to *R v Adams* in relation to the use of double effect as a working principle in English law. Ognall J's focus on intention and foresight was inappropriate. Significant focus should have been given to the patient's will-rights: this was not the case here and the patient in *R v Cox* should have been able to waive the benefit to his own life.

116 See Daniel Fenwick, *A Gewirthian Conception of the Right to Enabled Suicide in England and Wales* (unpublished) PhD thesis (Durham University, 2015).

117 ibid.

118 Deryck Beyleveld, 'The Principle of Generic Consistency as a Supreme Moral Principle' (2011) 13(1) *Human Rights Review*, 1–18, pp 14–15.

In the context of cases where double effect was not relied upon, were the approaches adopted suitable indirect applications of the PGC? To revert to *Re A*, where the defence of necessity was relied upon, instead of double effect, while the conclusion of the court in relation to the adoption of the doctrine of necessity reflects the grave nature of both the suffering that applies to terminal illness and the gravity of the decisions that are made in respect of the dying process, it could be argued that insufficient weight is given in the judgment to the agency of the patient and his ability to exercise his will-rights, including the right to waive the benefit of his rights, as enshrined under the PGC. This failure to sufficiently recognise a patient's will-rights was also apparent in *Nicklinson* at the Supreme Court.[119] Was the approach of the Court of Appeal in *Re A* sufficient in the context of its compatibility to the PGC? It is suggested that the court was correct, in this instance, to rely on the defence of necessity instead of relying on double effect. This is due to the fact that the defence of necessity is supported under the indirect application of the PGC. It does not rely on sanctity of life and can be justified under Gewirth's hierarchy of rights. While the defence of necessity worked at a practical level, at a more fundamental level, there is a question as to whether there should have been a need for this defence to have been invoked at all. Using this defence suggests that there was some action that had illegal or criminal or immoral connotations. In effect, the doctors needed to defend their position so that they would not be liable for the commission of a crime. In *Re A*, although the defence of necessity had to be used as a legal mechanism to escape any form or murder/manslaughter conviction, and it answered the needs of pragmatism, at a principled level it should not have been required.

The approach in *Woollin* is welcomed. The lack of reference to double effect is concurrent with the PGC. It does the patient some service in so far as, by removing the potentially arbitrary vagueness of double effect, it assigns more agency to patients and allows for the exposition of greater 'truth' in the decisions made. *Woollin* removes the hiding place of the semantics of foresight and intention and puts greater emphasis on the will-rights of mentally competent patients. This approach can be complemented by the adoption of defence of necessity in English law. English law has not given full effect to Article 9 and it has not done all that is required to bring to fruition the substance of this Article. Lord Steyn's ignoring of the double effect principle was sensible and accords with the tenets of the PGC. Even though Lord Steyn was correct not to rely on double effect, insufficient clarity exists as to the current state of the law. The aftermath of *R v Woollin* and the murkiness of the law means that something else that is needed that could provide some prescription in a PGC-compliant manner.

In summary, double effect is not compliant with the PGC due, in principle, to the fact that an agent who is a mentally competent patient has will-rights and those will-rights allow the patient to waive the benefit to the right to life itself. This position is contrary to sanctity of life and so is contrary to double effect. Clarity is needed in the law, given the inappropriateness of double effect's reliance

119 *Nicklinson* (Supreme Court) (n 50).

on sanctity of life, and given also the fact that reliance has confusingly been placed on necessity as a defence to murder and as a consequence of Lord Steyn's approach to intention in *R v Woollin*, which negates double effect.

Question 3: Is there an alternative approach that will provide greater compliance with the framework?

It is concluded, following the analysis in relation to question 2, that under the PGC the principle of double effect is not a defensible principle. As explained in question 1, the position of double effect is not set in stone, as the law governing palliative care is currently unresolved. It is now necessary to consider what is to be replaced in order to resolve the issue in a manner that complies with the PGC. Suggestions for future legal developments are presented by firstly identifying appropriate responses in a polity in which the PGC is the supreme constitutional norm. This will allow for the exploration of what issues are legitimately or appropriately left to legislative or judicial development. This third methodological section involves asking two questions: (a) what would happen in Gewirthia in the context of palliative care? (b) what can we do in English law (either by the legislature or the judiciary) to give effect to the rights that are protected under the PGC?

In relation to part (a) and the approach taken in a Gewirthian society, the starting point is consideration that, under the PGC, a right to pain relief exists. However, in the context of part (b), in order to give effect to this right in a non-Gewirthian society, action is needed by either the legislature or the judiciary in the form of legislation or a development of the common law. Part (b) also involves further consideration of the problems with the existing law and what the legislature or the judiciary could to protect the rights identified, such as the right to pain relief, as rights that will give effect to the PGC.

Position in Gewirthia

Let us, for a moment, consider what type of legal principles we would adopt in an ideal world and in an ideal legal system if we were to deal with the problem of life-shortening pain relief from the perspective of the PGC. In Gewirthia, where the PGC is the constitutional norm, the patient's generic rights are the starting point and the PGC can be applied directly.[120]

In the context, firstly, of a mentally competent adult, there is a basic generic right to pain relief because pain inhibits purpose no matter what the purposes are. The right to life is subject to will (so is the right to pain relief). Where such pain relief within Gewirthia is requested, there is no conflict of rights: there is a straightforward direct application of the PGC. The only potential problem with the administration of this pain relief in Gewirthia might relate to resource

120 See Deryck Beyleveld and Roger Brownsword, 'Principle, Proceduralism, and Precaution in a Community of Rights' (2006) 19(2) *Ratio Juris*, 141–168.

allocation restrictions, or monetary legal capacity for the purchase of medication for this pain relief. The same starting point applies to a mentally incompetent patient who is in severe pain; she has a right to the pain relief, which may shorten her life.

All is not fully homogenous, however in this idyllic land. In Gewirthia, there will still be people with religious and contingent beliefs. Gewirthia doesn't assume that all agents are mono-cultural. It doesn't assume that everybody who lives in this state is some idealised person who has no beliefs other than those that are immediately necessitated by the PGC. We are still agents. We are still able to have our individual values. We accept that all our values are subject to the PGC, but we still have them within our cultural context. Gewirthia A and Gewirthia B will have different approaches where the laws may differ. But the response in all Gewirthias will be the direct application of the PGC in so far as is possible. The direct application must lead to the conclusion that there is a basic generic right to freedom from pain. But the operationalisation of the PGC, whether by common law or statute or some procedural mechanism, will differ from one Gewirthian society to another.

In all these Gewirthias, there is no use of double effect or even doctrine of necessity. Gewirthians adopt a procedure in cases involving life-shortening decisions in palliative care in which the PGC is applied. These procedures do not consider sanctity of life, but are fully compliant with the values of the PGC. Gewirthian society accepts that all agents have a right to life as well as a right to die. They are not overly concerned about life shortening procedures for terminally ill patients because they consider that all agents can waive the benefit to their right to life.

Proposed approaches in non-Gewirthian (English) society/law

The question of what happens in an idealised world (Gewirthia) has been considered. Now we need to assess how far removed from that idyll the English law of today actually is and how we can get closer to it. The new approaches to be considered in non-Gewirthia (England) evolve from two different stances, one of principlism and one of pragmatism. The principled stance advocates new legislation where the PGC-compliant right to pain relief is laid down in the law and, recognising the practical difficulties of implementing this principled stance, a more moderate stance is proposed where, for pragmatic reasons, in the event that legislation is not passed, courts will be guided by Lord Steyn's approach and/or Pattinson's suggested use of doctrine of necessity to replace double effect will be supported.[121]

Approach 1 (Principled stance): new Act of Parliament, incorporating a right to pain relief

At the moment, the approaches in English law include conflicting perspectives. At one level, in situations involving end-of-life treatment, it can come to pass that relations, doctors, and, occasionally, patients can come to a joint decision to

121 Pattinson, *Revisiting Landmark Cases in Medical Law* (n 97) pp 33–34.

increase pain relief in the knowledge, but not the implicit intention that such pain relief can result in death. There is no particular focus on the autonomy of the patient and of the patient's right to assert his right to die in a manner that reflects his will-rights and includes his right to waive the benefit to life itself. This status quo is comfortable for all participants to some degree because it allows for pain relief and the consequent hastening of death in a manner that does not necessarily trouble action. This perspective, however, does not support a PGC-compliant response to end-of-life/palliative care that would promote the autonomy of the mentally competent patient, recognise his right to waive the benefit to life itself and appreciate the fact that the patient has the autonomy to knowingly take pain relief in the full knowledge that his death might be hastened. Thus, in any iteration of a PGC-compliant world, either in Gewirthia or in the England of today, the concept of double effect is redundant and its place at the table of legal discourse, deliberation and judgement is inappropriate. English society has basically moved on from double effect. It is reflective of a more multicultural society and English law cannot reflect the beliefs of one sector.

How much closer would we get to Gewirthian practice if Parliament were to adopt new legislation? Legislation, in theory, could get us far closer to the operation of the principles of the PGC than current common law practice, but there are practical (rather than legal) limitations on the legislature that limit its ability to enact new legislation. Attempts have been made to introduce new approaches to palliative care in the Parliamentary arena. In recent years, the Access to Palliative Care Bill[122] has been introduced as a potential means for addressing some of the issues concerning palliative care. The Bill aims to make provision for equitable access to palliative care services; for advancing education, training, and research in palliative care; and for connected purposes. The Bill is currently on its third reading in the House of Lords and its provisions are supported by this book in so far as they aim to provide more joined up services for those who require such palliative care. However, this Bill doesn't go far enough as it doesn't situate palliative care within the broader human rights framework. Neither does it sufficiently address the cultural and religious context of patients or healthcare professionals. It does not address the potential use of double effect in the courts and the role of sanctity of life in English medical law. What is needed is real change in the law that could result in an indirect application of the PGC: this change could also provide some much-needed clarity to the law governing palliative care.

A new Act is now proposed, which could be called the Rights of the Dying and Seriously Ill Act. It would take account of social, cultural, and religious differences that exist but would, ultimately, aim to act as an indirect application of the PGC. The new Act would disregard double effect and would incorporate a right to pain relief. The Act would shift the focus from the need to avoid murder to a positive affirmation of the duty of the doctor to act in accordance with the will-rights of

122 See 'Bill Stages-Access to Palliative Care Bill [HL] 2015–16', available at: http://services.parliament.uk/bills/2015-16/accesstopalliativecare/stages.html (accessed 27 January 2017).

the mentally competent patient. This Act has the potential to give greater voice to the rights of mentally competent people to determine the level of medical intervention that is required to 'ease their passage'. The main difference between Gewirthia and English society into the future is that the latter clings to some sort of sanctity of life viewpoint, a sense of *God Gives and God takes away*. For such reasons recent Bills on Assisted Dying have failed. The worry in society about the *slippery slope*, the danger that such legislation could pave the way for the killing of conceivably burdensome individuals, will impact upon the enaction of such legislation in a way that would not happen in Gewirthia, where all agents are treated equally and where a right to die is seen to be a manifestation of an agent's will-rights.

This new Act will be considered in conjunction with human rights instruments (such as the HRA/ECHR), which should be used in a manner that is compliant with the PGC. If we want to be PGC-compliant, we need to be rights focused. If a law exists that says that we have a right to pain relief, then there is no need for either necessity or double effect. The law solidifies the right of patients to have access to pain relief that could shorten their life and any action taken on the part of healthcare professionals, subject to constraints, would not be illegal. If such legislation were in place, this would leave judges with a much clearer canvas upon which to make judgments in this area, but it would also lessen the potential for contentious argument. Once this legislation is in place, application and interpretation of the relevant provisions would invalidate double effect in English law and would work as a suitable mechanism in indirectly applying the PGC. The seminal messages of the proposed Act can be summarised as follows:

1 The patient has a right to pain relief and this right exists, even if it shortens the life of the patient.
2 In line with acting in accordance with the patient's right to pain relief, it is lawful and permissible for doctors to administer pain relief that has the potential to hasten death.

In the future, in cases dealing with palliative care that might come before the courts, following the implementation of the Rights of the Dying and Seriously Ill Act, the administration of potentially life-shortening pain relief as a form of palliative care is allowed.

It is clear that if a palliative care case were to come before the courts in an era where the new Act was in place, then the courts would be guided by the clarity given by the Act to a specific right to pain relief and the right of the doctor to administer such pain relief. That is not say that double effect would be wholly negated. In practice, its use would trumped by the Act's assertion that a right to pain relief exists. In effect, this right to pain relief means that a doctor can legitimately administer palliative care drugs to the patient in the knowledge that the Act will permit this action so as to allow the doctor to act in accordance with the will-rights of the patient. Judges interpret the right to pain relief in line with the specific context of the case, following the implementation of the Act. Judges, into the future, will need to develop a shared understanding about what is permissible or appropriate in terms of this right to pain relief.

What are the possible ways in which judges could interpret this new Act into the future and what challenges might be posed in relation to judicial interpretation? In interpreting this right, judges will have to balance it with other rights, which could potentially be problematic. They will seek clarification as to the constraints to be applied. The Act leaves the matter of constraints to judicial interpretation in order to allow for organic development to occur. However, this could cause some difficulties at a practical level. Possible challenges to the Act include lack of prescription in terms of what is meant specifically by the right to pain relief and the conflict between the Act and previous case law that adopts a double effect/sanctity of life perspective.

Notwithstanding these possible challenges and difficulties, the Act balances rights appropriately in order to ensure that medical decisions, in immediate circumstances, are taken that support the rights of patients. This legislation does not explicitly prevent use of the principle of double effect, it merely means that if the doctor intends to kill (so cannot use that principle), then he may still have a defence. The action of the doctor, in this instance, relies upon the new statute that confers a right to pain relief. By negating the sanctity of life aspect of double effect and by focusing on the application of the Act, the PGC is indirectly applied. Legislative change will require using public reason and its deliberative process to come to an agreed perspective about the key elements of any new Act. Arguments presented in favour of retaining double effect would have to be translated to become palatable to a wider audience and reciprocal arguments would need to be made by all parties. The most salient consideration within these deliberations will be the need to ensure that the Act complies with the PGC. The suggested layout of the proposed Act supplied here offers a good faith attempt at applying the PGC.

Approach 2 (Pragmatic stance): alternative to the adoption of a new Act (given the potential difficulty in passing such legislation)

The optimum approach to give effect to the PGC in English society in the context of palliative care is this proposed change in legislation. However, due to the collapse of the Assisted Dying Bill, which was similar to this proposal, it is probable that such an Act would face severe difficulties in being passed by Parliament, but, perhaps, the mooted British Bill of Rights could present opportunities for new rights to be tied to culturally recognised values. Within the legislature there is little political will for change, as is evident in the vast array of unsuccessful Private Member's Bills.[123] The more the existing laws are manipulated, the more problematic they become. Ultimately pragmatism may prevail, rather than principle. The judiciary may, however, be able to act more proactively than the legislature. In the first instance, they could declare definitely (particularly in the Supreme Court) that the principle of double effect should not be relied upon and, instead, the approach taken by Lord Steyn in relation to the concept of intention ought to be used, where intention of murder can be inferred, even though there was no desire to kill

123 See, for example, *Assisted Dying (No 2) Bill 2015–2016.*

or cause serious bodily harm to the victim when the defendant's voluntary act results in death. The wide interpretation of intention should be used by the courts, thus allowing for greater consistency and a greater focus on the will-rights of patients.

Equally, judges could adopt Pattinson's suggestion that the doctrine of necessity should be used in order to indirectly apply the PGC.[124] Necessity, as formulated as part of the newly proposed statute, would allow for a more suitable response than current English law due to the fact that it can be justified under the PGC and, unlike double effect, it does not rely on sanctity of life and gives sufficient consideration to the will-rights of patients. In Pattinson's recent hypothetical appeal judgment of *R v Adams*,[125] the Court of Appeal states that 'English law recognises the lawfulness of proper and necessary pain relief, even where one of its effects is to hasten death, under the doctrine of necessity'. Pattinson, therefore, argues that necessity is a more appropriate tool than double effect. It is a tool that is supported by the PGC and, consequently, the framework adopted. This chapter supports Pattinson's contention (in his hypothetical judgment) that necessity, as a defence, applies where the only way for a doctor to ease pain will result in the hastening of a patient's death. Pattinson puts forward the view that the easing of pain, contingent on the ability of the patient to consent or to refuse consent, is preferential to preserving life at all costs.[126] He considers that double effect does allow for the harmful effect (death) when bringing about a greater good (easing of pain), but he makes a very valid point that if the logic of double effect is followed, then a doctor who acts in line with multiple purposes could, in one instance, commit murder and, in another instance, not commit murder according to a perception of foresight or intention.[127] The point here is that the same treatment could be given, but the purpose of the treatment has the potential to determine whether he is murderer or pain-reliever. The existence of this principle does not help either doctor or patient because it allows for the masking of treatment that might have life shortening consequences in philosophical viewpoints of foresight and intention, instead of supporting the will-rights of the patient and, ultimately, the agency of the patient.

Pattinson's hypothetical Court of Appeal comes to the conclusion that necessity (unlike double effect in *R v Adams*) defends a doctor's actions where it is not shown beyond reasonable doubt that he did not realistically think that providing the painkilling drugs to the dying patient was a suitable and essential way of dealing with the suffering and pain of the dying patient.[128] This hypothetical judgment finds that the defence of necessity is a stronger mechanism than reliance on *mens rea* and *actus reus*. The principle of double effect is not applied to the understanding of what constitutes intention. The defence of necessity does not ask

124 Pattinson, *Revisiting Landmark Cases in Medical Law* (n 97) pp 33–34.
125 *R v Adams* (n 53); Pattinson, *Revisiting Landmark Cases in Medical Law* (n 97) p 50.
126 Pattinson, *Revisiting Landmark Cases in Medical Law* (n 97) p 52.
127 ibid.
128 ibid.

the law to deal with pain-relief that shortens life as if it had no effect on the patient's death even where there is evidence to the contrary.[129]

It is appropriate now to extend the discussion to further comment on issues/options that might arise in the future (where the idealised Act has not been enacted) when cases dealing with palliative care are judicially interpreted and this interpretation is subject to criticism. If the principled approach is not invoked and the pragmatic stance is adopted, what challenges could judges face in future cases in applying either a wide interpretation of 'intention'/the approach adopted by Lord Steyn in *R v Woollin* or the doctrine of necessity?

Under this first pragmatic approach to future English law, there will no reliance on the principle of double effect by judges. Instead, there will be a wide interpretation of 'intention', in line with Lord Steyn's judgment in *R v Woollin.*[130] There will also be an improved interpretation of Article 9 and Article 2 ECHR within the context of palliative care, where the Articles are used and interpreted in order to give a greater focus to the will-rights of patients. However, it is also likely that this interpretation might be subject to some challenge. In appeal courts, judges may be reluctant to apply a wide interpretation to intention, may continue to distinguish between intention and foresight and may still implicitly use the principle of double effect, which has not been debarred or limited by any legislation. For example, even if this wide interpretation of intention is accepted, it could still be held in appeal courts that the principle of double effect still applies and that it supports the religious beliefs of the patient who would have wished this principle to have been invoked. Equally, unless the doctrine of necessity is accepted in the Supreme Court as a definitive approach to palliative care in English law, its application will continue to be subject to challenges and doubt over its role in this context, thus, leaving judicial acceptance and application of it open to challenge in future courts. In the same manner as in the above instance concerning adoption of a wide interpretation of intention, judges (particularly in appeal courts) could, indeed, continue to decide upon these issues from the perspective of double effect, in the absence of legislation or, at the very least, in the absence of a definitive judgment in the highest court in the land.

It can be seen that the pragmatic approach is subject to more challenge at the level of judicial interpretation than the principled approach. However, both approaches offer principled and pragmatic mechanisms that comply with the PGC and that provide the judiciary with clear guidance that is not subject to subjective semantic interpretation between intention and foresight. As such, these approaches go some way towards resolving palliative care dilemmas in English courts.

Conclusion

The PGC, in this context, is, therefore, opposed to reliance upon Catholic doctrine over secular and other religious beliefs. It thereby does act as a constraint on legal adoption of some religiously inspired principles. Arising from that conclusion,

129 ibid.
130 *R v Woollin* (n 42).

it is feasible to allow a doctor to give lethal treatment to a suicidal patient when such treatment is requested by a patient who is suffering and dying. Of course, such action could be subject to misuse and abuse. The doctor could put undue pressure on a patient, family could reinforce the message that the patient is somehow a burden on themselves or on society or on the family. The patient's medical condition may be such that it is unclear if a decision has been made entirely of free will and there may be situations in which the legal capacity to make such a decision might be questionable. However, the PGC gives a suffering patient an entitlement to act in accordance with their own agency. Society might not like that action. We may fear it, but if we accept the PGC as the supreme moral principle, we cannot object to the governing principle that ascribes agency to people. Actions are aligned to freedom, obligations and responsibilities. The freedom to assert the wish to die, the obligation of the doctor to act in accordance with the patient's autonomous wish, and the responsibility to act according to the PGC fall within the circle of difficult decisions that are taken by, on behalf of and with people who are gravely ill. The protective mantle of double effect can provide a semantic smokescreen that is not palatable to some. The PGC casts this smokescreen aside and allows for action that may not satisfy society's desire to leave the business of dying to an agency outside of the agents themselves.

Somewhere in all the talk of foresight and intention and proportionality there are people and patients for whom decisions are made on the basis of a religious principle that might or might not have relevance for them or resonate with their own beliefs. At the very least, for people dealing with patients who are seriously ill or for those seriously ill patients themselves, a broader moral barometer is needed that is reflective of the plurality of belief about human life, human dignity, human capacity for life, or belief about suffering or death that exists in the mind of the patient. Within that cauldron of moral uncertainty, the PGC can come into play.

This book uses a framework in order to assess the suitability of religious principles or religious arguments in English medical law. The chapter measured the usefulness or otherwise of the principle in medical law and ethics and cited and analysed case law in respect of palliative care. The approach adopted by judges towards the principle was set out and its position within the secular neutrality of the court, was discussed. *R v Woollin*[131] has brought a new reality into deliberation about double effect. Prior to this, debate has been centred upon degree of proportionality, degree of foresight, and degree of intention in double effect.

This chapter clearly explained why double effect cannot be justified or used as a working principle in English medical law. It cannot be compatible under the superior moral principle (the PGC). It is advocated that the principle of double effect should not be relied upon and, instead, two possible approaches exist: the new Rights of the Dying and Seriously Ill Act would confer a PGC-compliant right to pain relief. Alternatively, in the absence of acceptance of this legislation, judges will directly disallow double effect and will continue to adopt the approach taken in relation to intention by Lord Steyn's in *R v Woollin*. Support is also given

131 *R v Woollin* (n 42).

to the use of the defence of necessity, as an indirect application of the PGC and as allowing, consequently, for a more suitable response than current English law.

References

Assisted Dying (No 2) Bill 2015–16, available at: http://www.publications.parliament.uk/pa/bills/cbill/2015-2016/0007/cbill_2015-20160007_en_1.htm (accessed 27 January 2017).

Beyleveld, Deryck, 'The Principle of Generic Consistency as a Supreme Moral Principle' (2011) 13(1) *Human Rights Review*, 1–18, pp 14–15.

Biggs, Hazel, *Euthanasia, Death with Dignity and the Law* (Hart, 2001).

Biggs, Hazel, 'Decisions and Responsibilities at the End of Life: Euthanasia and Clinically Assisted Death' (1996) 2(3) *Medical Law International*, 229–245.

Biggs, Hazel, 'Euthanasia and death with dignity: still poised on the fulcrum of homicide' (1996) Dec *Criminal Law Review*, 878–888.

'Bill Stages-Access to Palliative Care Bill [HL] 2015–16', available at: http://services.parliament.uk/bills/2015-16/accesstopalliativecare/stages.html (accessed 27 January 2017).

Congregation for the Doctrine of the Faith, Instruction on Respect for Human Life in its Origin and on the Dignity of Procreation Donum Vitae (22 February 1987), Introduction, No. 5: AAS 80(1988), 76–77; cf. Catechism of the Catholic Church, No. 2258.

Devlin, Patrick, *Easing the Passing: The Trial of Dr John Bodkin Adams* (The Bodley Head, 1985).

Fathers of the English Dominican Province (translators), *Summa Theologicia of Saint Thomas Aquinas* (Benziger Bros, 1947).

Fenwick, Daniel, A Gewirthian Conception of the Right to Enabled Suicide in England and Wales, (unpublished) PhD thesis (Durham University, 2015).

Foster, Charles, 'Airedale NHS Trust v Bland' in Jonathan Herring and Jesse Wall (eds), *Landmark Cases in Medical Law* (Hart, 2015).

Foster and Others, 'The Double Effect Effect' (2011) 20(1) *Cambridge Quarterly of Healthcare Ethics*, 56–72.

Gury, JP, *Comtempendium Theologicae Moralis*, 2 vols, F Pustete 1874: 1.8 as cited in Foster and Others (n 1).

John Paul II, Pope, *Evangelium Vite*, 25 March 1997, available at: http://www.vatican.va/holy_father/john_paul_ii/encyclicals/documents/hf_jp-ii_enc_25031995_evangelium-vitae_en.html (accessed 27 January 2017).

Katme, Majid, 'The Sanctity of Human Life is a Basic Concept in Islam' (Society for the Protection of the Unborn Child), available at: https://www.spuc.org.uk/about/muslim-division/euthanasia (accessed 27 January 2017).

Keown, John, *The Law of Ethics and Medicine: Essays on the Inviolability of Human Life* (OUP, 2012).

Keown, John, *Euthanasia, Ethics and Public Policy: An Argument Against Legislation* (CUP, 2002).

Keown, John, 'Beyond Bland: A Critique of the BMA Guidance on withholding and withdrawing medical treatment' (2000) 20(1) *Legal Studies*, 66–84.

Keown, John, 'Restoring Moral and Intellectual Shape to the Law after Bland', (1997) 113 *Law Quarterly Review*, 282–503.

Law Commission, 'Murder Manslaughter and Infanticide' (Law Com No 304, 2006), available at: https://www.gov.uk/government/uploads/system/uploads/attachment_data/file/228782/0030.pdf (accessed 27 January 2017).

Pattinson, Shaun D, *Revisiting Landmark Cases in Medical Law* (Routledge, 2018).

Pattinson, Shaun D, *Medical Law and Ethics* (5th ed, Sweet and Maxwell, 2017).

Rosner, Fred, 'The Beginning of Life in Judaism', available at: http://www.myjewishlearning.com/beliefs/Issues/Bioethics/Abortion/Fetus_in_Jewish_Law/Beginning_of_Life.shtml?BFIS (accessed 27 January 2017).

Sheldon, Sally and Wilkinson, Stephen, '"On the Sharpest Horns of Dilemma" Re A (Conjoined Twins)' (2001) 9(3) *Medical Law Review*, 201–207.

The Holy Bible (OUP, 1991).

Wells, Celia, 'Patients, Consent and Criminal Law' (1994) 1 *Journal of Social Welfare and Family Law*, 65–78.

Williams, Glenys, 'The Principle of Double Effect and Terminal Sedation' (2001) 9(1) *Medical Law Review*, 41–53.

World Health Organisation, 'WHO Definition of Palliative Care', available at: http://www.who.int/cancer/palliative/definition/en/ (accessed 27 January 2017).

4 Adult Jehovah's Witnesses and refusal of blood transfusions in English medical law

Introduction

One of the purposes of this book is to examine the impact of religious belief on autonomous decisions in medical law and to explore the interconnection between these variables through case studies. Human rights law, domestic law, medical procedures, and protocols all attest to the fact that a legally capacitated adult patient can refuse treatment, even if such a refusal has a negative impact upon the patient's health. The right to refuse medical treatment is, thus, enshrined in the spirit and practice of medical law. Why, then, does this book consider in depth the refusal of blood transfusions by Jehovah's Witness patients, given that such refusal is permitted under current law, in the case of adults who have legal capacity? This is an area in medical law that deals with the manifestation of religious belief in life or death contexts. It grasps the public imagination and perplexes people: they cannot understand why anyone would refuse a life-transforming and life-saving intervention. Medical personnel are confronted with this as a practical reality. It has even formed the basis of recent 2016 guidelines to surgeons.[1] This issue provides an exemplar for using the framework as a mechanism to support the arbitration of cases where mentally competent patients make decisions, in line with the exercise of their generic rights. This chapter aims to situate the problems that arise when adults refuse blood transfusions within the context of theological positioning, English case law, Strasbourg jurisprudence, and the PGC. The current law in respect of adults, as will be seen, is broadly compliant with the PGC. The way in which legally capacitated adults are permitted to exercise their will-rights will be contrasted in the next chapter with the manner in which the exercise of the will-rights of mentally competent adolescents/children is more strongly impeded by the paternalism of the courts.

A number of terms are used throughout the text that merit definition and brief explanation, as follows:

Legal capacity: 'legal capacity' in this context is taken to mean satisfaction of the legal test to be recognised as mentally competent.

1 See Royal College of Surgeons of England, *Caring for Patients who Refuse Blood* (Royal College of Surgeons of England, 2016).

Mental competence: a patient is mentally competent when they have sufficient cognitive faculties to be able to make a decision in relation to a particular situation or context.[2] This definition sees mental competence as something that is defined within the sphere of cognitive functioning. A mentally *incompetent* person is someone who lacks the cognitive faculties to enable them to make a decision for a particular situation or context. A distinction exists in the law between being recognised as having legal capacity and apparently having the cognitive-functional abilities to make a decision (mental competence).

Jehovah's Witnesses and blood transfusions: shifting sands

Jehovah's Witnesses are a millenarian restorationist Christian religious denomination whose believers strictly adhere to their interpretation of the Bible, as well as their belief in Armageddon/the end of the world.[3] Adherents of the faith refer to their belief structure as 'the truth'. Beackford points out that Jehovah's Witnesses have a relatively low rate of doctrinal modification and that the denomination promotes strict consistency of belief.[4] The beliefs of Jehovah's Witnesses have been subject to legal discourse as a result of their controversial practices. One of these beliefs is the refusal to accept blood transfusions and that contentious stance forms the basis of the content of both this chapter and the subsequent chapter.

Rhodes points out that it has been the position of the Watchtower Society for a long time that Witnesses have a duty to refuse blood transfusions, even in situations where the refusal would result in inevitable death.[5] According to Rhodes, pre-reform, The Watchtower Society taught that parents should ensure that their children do not receive blood transfusions.[6] Witnesses reject blood transfusions because they regard it as 'eating blood', thus contravening their interpretation of the Bible. As a consequence, many Witnesses have a signed card in their possession indicating their lack of consent to a transfusion.[7] According to Genesis 9.4: 'But flesh with the life thereof, which is the blood thereof, shall ye not eat'. This verse is used to justify their understanding that to accept a transfusion would be the same as eating blood. This interpretation of the Bible is rejected by the majority of non-Witnesses. Additionally, the Watchtower Society contends that their position is supported in Leviticus 7: 26–27, which says that 'And wherever you live, you must not eat the blood of any bird or animal. Anyone who eats blood must be cut off from their people'.

2 Shaun D Pattinson, *Medical Law and Ethics* (5th ed, Sweet & Maxwell, 2017) p 136.

3 See Clayton Ó Néill, 'Jehovah's Witnesses and Blood Transfusions: An Analysis of the Legal Protections Afforded to Adults and Children in English European Human Rights Contexts' (2017) 24(4) *European Journal of Health Law*, 368–389, p 370.

4 James A Meckford, *The Trumpet of Prophecy: A Sociological Study of Jehovah's Witnesses* (Blackwell, 1975), p 92, pp 98–100.

5 Ron Rhodes, *Reasoning from the Scriptures with the Jehovah's Witnesses* (Harvest House Publishers, 1993) p 376.

6 ibid. p 377.

7 ibid. p 378.

However, it is worth noting that the stance on this subject has moved from one of intransigence to one that is slightly more accommodating. In 1961, anyone who accepted a blood transfusion would 'be cut off from God's people by excommunication or dis-fellowship.'[8] The recent modified approach is evident in the 15 June issue of the *Watchtower* where it was stated that 'fractions of all primary components' are now permitted.[9] The article also notes that '...when it comes to fractions of any of the primary components, each Christian, after careful and prayerful meditation, must conscientiously decide for himself'.[10]

McCormick indicates that the position of the Church in respect of blood transfusions may evolve in the future.[11] The softening process towards transfusions is related to the current teaching that those who receive a blood transfusion, but who subsequently repent, will not be dis-fellowshipped. Barker points to this as being a positive development. However, he also discusses the ambiguities behind this stance. No definitive standards currently exist as to determination of repentance for receiving transfusions and discretion is left to individual elders in this regard.[12] This leads to decisions made being based upon subjective stances of these elders, where some can show mercy and understanding, but where others can adopt more intransigent positions, resulting in the involuntary disassociation from the Jehovah's Witnesses of people who have undertaken blood transfusions. In summary, notwithstanding some softening of intransigent positions, for many Jehovah's Witnesses the refusal to accept blood transfusions is an important tenet of their faith and has consequential implications for their healthcare needs.

Question 1: How have English law and the ECtHR dealt with the issue of adult Jehovah's Witnesses who refuse blood transfusions?

The law has treated cases involving Jehovah's Witness adults and their refusal to take blood transfusions with some degree of consistency. It is shown in the forthcoming cases that what has been consistently upheld is the almost sacrosanct autonomy of the adult who has legal capacity to refuse medical treatment. What shifts the consistency of these legal decisions is when the decision-making ability of an adult is in question when, for example, undue influence is exerted. This chapter will now consider how English law and Strasbourg jurisprudence have dealt with the issue of a patient refusing a potentially life-giving blood transfusion, based on religious belief.

8 Watch Tower Bible and Tract Society, *The Watchtower* (15 January 1961) p 64.
9 ibid.
10 Watch Tower Bible and Tract Society, 'Questions from readers' (15 June 2000) pp 29–30.
11 Thomas R McCormick, 'Ethical Issues Inherent to Jehovah's Witnesses', (2008) 3 *Perioperative Nursing Clinics*, 253–258, p 253.
12 Jason Barker, 'New Watchtower Blood Transfusion Policy' (Watchman Fellowship) available at: http://www.watchman.org/articles/jehovahs-witnesses/new-watchtower-blood-transfusion-policy/ (accessed 27 January 2017).

Adults are autonomous individuals in the eyes of the law: they are entitled to refuse treatment unless they fail to satisfy the legal capacity test under the Mental Capacity Act 2005 (MCA). This Act is applied to adults and it aims to safeguard people who may lack the legal capacity to made decisions about their medical treatment/care. The MCA, in s 1, imposes key principles, as follows:

1 The following principles apply for the purposes of this Act.
2 A person must be assumed to have capacity unless it is established that he lacks capacity.
3 A person is not to be treated as unable to make a decision unless all practicable steps to help him to do so have been taken without success.
4 A person is not to be treated as unable to make a decision merely because he makes an unwise decision.
5 An act done, or decision made, under this Act for or on behalf of a person who lacks capacity must be done, or made, in his best interests.
6 Before the act is done, or the decision is made, regard must be had to whether the purpose for which it is needed can be as effectively achieved in a way that is less restrictive of the person's rights and freedom of action.

These principles provide a useful frame of reference to those involved in the medical care of patients who may lack legal capacity.

Under the Act, a two stage legal capacity test exists, as apparent in s 2 and 3 of the Act. The *first stage* (s 2) states that the patient only lacks capacity if 'he is unable to make a decision for himself in relation to the matter because of an impairment of, or a disturbance in the functioning of, the mind or brain' (s 2(1)). Under s 2(2) '[i]t does not matter whether the impairment or disturbance is permanent or temporary'. *Stage two* of the test is exemplified in s 3, as follows:

> [A] person is unable to make a decision for himself if he is unable—
> (a) to understand the information relevant to the decision,
> (b) to retain that information,
> (c) to use or weigh that information as part of the process of making the decision, or
> (d) to communicate his decision (whether by talking, using sign language or any other means).

Under this two-stage test, legal capacity can change over time. A patient might be lacking in legal capacity at one point, but he might be able to make the same decision in a different period of time (s. 3 (3)). There is a requirement to understand the information that is relevant to the particular context/task; the general understanding in a non-specific context is not at issue under the Act.[13]

It is important to stress that the issue of the blood transfusion is not related to the issue of legal capacity and the MCA legal capacity test doesn't interrogate this

13 Pattinson (n 2) p 140.

issue or arbitrate upon it. It just interrogates the legal capacity of the individual. The first stage of the test seeks to identify if any impairment exists and the second stage asks whether or not this impairment is sufficient for the person to lack legal capacity in a specific content. This stage means that a patient who is functionally unable to make a decision under the s 3 stage 2 limb of the capacity test will still have legal capacity under the MCA test if that inability is not due to an impairment in the functioning of the mind or brain.

In a situation where a patient is deemed to lack legal capacity by failing this two-stage test, then a test to determine his best interests is applied. This best interests test is found under s 4 of the Act and is governed by a number of factors which seek to ensure that all actions taken support, as far as is practicable, the best interests of the legally incapacitated patient. A fuller account of the factors involved in and the application of the best interests test can be found later in this chapter.

Valid consent to medical treatment is predicated upon the existence of a number of conditions, including the legal capacity to consent (which tracks mental competence) and the requirement that consent be informed, voluntary and free.[14] The same must apply to refusal of treatment. This refusal must be free, voluntary, informed, and based upon the patient having sufficient mental competence to make the decision. Medical personnel must give appropriate information to empower the person to 'weigh up the necessity or usefulness of the aims and methods of the intervention against the risks and the discomfort or pain it will cause'.[15]

It has long been established in medical care that adult patients with legal capacity can consent to or refuse medical treatment. It has, equally, been established that less weight, however, has been given to the refusal of patients to treatment than to their consent.[16] This reticence to accept the decision of patients who refuse treatment is seen to derive, primarily, from the courts' apprehension at the prospect of accepting decisions that they see as being against the best interests of the patient. There is, therefore, a conflict between well-meaning judicial paternalism and the recognition that a legally capacitated patient has a right to refuse treatment.

Two relevant general cases relating to consent, legal capacity, best interests, and medical law

The acute impact of religious belief on decision-making is seen in *Wye Valley NHS Trust v B*.[17] This case concerned whether or not it was permissible for a doctor treating a 73-year-old patient (Mr B) to act against the patient's wishes by

14 Deryck Beyleveld and Roger Brownsword, *Consent in the Law* (Hart, 2007) chapter 1.

15 Council of Europe, *Convention on Human Rights and Biomedicine*, explanatory report at [36], as cited in Beyleveld and Brownsword, *Consent in the Law* (n 14) p 7.

16 Beylevld and Brownsword, *Consent in the Law* (n 14) p 26.

17 *Wye Valley NHS Trust v B* [2015] EWCOP 60.

amputating his leg in order to save his life. The reality was that, if Mr B's leg were not amputated, he would die within a few days, while if he were to receive the amputation he would likely live for quite a number of years.[18] A longstanding mental illness meant that Mr B lacked the legal capacity to make decisions for himself. Therefore, the operation could only be undertaken if in the patient's best interests.[19] In evaluating the merits of the courses of action to be taken, Peter Jackson J stated that:

> The starting point is a strong presumption that it is in a person's best interests to stay alive. But this is not an absolute, and there are cases where it will not be in the patient's interests to receive life-sustaining treatment.[20]

The judge also referred to Baroness Hale in *Aintree* in relation to best interests, whose purpose, according to her, was to give clarification to the patient's perspective and determination of meaningfulness of future life.[21] Peter Jackson J stressed that, if the patient lacks legal capacity, it is very important to give proper weight to the patient's wishes, beliefs, and feelings, when applying the best interests test.[22] Interestingly, the judge noted that patients with illnesses such as Mr B often possess 'religious delusions'.[23] Mr B developed paranoid schizophrenia in his mid-20s and for many years experienced auditory hallucinations—he heard voices of angels and the Virgin Mary.[24] He described hearing angelic voices that told him when he could take medication. The judge expanded upon this, as follows:

> Delusions arising from mental illness may rightly lead to a person's wishes and feelings being given less weight where that is appropriate. However, this cannot be the automatic consequence of the wishes and feelings having a religious component. Mr B's religious sentiments are extremely important to him, even though he does not follow an established religion. Although the point does not arise for determination in this case, I approach matters on the basis that his Article 9 right to freedom of thought and religion is no less engaged than it would be for any other devout person.[25]

Accordingly, Peter Jackson J noted that this case reflected the notion that patient values or beliefs ought not to be 'routinely undervalued'.[26] In relation to legal capacity, the judge was satisfied that Mr B lacked capacity.[27] The judge explained

18 ibid. at [1].
19 ibid.
20 *Wye Valley* (n 17) at [7].
21 *Aintree University NHS Trust Foundation v James* [2013] UKSC 67 at [39]. See *Wye Valley* (n 17) at [8]. *Re J* [1991] Fam 33.
22 *Wye Valley* (n 17) at [10] and [11].
23 ibid. at [14].
24 ibid. at [19].
25 ibid. at [14].
26 ibid. at [15].
27 ibid. at [34].

that if the operation were carried out, Mr B's 'religious sentiments will undoubtedly continue and he will believe that the amputation was carried out against the Lord's wishes'.[28] In the event of a successful surgery, no possibility of Br B returning to his previous life existed.[29] Following consideration of the evidence, Peter Jackson J said that the amputation was not in Mr B's best interests.[30] It would not be appropriate to deny Mr B his remaining independence or his dignity in order to substitute it with a future that he did not want. Therefore, the judge dismissed the application.

This finding substantiates the depth of consideration that must be given to patients' beliefs when applying the best interests test. There is a vindication here of the importance of longstanding and deeply held belief, even when the patient lacks legal capacity. This vindication has, of course, relevance to cases involving Jehovah's Witness adult patients into the future, particularly where such patients are found to lack legal capacity.

One of the most significant medical law cases of the 21st century was the *Montgomery v Lanarkshire Health Board*[31] Supreme Court decision. This case has had a major impact on the reconfiguring of the relationship between healthcare professionals and their patients. It puts *informed consent* at the epicentre of the decision-making process. What were the facts of the case? A baby was born with severe disabilities and, as a consequence, the mother claimed that the doctor was negligent. Mrs Montgomery, who had diabetes, had a number of concerns about vaginal delivery, but it was the policy of the doctor not to routinely advise women with diabetes about the possible complication of shoulder dystocia because, if informed of this small risk, such women could decide to have a Caesarean section, which the doctor felt was, ultimately, not in the interests of the patient. During the birth, which was carried out by vaginal delivery, shoulder dystocia occurred, and the baby was born with significant disabilities. Mrs Montgomery took a case stating that she would have opted for a Caesarean section if she had known of the small risk of shoulder dystocia.

Originally, the case was decided against the mother. Prior to this Supreme Court case, the leading authority was *Sidaway v Board of Governors of the Bethlem Royal Hospital and the Maudsley Hospital*,[32] where it was decided that the *Bolam*[33] test should be applied in deciding whether or not a doctor has acted in breach of his/her duty of care when omitting to warn a patient of particular risks. Accordingly, this approach was applied in the original case, and it was concluded

28 ibid. at [37].
29 ibid. at [37].
30 ibid. at [42].
31 *Montgomery v Lanarkshire Health Board* [2015] UKSC 11.
32 *Sidaway v Board of Governors of the Bethlem Royal Hospital and the Maudsley Hospital* [1985] AC 871.
33 *Bolam v Friern Hospital Management Committee* [1957] 2 All ER 118. According to McNair J (at 122), 'A doctor is not guilty of negligence if he has acted in accordance with a practice accepted as proper by a responsible body of medical men skilled in that particular art'.

that Mrs Montgomery had not made it clear that she would have opted for a C-Section if she had been given all relevant information, leaving causation unproven.

However, the Supreme Court found to the contrary. They believed that the *Bolam* and related *Sidaway* tests were no longer suitable instruments. According to Lord Kerr and Lord Reed, the doctor-patient relationship in *Sidaway* did not reflect reality: it would be incorrect to assume that patients are uninformed or wholly dependent on information provided by doctors. Following *Montgomery*, a greater focus is now placed on self-determination and autonomy.[34] The world has moved on and a duty exists for doctors to ensure that patients are aware of material risks associated with treatment. Lord Kerr and Lord Reed declared that:

> The doctor is therefore under a duty to take reasonable care to ensure that the patient is aware of any material risks involved in any recommended treatment, and of any reasonable alternative or variant treatments. The test of materiality is whether, in the circumstances of the particular case, a reasonable person in the patient's position would be likely to attach significance to the risk, or the doctor is or should reasonably be aware that the particular patient would be likely to attach significance to it.[35]

Thus, shifts within the doctor-patient relationship and shifts within the way in which a patient is perceived to have a role in decision-making left *Bolam* and *Sidaway* unsatisfactory instruments. The Supreme Court found in favour of Mrs Montgomery, essentially confirming her right to information and finding that her wishes, beliefs, and opinions should, at the very least, be taken into account in medical actions. This finding shifts the goalposts considerably from the patient as passive recipient of medical decisions imposed upon her by informed practitioners to the patient as co-decision-maker, within a context where informed consent is a key ingredient within the decision-making process. Obviously, this shift is of central relevance to other chapters in this book. For example, in cases involving the circumcision of a young baby, there can be no informed consent.

Specific cases relating to Jehovah's Witnesses who refuse blood transfusions

Newcastle upon Tyne Hospitals Foundation Trust v LM and Nottingham Healthcare NHS Trust v RC: certainty in the law?

A recent relevant case has emerged that copper-fastens the idea that courts respect and act according to the opinions of adult patients: *Newcastle upon Tyne Hospitals Foundation Trust v LM.*[36] In this case, the Hospital Foundation Trust applied for

34 *Montomery* (n 31) at [74]–[80].

35 ibid. at [87].

36 *Newcastle upon Tyne Hospitals Foundation Trust v LM* [2014] EWHC 454 (COP). Note that LM died shortly before the judgment was read.

a declaration that they could lawfully withhold a blood transfusion from 63-year-old LM. LM had practised as a Jehovah's Witness since the 1970s. She was a paranoid schizophrenic who suffered from depression.[37] The medical opinion was that, if she did not receive a blood transfusion, she might not survive another day, and, even if she received the transfusion, it would still be quite possible that she would die.[38] The Trust made the argument that LM had clearly refused the transfusion and that her wishes should be respected. Following the hearing, Mr Justice Peter Jackson allowed the application and said that:

> It shall be lawful for the doctors treating LM to withhold blood transfusions or administration of blood products notwithstanding that such treatments would reduce the likelihood of her dying and might prevent her death.[39]

At the Court of Protection, Mr Justice Jackson noted that the judgment concerned three issues: was LM capable of making the decision not to allow a blood transfusion? If she did have legal capacity, did it apply to her later circumstances?[40] On the other hand, if both of these questions were answered in the negative, was the application of the Trust to refuse to give a blood transfusion in her best interests?[41] If an advance refusal had been undertaken, it would have given more clarity to her decision to refuse a transfusion.[42] Subsequently, her condition deteriorated and she lacked legal capacity to make a decision.[43] The judge noted that '[a]lternatively, if it was a matter of best interests, the Trust did not wish to act against her wishes, being concerned to respect her individual dignity'.[44] Mr Justice Jackson found that LM was capable of refusing or accepting a blood transfusion.[45] He also said:

> In the alternative, if LM had not made a valid, applicable decision, I would have granted the declaration sought on the basis that to order a transfusion would not have been in her best interests. Applying s.4 (6) in relation to the specific issue of blood transfusion, her wishes and feelings and her long-standing beliefs and values carried determinative weight. It is also of relevance that a transfusion might not have been effective to save her life.[46]

As such, this decision vindicates the right of patients such as LM to refuse treatment on the basis of their own autonomy and self-determination (which, in this

37 ibid. at [6].
38 ibid. at [1].
39 ibid. at [2].
40 ibid. at [4].
41 ibid. at [4].
42 ibid. at [12].
43 ibid. at [13].
44 ibid. at [20].
45 ibid. at [21].
46 ibid. at [23].

case, was founded upon religious belief). The patient's wishes were treated respectfully, and the decision supported the carrying out of these voluntary wishes. Equally, the decision allowed for the manifestation of religious belief, even when such manifestation had the potential to result in the death of the patient.

Another relevant case is *Nottingham Healthcare NHS Trust v RC*.[47] It concerned a person who had been raised by Jehovah's Witness parents, but was never baptised. In February 2014 RC severely slashed his brachial artery and subsequently refused a transfusion. He signed an advance decision, stating that he should never be administered blood transfusions or blood components in any situation, even if there were a risk to his life.[48] Proceedings were commenced in relation to his legal capacity to refuse blood products and to self-lacerate, the validity of the advance decision and the lawfulness of the decision not to impose blood transfusions on RC. In his deliberations, Mr Justice Mostyn referred to John Stewart Mill's 1859 essay *On Liberty*:

> That the only purpose for which power can be rightfully exercised over any member of a civilised community, against his will, is to prevent harm to others. His own good, either physical or moral, is not a sufficient warrant … Over himself, over his body and mind, the individual is sovereign.[49]

He pointed out that every person with legal capacity has the right to either harm or kill themselves. He also referred to Judge LJ in *St George's Healthcare NHS Trust v S*[50] who said that '[e]ven when his or her own life depends on receiving medical treatment, an adult of sound mind is entitled to refuse it'. Mr Justice Mostyn also made reference to *LM*,[51] as discussed. He paid particular attention to the statement that '[t]here is no obligation on a patient with decision-making capacity to accept life-saving treatment, and doctors are neither entitled nor obliged to give it'.[52]

Consequently, the judge gave little weight to the fact that a 'tenet of RC's religious faith prevents him from weighing the advantages of a blood transfusion should his medical circumstances indicate that one is necessary'.[53] He was very satisfied that RC did not lack legal capacity to refuse blood products being administered to him. He concluded by saying that '[t]o impose a blood transfusion would be a denial of a most basic freedom' and that the decision to withhold the treatment was lawful.[54] This decision supported patient autonomy and the freedom to reject medical treatment. It also supported the patient's right to manifest religious belief and to seek treatment that gave credence to those beliefs.

47 *Nottingham Healthcare NHS Trust v RC* [2014] EWCOP 1317.
48 ibid. at [5].
49 John Stewart Mill, *On Liberty* (2nd ed, Ticknor and Fields, 1863) pp 14–15.
50 *St George's Healthcare NHS Trust v S* [1969] Fam 28, 43.
51 *LM* (n 36).
52 *RC* (n 47) at [24].
53 ibid. at [35].
54 ibid. at [42].

Taken together, therefore, both cases (*LM* and *RC*) showed evidence of the courts respecting the decisions made by patients, based on their religious beliefs, about their own medical treatment. Self-determination, in terms of treatment or non-treatment, is respected. Essentially, these cases illustrate that the courts permit adults to be the architects of their own medical destiny and their own futures (unless they lack the legal capacity to do so). In so doing, the courts give definitive protection to the manifestation of religious belief in this context. These cases go some way to pointing to a general indication that the position of the courts and the legal system in England broadly adequately protects the manifestation of religious beliefs in the context of adult patients.

Jurisprudence of the European Court of Human Rights

What is the position of the rights of mentally competent adults to refuse blood transfusions within the broad European human rights context? A number of relevant cases exist. The most seminar European Court of Human Rights (ECtHR) case is *Case of Jehovah's Witnesses of Moscow and Others* v *Russia*.[55] This case concerned the banning of Jehovah's Witnesses' practices in Russia, as a result of the introduction of the Russian Religious Act. Some of the reasons for banning the manifestation of Jehovah's Witnesses' practices included the following: alleged coercion in relation of minors being loyal to the organisation and the position on the refusal of blood transfusions which was regarded by the Russian government to have a undesirable impact on health and life. In the ECtHR case, Lord Donaldson's statement in *Re T* was referred to: 'every adult has the right and capacity to decide whether or not he will accept medical treatment, even if a refusal may risk permanent injury to his health or even lead to premature death'[56] and that '[i]t matters not that those others sought, however strongly, to persuade the patient to refuse, so long as in the end the refusal represented the patient's independent decision. If, however, his will was overborne, the refusal will not have represented a true decision'.[57]

Focus was placed by the Court on the fundamental concepts of dignity, human freedom, autonomy and self-determination—these are key aspects underpinning the promises of the Convention.[58] Thus, '[t]he ability to conduct one's life in a manner of one's own choosing includes the opportunity to pursue activities perceived to be of a physically harmful or dangerous nature for the individual concerned'.[59] The Court stated that even if death were the result of a refusal of a blood transfusion, imposing a transfusion on a legally capicitated patient without consent would intervene the patient's Article 8 ECHR right to physical integrity.[60] The Court stated that a legally capicitated adult patient has the right

55 *Case of Jehovah's Witnesses of Moscow and Others* v. *Russia* (Application no 302/02).
56 *Re T (adult: refusal of medical treatment)* [1994] 4 All ER 649 at p 664.
57 ibid. p 664.
58 *Case of Jehovah's Witnesses of Moscow and Others v. Russia* (n 55) at [135].
59 ibid.
60 ibid.

to accept or refuse treatment, to accept or refuse a blood transfusion.[61] This must be a meaningful decision that reflects the values and beliefs of the patient, regardless of how foolish these decisions might be viewed by broader society.

It was concluded by the European Court that the Russian Courts showed insufficient 'relevant and sufficient reasons' or relevant evidence to validate their limitations on autonomy, religious belief and physical integrity.[62] This meant that the Articles 9 and 11 (freedom of assembly and association) ECHR were infringed and, specifically, that refusing blood transfusions could not be used to justify the banning of the religious manifestation of Jehovah's Witnesses' beliefs in Russia/ Europe.

These findings were vindicated in a subsequent Russian 2013 case: *Avilkina and Others* v *Russia*.[63] This case concerned applicants who argued that their Articles 8 (right to respect for private and family life) and Article 14 (prohibition of discrimination) ECHR rights were breached because their medical files and confidential information were disclosed to prosecution authorities in Russia due to their refusal of blood transfusions in public hospitals. It was argued by the applicants that this confidential information fell within the sphere of Article 8. The European Court agreed with the applicants and claimed that their Article 8 rights were disproportionately infringed.[64] This case highlights the connection between the right to manifest religious belief and the requirement to safeguard private and family life. Therefore, both rights can interconnect: they are not entirely separate.

These Russian cases highlight the power of the ECtHR and, indeed, the Convention in protecting the rights of mentally competent adult patients who wish to manifest their religious beliefs. The ECtHR recognised the role of self-determination in relation to making medical decisions, even when this self-determination negatively impacts upon their heath or does not comply with what one might regard as a sensible medical decision.[65] These decisions are welcomed because they vindicate the right of a mentally competent patient to act in accordance with his or her wishes/beliefs when making medical decisions.[66]

61 ibid. at [136].
62 ibid. at [142].
63 *Avilkina and Others* v. *Russia* (application no. 1585/09).
64 ibid. at [32].
65 See Ó Néill (n 3) p 387.
66 Another relevant ECtHR case was *Hoffmann* v. *Austria* [1994] 1 FCR 193. This concerned a housewife who was once a Roman Catholic and became a Jehovah's Witness. She subsequently issues divorce proceedings against her husband. This was granted, and her former husband was denied custodial rights to his children. On Appeal, it was held by the Austrian Supreme Court that the lower court should have considered the children's education and the reality that they would be brought up as Jehovah's Witnesses by their mother. The decision reflected a concern that their membership of the Jehovah's Witness faith could potentially damage their health if a blood transfusion were required. However, when the case reached the ECtHR, the mother was successful. The Strasbourg Court held that by making a distinction mainly or solely on the basis of religious belief was not within the bounds of acceptability. Therefore, the Court held that a breach of Article 8 and also Article 14 existed.

The Strasbourg jurisprudence clearly protects the right of an adult with legal capacity to refuse medical treatment. It does not matter whether this is based on personal conviction or religious belief. The key issue is the fact that when a mentally competent adult patient who has legal capacity makes an autonomous choice, this decision is upheld by the courts. The situation, however, becomes more complicated when other factors (e.g. lack of legal capacity or undue include) come under scrutiny.

The consistency of Strasbourg's decisions must be seen in light of the fact that its jurisprudence has primarily arbitrated to date over fairly straightforward facts. The ECtHR, however, has not dealt, in any specific way, with more complicated cases such as those involving undue influence or the capacity of children to make decisions. It is clear that the both the ECtHR and English courts (in *LM* and *RC*) aim to ensure that legally capacitated adults can legitimately make their own medical decisions. However, English law has also endeavoured to decide upon a less simple case in *Re T* on the issue of undue influence. Less straightforward cases such as this become more clouded by legal, ethical and medical nuances that lead to somewhat less clarity in the response of the courts.

Borderline legal capacity not directly covered by the MCA

For some patients, the issue of whether they have legal capacity or not is not fully clear-cut or the issue of legal capacity is overridden by circumstances that are not covered by the MCA. The courts have used their inherent jurisdiction to protect 'vulnerable adults' who have borderline legal capacity. This specific jurisdiction acts within a context where the autonomy of a vulnerable adult has not been compromised by legal incapacity, but, rather, by some form of constraint, undue influence or some reason which deprives them of the legal capacity to make a relevant decision.[67] This issue of borderline legal capacity is not dealt with in any particular substance in this book, due to the fact that the case law that governs such patients has not yet related specifically to the manifestation of religious belief. It is referred to here, in a tangential manner, to elucidate the point that the law's treatment of these patients is not wholly appropriate. Into the future, situations may arise where patients who are assessed as having borderline legal capacity may make medical decisions, based upon their religious beliefs, including Jehovah's Witness belief, which end up in the courts.

The implementation of this inherent jurisdiction is to be seen in *DL v A Local Authority*.[68] This case concerned the determination of whether or not the inherent jurisdiction existed outside the context of the MCA in relation to vulnerable adults. The case concerned DL, who allegedly was physically and verbally abusive

67 See Emma Cave, 'Determining Capacity to Make Medical Treatment Decisions: Problems Implementing the Mental Capacity Act 2005' (2015) 36(1) *Statute Law Review*, 86–106, p 86. Also see Jonathan Herring, *Vulnerable Adults and the Law* (OUP, 2016) chapter 4.

68 *DL v A Local Authority* [2012] EWCA Civ 243.

to his elderly parents. It was also alleged that DL was coercing his parents into transferring the proprietorship of their house into his own name. Proceedings were initiated by the local authority under the inherent jurisdiction of the High Court in order to safeguard the parents from DL: these proceedings could not be initiated under the MCA because the parents did not lack legal capacity under the MCA test. The local authority claimed that the parents lacked legal capacity, not because they failed the MCA test, but as a consequence of the undue influence placed on them. According to MacFarlane LJ:

> … In the absence of any express provision, the clear implication is that if there are matters outside the statutory scheme to which the inherent jurisdiction applies then that jurisdiction continues to be available to continue to act as the 'great safety net'…[69]

As such, it was held that an inherent jurisdiction still existed in English law post-MCA.[70] While this case does not deal with a Jehovah's Witness, it is important to include it in so far as it vindicates the right of the courts to apply its inherent jurisdiction to cases that fall outside the MCA. The fact that this possibility exists means that patients who are in any way at risk, including potentially Jehovah's Witnesses, will be able to have their cases decided upon beyond the limits, boundaries and borders of the MCA.

Additionally, *A NHS Trust v A*[71] demonstrated how the courts dealt with an adult who fell outside the scope of the MCA's protection. This case involved Dr A, who was refusing food as a result of the mistaken belief that this action could result in UK Border Control granting him a visa. This refusal was not determined to be based on mental illness but was, rather, related to a physical disorder, which may have arisen from a mental disorder, but did not fall within the two-stage MCA legal capacity test. The court used their inherent jurisdiction to determine that it would be within Dr A's best interests to authorise treatment. This treatment involved physical constraint and consequential deprivation of liberty. This patient should have been given additional support in his decision-making: it seems apparent that the court acted too quickly in determining his best interests. In doing so, it is possible that the court violated the patient's autonomy to some degree or, at the very least, was insufficiently mindful of his autonomous decisions. In the event that a Jehovah's Witness with borderline legal capacity was involved

69 ibid. at [61].

70 The judge stated that it should be retained and relied on *Re SA (Vulnerable adult with capacity: marriage)* [2005] EWHC 2941 (Fam) at [54], where it was stated that the inherent jurisdiction should be retained because it: … is in part aimed at enhancing or liberating the autonomy of a vulnerable adult whose autonomy has been compromised by a reason other than mental incapacity because they are… (a) under constraint; or (b) subject to coercion or undue influence; or (c) for some other reason deprived of the capacity to make the relevant decision or disabled from making a free choice, or incapacitated or disabled from giving or expressing a real and genuine consent.

71 *A NHS Trust v A* [2013] EWHC 2442.

in a case like this, it is possible that, following this case law, the court might give little weight to the exercise of patient autonomy and apply the best interests test to disallow the refusal of a blood transfusion.

Undue influence and adults

Another issue that has bearing upon determining the sufficiency of the current legal approach is the relationship between legal capacity and undue influence. No apparent consent or refusal is considered to be valid if a patient has just consented to action in light of coercion or undue influence.[72] A patient has been unduly influenced if the will of that patient has been 'overborne' by another person's will. Beyleveld and Brownsword provide a useful description of just what constitutes undue influence:

> ...bullying or intimidating external influence belongs with duress; and the agent who settles for a quiet life or who chooses to make a decision that will please another might well be exercising an independent judgement—but they are close to the focal question, namely whether the agent understood its own responsibility for making the final decision and was sufficiently able to hold the influence at arm's length to exercise control over that decision.[73]

The MCA, as it stands, does not address undue influence at all. It determines legal capacity and the consequences of incapacity. The issue of undue influence brings additional nuances of uncertainty into the process. *Re T*[74] is a case in point where it was found that an adult daughter was under the undue influence of her mother and, as a consequence, her refusal of a blood transfusion, following a Caesarean section, was set aside. *Re T* involved a pregnant woman who was not a Jehovah's Witness member, but was raised by her mother to follow many of the tenets of the faith. Her father and boyfriend applied for a declaration that it would not be unlawful to administer the transfusion without her consent. It was concluded by the judge that, as a result of the medication she was taking, T was not fully rational when she refused consent. A blood transfusion was consequently carried out. The decision to overrule the patient's wishes was taken due to the fact that T wasn't given the proper information, was incapacitated temporarily and was unduly influenced. Butler-Sloss LJ described in some detail the intrusive and pervading nature of such influence by saying that 'in equity it has long been recognised that an influence may be subtle, insidious, pervasive and where religious beliefs are involved especially powerful'.[75] To demonstrate the effect of religious belief on a person, Butler-Sloss LJ also made reference to Lindley LJ in *Allcard v Skinner*[76] who stated that 'the influence of one mind over another is very subtle,

72 ibid. p 129.
73 Beyleveld and Brownsword, *Consent in the Law* (n 14) p 170.
74 *Re T* (n 56).
75 ibid. p 120.
76 *Allcard v Skinner* [1887] 36 Ch.D. 145 at p 183. See *Re T* (n 56) p 119.

and of all influences religious influence is the most dangerous and the most powerful'.[77]

It is noteworthy that the High Court, in grave circumstances, can intervene to safeguard an adult who complies with the MCA test in order to provide protection to a vulnerable adult who is perceived to be unable to make an autonomous decision due to coercion or undue influence. The same caveat applies here as in the discussion of borderline legal capacity above, namely the danger that the courts can impose their decision on the patient. In *Re T*, which predated the MCA, Lord Donaldson recognises that a conflict of interests exits in this case: the interests of the patient as well as the interests of the society in which s/he lives. He points out that self-determination is an important part of a patient's interests, even if the decision will cause the patient to die prematurely.[78] He described self-determination as 'the patient's interest… to live his own life how he wishes, even if it will damage his health or lead to a premature death'.[79] Lord Donaldson calls into question two facts: the strength of will of the patient and the relationship of the 'persuader' to the patient. He recognises that there is a very strong relationship between a parent and a child.[80] In this case, it was found that T was temporarily legally incapacitated as a result of the undue influence. This meant that her wishes were set aside, leading to some disquiet about the rapidity with which this finding of undue influence led to the annulling of her self-determination. This gives rise to an overall concern that the deeply felt wishes of the patient, including those that derive from religious belief, in the particular case of patients who are unduly influenced are not given wholly sufficient protection in the courts.

Summary of current law

In summary, the two-tier MCA test provides a mechanism to determine the legal capacity of adults. The position under English law is supported by the Strasbourg jurisprudence. Current law, in the main, respects the autonomous decisions of

77 ibid. at p 183. The legal test for determining when an influence is undue is described in *Barclays Bank plc v O'Brien* [1994] 1 AC 180 and *Royal Bank of Scotland v Etridge* [2001] UKHL 44. provide clarity. Lord Browne-Wilkinson in *O'Brien* said that two categories of undue influence exist. The second category is further divided into two parts. The categories were actual undue influence (identified as 'Class 1') and presumed undue influence ('Class 2') He divided presumed undue influence into class 2A and 2B. Class 2A involves influences arising from relationships (doctor-patient etc.) which will always result in undue influence being presumed. Class 2B involves influence resulting from relationships that have developed in such a manner that a presumption of undue influence should exist. However, in *Etridge* it was held by the House of Lords that, while a difference exists between actual and presumed undue influence, it should not function in the manner put forward in *O'Brien* because of the fact that class 2B can be misinterpreted. See ibid. at [107]. Lord Hobhouse said that 'it is not a useful forensic tool'.

78 ibid. p 153.

79 *Re T* (n 56) at [59].

80 ibid. at [113–114].

legally capacitated adults to refuse blood transfusions, although there is some evidence of the imposition of paternalism in the approach taken to borderline legal capacity/undue influence. Into the future, it is likely that, in the decision-making process, even greater consideration will be given to patients' beliefs and the degree to which their consent is informed.

Question 2: Re adults: why is this current law sufficient or insufficient in the context of the PGC?

This section seeks to determine if the current law dealing with Jehovah's Witness adults who refuse blood transfusions complies with the PGC. To do this, it is, firstly, determined if the two-stage MCA legal capacity test is in line with the PGC. For patients who are deemed to be legally incapacitated under this test, the compliance with the PGC of the MCA's best interests test is then gauged. In addition to this, English law's approach to undue influence and borderline legal capacity in this specific context is scrutinised in order to ascertain its appropriateness and/or to determine if a conflict exists between the law's paternalistic approach and the autonomy of the patient. This examination leads to a conclusion that the current approach of English law in respect of adults is broadly compliant with the PGC, notwithstanding some reservations.

Compliance of relevant case law on adult Jehovah's Witnesses who refuse blood transfusions

The MCA is founded upon a number of fundamental principles, set out in s 1 (as previously summarised). These principles are congruent with the PGC because they aid the exercise of autonomous decisions.[81] The primary reason why the two-stage legal capacity is, equally, compliant with the PGC lies in the fact that its approach tracks mental competence in an appropriate manner.

To illustrate the sufficiency of the law's approach in terms of its compliance with the PGC, attention is now given to the cases of *LM*[82] and *RC*.[83] In *LM*, the processes that the court adopted to determine capacity (the utilisation of the MCA legal capacity test), tracked LM's mental competence in an appropriate manner. Peter Jackson J found that, in line with the s 2 (1) MCA, there was no evidence

81 The assumption of legal capacity under s 1 (2) MCA ties in with the idea that an adult is an apparent agent and the presumption that he can act in accordance with his will-rights. In the context of Jehovah's Witnesses, s 1 (4) is particularly interesting. It is appropriate that decisions that seem 'unwise' are permissible and this complies with the PGC, as long as the apparent agent does not interfere with the generic rights of others. The focus on best interests in s 1 (5) also represents a suitable way of acting because in accordance with the PGC's protection of people who are mentally incompetent. Additionally, the fact that the least restrictive approach should be taken in acting in the best interests of a legally incapacitated patient complies with the PGC's idea that actions should be taken that allow for the patient to exercise their generic rights.

82 *LM* (n 36).

83 *RC* (n 47).

'that her underlying mental illness rendered her unable to make a decision'.[84] He further found that s 1(2)'s presumption of capacity was not displaced and s 3's criteria for legal capacity were in the 'balance of probabilities met'.[85] This led him to the conclusion that LM 'understood the nature, purpose and effects of the proposed treatment, including that refusal of a blood transfusion might have fatal consequences'.[86] Of crucial importance is that the judge indicated that LM's decision in advance of loss of legal capacity held for differing circumstances. Thus, the court's approach allowed for action that was in line with LM's actual wishes.

Applying the PGC to this case involves consideration of LM as an apparent agent with generic rights. Prior to her losing her legal capacity, she made her decisions in line with her will-rights: these will-rights are the behaviours that are expected of an agent: they enabled LM to make voluntary decisions.[87] She was a being who had reached a threshold of mental competence. It must be concluded, thus, that she was an apparent mentally competent agent who could exercise her will-rights and, therefore, could legitimately refuse treatment. To deny LM, at this stage, as a mentally competent adult, the right to make a decision to refuse a blood transfusion would be to unjustly interfere with her will-rights and would, therefore, contravene the PGC.

As her condition deteriorated, LM lost legal capacity, indicating a change in her circumstances. However, the PGC requires us to still give effect to the will-rights of LM when she was an apparent mentally competent agent: she had previously articulated these wishes very clearly. The way that she lived, in accordance with her Jehovah's Witness faith, was patently in line with her purpose-fulfilment. Although there was a change in characteristics of agency seen in LM, there was no change in the purpose with which she lived her life and so the judgment in this case is fully supported by the PGC and is sound. The stance here in English law is a progressive one. It gives effect to the will-rights of the apparent agent, even though a change of circumstances existed, and it is an example of the law being used in a purposeful and PGC-compliant manner.

The judgment in *RC* was also a PGC-compliant one and the MCA capacity test successfully provided a tracking measure for RC's mental competence. Mostyn J referred to the need to apply aspects of the legal capacity 'very cautiously and carefully when religious beliefs are in play'.[88] He infers that we shouldn't relate a religious belief to a question of legal capacity.[89] The judge correctly determined that an adult is entitled to refuse treatment, even if it results in his or her death. It is evident from the doctor's report that RC was of sound mind and knew the decision he was making. It is a deep-rooted right that a mentally competent adult has autonomy to refuse treatment and that this autonomy, to quote John Stewart Mill, 'is sovereign'. This emphasis on autonomy is in line with the will-rights of

84 *LM* (n 36) at [21].
85 ibid.
86 ibid.
87 See chapter 2.
88 *LM* (n 36) at [34].
89 ibid.

the PGC (but the PGC goes further than Mill in so far as the PGC includes a definition of harm).[90] The PGC finds that denying the patient (RC), who did not lack capacity, permission to refuse a blood transfusion would be at variance with his generic rights which, under the PGC, he can waive. RC can waive the benefit to his right to life under the PGC and can, therefore, make the decision to refuse treatment.

The MCA test for legal capacity, in the context of these cases is compatible with the PGC because it allows for apparent agents to exercise their generic right to waive the benefits to these rights and the criteria used in the second stage of the test adequately reflect the PGC's idea of mental competence as being task-specific. Notwithstanding this affirmation of the MCA in terms of its broad compliance with the PGC in the case, there are, nonetheless, some difficulties with it, as articulated by Cave.[91] It is accepted that there are gaps in the MCA that are, to a degree, plugged by the courts' inherent jurisdiction, as apparent in *DL*.[92] Cave's concern that the MCA fails to keep abreast of human rights developments and fails to adequately address the issue of disability are legitimate, but discussion of these issues falls outside the scope of this chapter because, to date, such matters have not arisen to any great degree in Jehovah's Witnesses cases.[93]

Is the best interests test PGC-compliant in situations where English law determines that the patient lacks capacity?

As explained, the best interests test, under s 4 MCA, only comes into play when the patient has been determined to lack capacity. To what degree does this test track the generic needs of mentally incompetent patients and so comply with the PGC?

It is argued that the use of the best interests in s 4 is, for the most part, compliant with the PGC. The consideration by the courts of all the relevant circumstances and factors set out in s 4 tracks the generic needs of mentally incompetent patients. This is a good attempt at giving effect to the patient's generic rights. The values of legally incapacitated patients must be respected.[94] In terms of people

90 See Alan Gewirth, *Human Rights: Essays on Justification and Application* (University of Chicago Press, 1982) p 236.

91 Cave, 'Determining Capacity to Make Medical Treatment Decisions: Problems Implementing the Mental Capacity Act 2005' (n 67).

92 ibid. pp 90–91.

93 ibid. pp 91–92.

94 The patient's viewpoints are given some consideration under s 4 (6) (a), where the decision-maker must consider 'the person's past and present wishes and feelings'. Section s 4 (6) (b) also states 'the beliefs and values that would be likely to influence his decision if he had capacity'. Additionally, under s 4 (6) (c), the court considers 'the other factors that he would be likely to consider if he were able to do so'. There is also evidence that the substituted judgment test also provides judges with a directional line of stewardship in the event that the best interests test is inconclusive. (See Pattinson (n 2) pp 147–148.) This requires judges when an advance decision is absent to apply the values that the patient possessed when he had been deemed to have legal capacity.

with strong religious convictions, the strength of those convictions can still apply to decisions made in what is determined to be in their best interests, even if the person lacks legal capacity. Just because these patients are legally incapacitated doesn't mean that they cannot have values or that their religious beliefs should not be respected. All relevant circumstances, under s 4, in the case of Jehovah's Witnesses, could include an acknowledgement of the patient's adherence to the tenets of their religious beliefs in respect of the refusal of blood transfusions. Consideration of s 4's factors, therefore, represents an attempt to make the most appropriate decision for the patient that respects his wishes prior to being legally incapacitated.

However, the guidance given in the MCA as to how the best interests of the patient can be safeguarded is somewhat vague, and this vagueness has the potential for the values of the court or other people to creep into the decision-making process and, perhaps, ultimately, to override those of the patient.[95] What potentially also limits the effect of tracking of the generic needs and consequent compliance with the PGC is where disproportionate attention is given to the views of others (s 4 (7)). As such, there is an acknowledged danger that consideration of the subjective or paternalistic or well-meaning preferences of those others could potentially impede the exercise of the rights of the patient. Herring suggests, for example, that the opinions of a family who oppose the blood transfusion should not 'carry the day'.[96] He makes the strong point that the viewpoint of family members can only be taken into account if they assist in determining best interests.[97] They cannot be used to justify making an order that would be contrary to the patient's best interests.

There is rarely consensus between parties as to what constitutes best interests. A doctor might see a conflict between his need to give treatment and the Jehovah's Witness patient's right to refuse this treatment.[98] For the doctor and the patient, the future, which could include the death of the patient arising from the non-treatment, could be more significant than the present. Interests of third parties could include siblings who have differing opinions than those of the patient, but who can offer some shared history and some shared values with the patient. It is also conceivable that judges can use best interests as a fudge or delaying tactic to prevent a decision being made that would contravene what the judge feels is in the patient's best interests. However, this way of using the best interests test is not

(See Pattinson (n 2) p 148.) For example, in the case of *Aintree* (n 21), a patient's medical situation had deteriorated beyond that considered in the Court of First Instance and Lady Hale suggested that, in considering what the patient's view might have been, there was a need to also consider that those views might 'well have changed in the light of the stresses and strains of his current predicament' (at [45])

95 See Jonathan Herring, *Medical Law and Ethics* (6th ed, OUP, 2016) p 218.

96 ibid. Herring summarises a number of criticisms of the best interests test, including its vagueness, its individualistic nature and the need to ensure that the best interest standard should 'take into account the values and principles of the individual person'. Also see Beyleveld and Brownsord, *Consent in the* Law (n 14) pp 117–118 where they point out some difficulties with the best interests test.

97 ibid.

98 Beyleveld and Brownsword, *Consent in the Law* (n 14) pp 117–118.

compliant with the PGC. The judge must be sure that she identifies the fact that, because the patient lacks legal capacity at that moment in relation to the relevant decision, the religious convictions that the patient had before the onset of lack of legal capacity are not negated. Therein lies the difficulty for the judge, in line with s 4 (6), to ensure that the decision made adequately protects the values and beliefs of the patient and does not overly emphasise the influence of others. A failure to do this is not an appropriate compliance with the PGC.

The issue for adults who lack legal capacity is to ensure that the values and, in this case, the religious beliefs of the patient are respected, in accordance with their rights under the PGC. The right to express these values is not annulled because of legal incapacity, but, obviously, particular caution has to be adopted in terms of decisions made to uphold these rights and to ensure that values of others do not trump the values of the patient.

The finding in *Montgomery* in relation to importance of informed consent is fully compliant with the PGC and it provides a positive pathway for deliberations on such cases into the future. By allowing for informed consent and by rejecting medical paternalism, patients (apparent agents) are acting in accordance with their will-rights, as they are given the opportunity to exercise their freedom and well-being. Equally, the way in which the best interests test was used in *Wye Valley* also complies with the PGC, by recognising the importance of deeply held-belief and so allowing for the exercise of the patient's rights under the PGC.

Is English law's approach to undue influence in relation to Jehovah's Witnesses who refuse blood transfusions PGC-compliant?

If undue influence is proven to be a factor in the decisions made by the patient, then this renders those decisions involuntary[99] and so would be contrary to the patient's generic conditions of agency. Such a patient would be denied the necessary freedom and well-being that are required to justifiably make the relevant decision. It is important to consider the applicability of English law's approach in determining undue influence to ascertain whether or not such influence is a coercive one that denies patients the freedom to exercise their generic rights.

In relation to the compliance of the judgment in *Re T*, there are two possible ways of assessing it from the point of view of the PGC. Firstly, if the undue influence impacted upon T's mental competence and, so, impacted upon her decision-making ability, then her generic rights would be compromised by her susceptibility to the undue influence placed upon her by her mother.[100] Her lack of mental competence in that specific instance indicates that T could not refuse treatment/waive the benefits to her generic rights. Applying the PGC in this

99 Pattinson (n 2) p 126.

100 Determining the level of undue influence, according to Pattinson, summarising *Re T* (n 56), will include a need to take account of three factors: '(1) the relationship between the persuader and the patient, (2) the strength of the patient's will and (3) whether religious belief is involved (*Re T*)'. See Pattinson (n 2) p 129.

manner means that the judgment in this case could actually be correct because her decision may not have been fully autonomous, and her freedom and well-being may have been compromised.

Secondly, however, it is possible to come to an alternative conclusion if the issue of voluntariness and undue influence is examined more comprehensively in this case. Did T, as an apparent agent, comprehend her own responsibility for making the ultimate decision and was she in a fit position to gauge the merits of other people's influence in a balanced way so that she was able to, according to Beyleveld and Brownsword, 'exercise control over that decision'?[101] There is a possibility that a significant leap was made, in this case, between being unduly influenced and lacking legal capacity. This leap may have been disproportionate: T, although unduly influenced, may have still been mentally competent. As a mentally competent adult, the PGC would hold that T had will-rights, could waive the benefits of her generic rights (including life). If this were the case, the PGC would hold that the judgment was wrong because it did not assign will-rights to T, as an apparent mentally competent agent. It could be inferred that the judgment suited all concerned: as long as T was evaluated as lacking in legal capacity, then she could receive a blood transfusion and both she and her baby would be saved. If the issue of legal capacity were not invoked, then T as a mentally competent autonomous apparent agent (adult) would, thus, be entitled under law to refuse medical treatment, with potentially grave consequences for both herself and her unborn baby.

Pattinson suggests that feminists and those who hold religious convictions would view the decision to ignore the woman's expressed convictions, in this case, with some dismay.[102] Was the whole argument about undue influence, as Pattinson infers, not just somewhat convenient?[103] The 'convenience' here is understandable because the consequence of allowing T to make her own decision could have been calamitous. However, that caution should not have undermined T's right to act freely and voluntarily. Insufficient attention was given to the religious convictions of T herself. The strongly held convictions of the mother were not necessarily those held by T because there is evidence that she was not, actually, a practising Jehovah's Witness. The main criticism of the case relates to the fact that the existence of undue influence was seen automatically to lead to legal incapacity. That seems to be a bridge too far. Yes, there was undue influence, but that should not necessarily mean that T could not make up her own mind.

In supporting this second line of argument, we cannot say that, just because there is some evidence of undue influence, then the patient's decision automatically becomes involuntary. Basically, the doctrine of undue influence cannot be applied when it suits. We cannot decide that undue influence exists and so bring about a result that reflects our view of what would be good for the patient. A PGC-compliant response must give entitlement to the patient and give effect to

101 Beyleveld and Brownsword, *Consent in the Law* (n 14) p 170.
102 Pattinson (n 2) p 127.
103 ibid.

the patient's generic rights. The PGC, therefore, can arrive at different conclusions: if T had sufficient mental competence, then the PGC would find that she should be able to refuse treatment, in line with her will-rights. If, however, there were irrefutable evidence that she was unduly influenced, then her voluntariness would be impeded and compromised and, thus, she could not refuse the treatment. Additionally, while undue influence may be a factor in a case, it should not be seen to automatically undermine the legal capacity of a patient.

Thus, the current position of the law in respect of considering undue influence is somewhat unclear: in many ways, it makes a good attempt at promoting and safeguarding voluntary action and, as a consequence, is compatible with the PGC. However, there is a danger that arguably unfounded declarations of undue influence could impede the exercise of the generic rights of patients and this would breach the PGC.

Is the approach of current law to adults with borderline legal capacity compliant with the PGC?

There are situations where some people who should have legal capacity to make decisions with some support are, instead, obliged to submit to the decision of others.[104] This means that the approach of current English law to adults with borderline legal capacity has been, essentially, to act in a paternalistic way and to make decisions *for* the patients. There is little evidence in, for example in *A NHS Trust v A*,[105] of the facilitation of discourse and discussion that would support such patients in articulating their decisions and for such decisions to be given the gravitas of adequate consideration by the courts. This approach does not fully comply with the PGC because the muting of the voice of these marginally legally capacitated adults also mutes the expression of their generic rights, which is a derogation of the PGC. In addition to this, the paternalistic tendencies of the court, in this context, may also compromise a borderline legally capacitated patient's 'self-fulfilment', to be discussed in chapter 5, and so provide another derogation from the PGC.[106]

Question 3: Is there an alternative approach in the context of adults that will provide greater compliance with the framework?

Approach in Gewirthia

In Gewirthia, a right to refuse treatment exists, based upon identification that all agents have generic rights.[107] This right is, however, based upon mental competence and citizens in Gewirthia will have to have sufficient mental competence (and, consequently, legal capacity) in order refuse blood transfusions.

104 See Cave, 'Determining Capacity to Make Medical Treatment Decisions: Problems Implementing the Mental Capacity Act 2005' (n 67) p 104.

105 *A NHS Trust v* A (n 71).

106 Alan Gewirth, *Self-Fulfillment*, (Princeton University Press, 1998).

107 See Deryck Belyleveld and Roger Brownsword, 'Principle, Proceduralism, and Precaution in a Community of Rights' (2006) 19(2) *Ratio Juris*, 141–168.

Alternative approaches in non-Gewirthian English society/law

In summary, many of the current approaches adopted by English law comply with the PGC and minimal change is proposed. The fundamental principles of the MCA, as set out in s 1, are aligned with the PGC. No significant change is required to the MCA legal capacity two-stage test. The best interests test, while not perfect and if properly applied, does allow for action that reflects the values of the patient and also balances this with consideration of other circumstances, including the potential for generic harm being inflicted on the legally incapacitated patient. The protections, as enshrined in s 4 (6), that give a listening ear to other people are appropriate, but cognisance of other people's point of view will have to be appropriately balanced to ensure that decisions reached don't reflect the values of other people or of the courts to the detriment of the patient.

Judicial guidelines should now include guidance on how to apply the best interests test in order to guarantee that the opinions of others, however well meaning, are not given disproportionate weight. If judges were to adopt this PGC-compliant stance, it would ensure that patients' freedom and well-being were appropriately protected. Equally, there is a need to provide additional guidance as to how undue influence can be identified and dealt with, in the knowledge that the important *Re T* case existed prior to the enaction of the MCA. Judges are urged to be cautious when using the best interests test and when considering the concept of undue influence, in order to ensure that the most suitable approach is taken that best respects a patient's generic rights.

Cave has discussed the problems with implementing the MCA, in particular in relation to those who might be perceived to straddle both legal capacity and incapacity.[108] She argues that some form of additional support is needed by such patients in order to mediate the tricky ground of decision-making with them, for them and, ultimately, by them. This book reaffirms this call because her idea of empowerment is in line with the PGC. It would allow for a process that would make every effort to ensure the exercise of patients' generic rights and, therefore, would act as a good faith attempt at applying the PGC. An approach which ensures that the inherent jurisdiction of the courts is integrated with a supportive process would have the advantage of leading to greater patient empowerment and, consequently, a greater vindication of the principles of the PGC: it would allow for the patients to make their own decisions and to articulate them coherently to interested parties, thus, getting as close as possible to the operation of the PGC in this context.

In the context of Strasbourg jurisprudence discussed in question 1 above, there is no particular need for the ECtHR to alter its position in relation to adults as the Court's jurisprudence adequately supports the ability of patients with legal capacity to act in accordance with their will-rights.

108 Cave, 'Determining Capacity to Make Medical Treatment Decisions: Problems Implementing the Mental Capacity Act 2005' (n 67) p 90.

Conclusion

Examination of case law demonstrates that English courts have, for the most part, provided an appropriate response to cases involving adult Jehovah's Witnesses who refuse blood transfusions. Overall, the MCA's two-stage legal capacity test properly tracks the mental competence of adults and the best interests test, if properly applied, is broadly compliant with the PGC. In all cases, those involved with the decision-making are urged to be cautious and to try to ensure that decisions reached are supportive of the protection of the generic rights of patients, in line with the PGC.

References

Barker, Jason, 'New Watchtower Blood Transfusion Policy' (Watchman Fellowship) available at: http://www.watchman.org/articles/jehovahs-witnesses/new-watchtower-blood-transfusion-policy/ (accessed 27 January 2017).

Beyleveld, Deryck and Brownsword, Roger, *Consent in the Law* (Hart, 2007).

Belyleveld, Deryck and Brownsword, Roger, 'Principle, Proceduralism, and Precaution in a Community of Rights' (2006) 19(2) *Ratio Juris*, 141–168.

Cave, Emma, 'Determining Capacity to Make Medical Treatment Decisions: Problems Implementing the Mental Capacity Act 2005', (2015) 36(1) *Statute Law Review*, 86–106.

Council of Europe, 'Convention on Human Rights and Biomedicine', available at https://rm.coe.int/168007cf98.

Gewirth, Alan, *Self-Fulfillment* (Princeton University Press, 1998).

Gewirth, Alan, *Human Rights: Essays on Justification and Application* (University of Chicago Press, 1982).

Herring, Jonathan, *Medical Law and Ethics* (6th ed, OUP, 2016).

Herring, Jonathan, *Vulnerable Adults and the Law* (OUP, 2016).

Meckford, James A, *The Trumpet of Prophecy: A Sociological Study of Jehovah's Witnesses* (Blackwell, 1975).

McCormick, Thomas R, 'Ethical Issues Inherent to Jehovah's Witnesses (2008) 3 *Perioperative Nursing Clinics*, 253–258.

Mill, John Stewart, *On Liberty* (2nd ed, Ticknor and Fields, 1863).

Ó Néill, Clayton, 'Jehovah's Witnesses and Blood Transfusions: An Analysis of the Legal Protections Afforded to Adults and Children in English European Human Rights Contexts' (2017) 24(4) *European Journal of Health Law*, 368–389.

Pattinson, Shaun D, *Medical Law and Ethics* (5thed, Sweet & Maxwell, 2017).

Rhodes, Ron, *Reasoning from the Scriptures with the Jehovah's Witnesses* (Harvest House Publishers, 1993).

Royal College of Surgeons of England, *Caring for Patients who Refuse Blood* (Royal College of Surgeons of England, 2016).

Watch Tower Bible and Tract Society, *The Watchtower* (15 January 1961).

Watch Tower Bible and Tract Society, 'Questions from readers' (15 January 2000).

5 Children, Jehovah's Witnesses, and refusal of blood transfusions

Introduction

It has been demonstrated that current law, at both domestic and European level, gives some protection to the manifestation of the religious beliefs of adult Jehovah's Witnesses. The position of children who refuse blood transfusions on the basis of religious belief gives rise to a number of queries, recommendations, and concerns about the current insufficiency of focus on the rights of children (particularly adolescents) to act in accordance with such belief. This represents a likely denial of their will-rights, as apparent (mentally competent) agents. As in the previous chapter, this situation of children will be analysed through the methodological lens of the three questions. The chapter assesses the compliance of current law with the PGC and it makes some recommendations for change.

Question 1: How have English law and the ECtHR dealt with the issue of Jehovah's Witness children who refuse blood transfusions?

In medical situations that have not come before the courts, there is some incidental evidence that children's wishes to consent to or refuse treatment are listened to and acted on. For example, Joshua McAuley, a 15-year-old Jehovah's Witness, died after a road traffic accident, following the acceptance of his refusal of a blood transfusion.[1] Equally, the Department of Health said in 2009 that, where the wishes of the child conflicted with the wishes of the parent(s), the parental wish should not automatically be acceded to but, rather, physicians should seek guidance from the courts.[2] Cave indicates that cases governing refusal of consent to medical treatment by children, which had been prevalent in the 1990s, no longer come to the fore in legal attention.[3] This may be

1 See Emma Cave and Zenon Stavrinides, *Medical Practitioners, Adolescents and Informed Consent*, (University of Leeds, 2013), available at: http://www.law.leeds.ac.uk/assets/files/research/cfig/Medical-Practitioners-Adolescents-and-Informed-Consent-Final-Report-2013.pdf (accessed 27 January 2017) p 40.

2 ibid.

3 Emma Cave, 'Determining Capacity to Make Medical Treatment Decisions: Problems Implementing the Mental Capacity Act 2005' (2015) 36(1) *Statute Law Review*, 86–106.

due to a number of factors, including greater societal acceptance of the wishes of patients, a preference for persuasion, rather than litigation, and the development of a greater focus on partnership between doctor and patients, in accordance with General Medical Council (GMC) guidance.[4] From the point of view, however, of cases dealing with Jehovah's Witness children that have made their way through the courts, there is little evidence that the voices of children have been heard sufficiently. The current legal approaches evidenced in the case law, which are primarily paternalistic in nature, are now outlined.

The legal situation for children is somewhat different from that of adults. There are two particular groupings for whom distinct approaches are used, children who are 16–17 years old and children under 16. The Family Law Reform Act 1969 (FLRA) applies to the decisions of children in the 16–17 age range. Section 8 (1) states that the consent to medical treatment of these children is as effective as that of an adult. A presumption exists that such children can give consent unless it is shown that they cannot satisfy the MCA's two-stage legal capacity test under this section. For children who are under 16, *Gillick* and its developments are the test for legal capacity. A child under 16 can give consent to treatment if he/she has 'sufficient understanding and intelligence' under *Gillick*[5] (i.e. the original *Gillick*-competence test), but this has, however, been extended in developing case law. It is important to stress that the standard expected under *Gillick* is at a higher standard than the adult test of legal capacity.[6] Even in the event that children under 16 satisfy this test, their decisions are likely to be overruled in the courts. An explanation of this judicial paternalism might best be found in Nolan LJ's explanatory statement in *Re W* where he said that '[a]n individual who has attained the age of 18 is free to do with his life what he wishes, but it is the duty of the court to ensure so far as it can that children survive to attain that age'.[7]

In *Re W*, a child over 16 refused to be transferred to a specialist unit for treatment.[8] This refusal was overridden at both the High Court and the Court of Appeal. It was stated that the risk of irreversible harm or death meant that the refusal of a minor can be overridden by the court, in line with the best interests of the child. Parents also have the power to override the refusal of a child.[9] Another important case is *An NHS Foundation Hospital v P*.[10] In this case, a 17-year-old girl tried to commit suicide and refused treatment. She was deemed to satisfy the legal capacity test, but the provision of the treatment that she had refused was, nevertheless, considered to be lawful. Barker J referenced *Re W* by stating that '[w]here…a Gillick-competent child refuses to give her consent to the treatment,

4 ibid. p 104.
5 *Gillick v West Norfolk Area Health Authority* [1986] AC 112.
6 See also the case of *Re M (Medical Treatment: Consent)* [1999] 2 FLR 1097 which concerned a heart transplant where the refusal of the under 16 child was overridden simply due to the best interests test.
7 *Re W* [1993] Fam 64 p 94.
8 ibid.
9 ibid. at [84].
10 *An NHS Foundation Hospital v P* [2014] EWHC 1650 (Fam).

the court may, in the exercise of its inherent jurisdiction, override the child's wishes in her best interests and give its consent to her treatment.'[11] This case supported, therefore, what *Re W* says about the court's powers under its inherent jurisdiction to override decisions. A court or parent can overrule the refusal of a child under 16 if treatment is essential to stopping death or serious, permanent harm.[12] This was clarified in *Re R*[13] where a child under 16 had a changeable mental state and, when she was 'lucid',[14] she refused anti-psychotic drugs. Lord Donaldson, at the Court of Appeal, said that she did not satisfy the *Gillick*-competence test and he stated, *in obiter*, that even if *Gillick* were satisfied, the court would override her refusal due to the application of the best interests test.

A case that strongly illustrates the paternalistic tendency of the court is that of *F (Mother) v F (Father)*.[15] This was a case about two children who didn't want to be inoculated with the MMR vaccine. Their position was in accordance with the wishes of their mother, but against the wishes of their father. It was held that it was in the best interests of the children to receive the vaccine.[16] The views of these children, Cave believes, weren't given sufficient attention.[17] Under English law, their objection to the vaccine was not taken seriously enough and their level of understanding was set at too great a threshold. Cave notes that a balance had to be struck between the medical benefit of inoculation and the welfare considerations of non-consensual inoculation and that the court was wrong to simply consider one side of the argument.[18] She argues that there was a failure in the judgment to facilitate the children's legal capacity to make a decision.[19] She claims that this would not happen in the case of adults, where they could set out their own viewpoints and that these would, at least, be considered.[20] *F (Mother) v F (Father)* clearly shows that, in the case of children, a very high threshold of understanding exists and that there is a tendency for the courts to overrule children's decisions in a way that diminishes the validity of their voices. It is notable that *Gillick* was not applied or discussed in this case.

11 ibid at [12].
12 See *Re R* [1991] 4 ALL ER 177 in relation to a child under 16-year-old and *Re W* (n 7) in the context of a 16–17-year-old child.
13 ibid.
14 Shaun D Pattinson, *Medical Law and Ethics* (5th ed, Sweet & Maxwell, 2017) p 163.
15 *F (Mother) v F (Father)* [2013] EWHC 2683 (Fam).
16 It was Thesis J's opinion that the children were influenced by factors which impacted upon the weight that should be given to their beliefs and opinions. She said that a balance had to exist between their understanding of these issues and the influential factors and held that they did not possess a balanced level of understanding. Her decision was supported by the fact that medical advice encourages children to have the injection, even if there are a number of possible side effects. Finally, Thesis J considered the emotional effect of the decision being made for them but said that their parents must support and assist them, as a consequence of the decision.
17 Emma Cave, 'Adolescent Refusal of MMR Inoculation: F (Mother) v F (Father)' (2014) 77(4) *MLR*, 630–640.
18 ibid. p 640.
19 ibid. p 636 and p 640.
20 ibid. p 640.

For legally capacitated adults, the freedom not to accept blood transfusions is fully protected under Article 9 of the European Convention on Human Rights (ECHR). The same level of protection is not, however, given to children. Although children's right to express religious belief is protected under Article 9, the limitations of this Article apply. These limitations under Article 9 (2) are those that are 'prescribed by law and are necessary in a democratic society in the interests of public safety, for the protection of public order, health or morals, or for the protection of the rights and freedoms of others'. The use of Article 9's limitations as the basis of an argument prohibiting the refusal of blood transfusions has not been called upon sufficiently by the courts in English law to date, but its use has the potential to provide meaningful protection to vulnerable people and children.

Development of law concerning legal capacity and Jehovah's Witnesses children

There are three particular contexts in dealing with children: babies, younger children, and adolescents and each of these contexts involves differentiated approaches. In the context of infants, the case of *Birmingham Children's NHS Trust v B & C*[21] is relevant. The court indicated that, in the application of the best interests test, it was appropriate for a baby to have a heart operation even though the baby's parents refused to consent as a result of their religious beliefs, as Jehovah's Witnesses. Mr Justice Keehan stated that '[i]t is plain on the evidence before me that, whilst there are risks attached to him undergoing the TGA procedure, those are minimal risks, whereas starkly, if he does not undergo the procedure, his chances of survival are extremely poor'.[22] He also said that there 'no reasonable alternative to the administration of blood and/or blood products, they shall be at liberty to administer such blood and/or blood products without the consent of his parents'.[23]

The case illustrates the potential of the courts to act in what is perceived to be the best interests of the baby. It is clear that babies lack legal capacity to make these types of decisions. The courts override the decision of parents in these scenarios because of the potential injurious harm caused to the baby, who is unable to articulate his own wishes. It is strange that such a concern for the harm caused to the baby in this instance differs from the almost generic societal acceptance of the harm that is caused to a baby boy who is circumcised, and this anomaly will be fleshed out in the next chapter.

As the child gets older, the issue becomes more problematic and difficult to resolve. As stated, under English law, children are dealt with in a way that is primarily age-specific. Let us, firstly, consider the case of *Re L.*[24] In this case, a 14-year-old girl, who followed the tenets of the Jehovah's Witness faith, was scalded in a very hot bath. As a result of her beliefs, she rejected a blood transfusion.

21 *Birmingham Children's NHS Trust v B & C* [2014] EWHC 531 (Fam).
22 ibid. at [6].
23 ibid.
24 *Re L* [1998] 2 FLR 810.

However, the court did not allow her to refuse the transfusion.[25] Sir Stephen Brown P said that L lacked *Gillick* competency. This was partly due to the fact that, at the time, she did not have all of the vital information in relation to how she might die if the transfusion were not administered. The judge claimed that he limited experience of the world impacted upon her ability to make such a serious decision.[26]

The court sought a level of capacity within L that they felt was inhibited by her sheltered life and by the powerful and limiting influence that her Jehovah's Witnesses religious belief exerted on her. L needed to show that she was *capable* of understanding the consequences and not, simply, that she actually understood the consequences of her refusal. Pattinson argues that this approach resulted in an 'impossible threshold' because she was not informed of how she might die.[27] She didn't have the actual information to ever to be able to achieve that manner of understanding. Thus, her decisions were always going to be compromised by the fact that she was not provided with sufficient information. One could argue that this over-controlling approach was influenced by a paternalistic desire to save her life. I have argued elsewhere that '[t]he principle of the greater the decision the greater the level of legal capacity required was seen to be in play. But the genuine beliefs and wishes of L were insufficiently factored into the decision'.[28]

There is not universal acceptance of the reasoning in the judgment. For example, Jackson argues that it involves a misreading of the *Gillick*-competency test because the test is meant to judge the capability of a child to understand information and not whether she has been provided with enough information to allow her to make an informed decision.[29] Overall, this case demonstrates the veracity of Adhar and Leigh's statement that, even though the thoughts of a mature minor will be considered, the 'paternalistic instincts of the law triumph'.[30]

25 See Clayton Ó Néill, 'Jehovah's Witnesses and Blood Transfusions: An Analysis of the Legal Protections Afforded to Adults and Children in English European Human Rights Contexts' (2017) 24(4) *European Journal of Health Law*, 368–389.

26 *Birmingham Children's NHS Trust v B & C* (n 21).

27 Pattinson (n 14) p 165.

28 Ó Néill (n 25) p 385.

29 Emily Jackson, *Medical Law: Text, Cases and Materials* (3rd ed, OUP, 2013) p 270. Additionally, Grubb contends that, since it is the medical professions who have most of the control over the information provided, it would be disappointing if the lack of information would automatically mean that the person lacks mental competence. See Andrew Grubb, 'Commentary on *Re L (Medical Treatment-Gillick Competency)*' (1999) 7 *Medical Law Review*, 58–61, 60. Also see David Ziebart, 'Jehovah's Witnesses- Medical Care, Minors and the Religious Rite/Right' (2007) *The Denning Law Journal* 19 (1), 233. Ziebart, a practising Jehovah's Witness argues that refusal of treatment will be ignored if it is the court's contention that the administration of the treatment is in the best interests of the child, when considered objectively. He contends that the fact that a minor understands the decision they are making has no practical value at all. He argues that this is an unsatisfactory approach as it shows reluctance on the court's part to treat a child with mental competence in the same way as an adult.

30 Rex Adhar and Ian Leigh, *Religious Freedom in the Liberal State* (2nd ed, OUP, 2013) p 318.

The motif of insufficient attention to the wishes of the child extends further in the case of *Re E*.[31] This case concerned a 15-year-old Jehovah's Witness who refused a blood transfusion because doing so would not comply with his beliefs. The court held that he was not *Gillick*-competent due to the fact that he could not understand the implications of his decision.[32] In applying the best interests test the court considered his wishes and beliefs, but held that the significant influence placed upon him by his faith meant that his decision was not completely free.[33] Thus, in balancing the respect for the child's wishes with the opportunity for him to live, it was concluded that the transfusion ought to be administered. This arguably well-meaning decision, however, gave very little weight to E's religious beliefs.[34]

Thus, there is evidence in case law that children's voices are relatively unheard and that judges adopt paternalistic stances, based upon their perception of acting in accordance with a child's best interests. Whether this best interests fully reflects the child's commitment to the manifestation of his faith and conviction and his mental competence to make the relevant decision is, however, debatable, and the appropriateness of this position will be discussed now in the context of the PGC.

Question 2: Why is this approach, as it pertains to children, sufficient or insufficient in the context of the PGC?

Case law's compliance with the PGC

One of the main difficulties with the current law, from the perspective of the PGC, is the use, subsequent development, and dis-application of *Gillick*[35] in order to determine the legal capacity of children under 16. This test has been inappropriately dis-applied to debar decisions made by those who might otherwise have legal capacity. From a PGC point of view, this approach gives insufficient protection to a mentally competent child's will-rights, the benefits of which can be waived. This approach in English law is not PGC-compliant because a child's decision (a) can be overridden anyway by the courts (even when they have sufficient mental competence) and (b) the standard of maturity and understanding required is almost an impossible threshold to reach.[36]

When a mentally competent child exercises his will-rights, this happens in a task-specific context. This position confers a significant level of decision-making authority on such a child. Reverting to *Re E*, the PGC will likely hold that the

31 *Re E* [1993] 1 FLR 386.

32 When E reached the age of 18 he, again, refused blood transfusions. Given the fact that he had now reached the state of adulthood, this decision was accepted. The patient eventually died following this refusal.

33 See Ó Néill (n 25) pp 386–387.

34 ibid.

35 *Gillick* (n 5). Also see *Re W* (n 7) and *Re R* (n 12) in relation to *Gillick*'s dis-application.

36 See, for example, Pattinson (n 14) pp 163–166.

child had task-specific mental competence and that the case should not have been decided simply on best interests, but on the determination of the E's legal capacity. Thus, the decision of the court, in this case, and its reasoning, are at variance with the PGC.

An overly paternalistic approach was also adopted in *Re L* by bringing into play new requirements about a level of information that L was obliged to have, resulting in a dis-application of *Gillick*. The PGC would not require this level of information because its primary focus is on the purposiveness and voluntariness of such apparent agents. The fact that there was a likelihood that L was mentally competent means that, in accordance with the PGC, L should have been permitted to refuse the blood transfusion and exercise her will-rights or, at the very least, L's opinions should not have been so easily set aside.

In both *Re L* and *Re E*, the courts intervened in the child's decision to refuse the transfusion. Obviously, they did so out of concern for the consequences of the actions of the child and in order to safeguard what they regarded as the best interests of L and E. The central issue of these cases should have been a proper analysis of L and E's legal capacity to make this grave decision, not the use of the best interests test almost by default, as a consequence of *Gillick* and its dis-application. According to the PGC, the almost automatic intervention on the part of the courts to determine the good of the child, by the use of the best interests test, without sufficient consideration of the ability of a mentally competent child to make the relevant decision is, thus, inappropriate.

The starting point for judges should not be that they can simply override the decision if they don't like it. Outside the context of *Gillick*, the case of *F (Mother) v F (Father)* demonstrated the way in which case law has fostered the development of a judicial paternalism that is not compliant with the PGC.[37] The generic rights of the children, in this case, were not facilitated in any way and, in fact, were denied.

Accepting that no agent is required to give up any part of his well-being in order to maintain any part of any another agent's well-being means accepting that a Jehovah's Witness's desire to refuse a blood transfusion cannot be sacrificed to maintain the doctor's or the court's desire to safeguard life. The court can act as a potential rescuer of the vulnerable child, but it must be mindful of the fact that the well-being of the mentally competent child is, perhaps, not amenable to this rescue and such a rescue could, in fact, be a derogation from the PGC. If a test for legal capacity is not sufficiently rigorous and objective, then the patient's viewpoints might be negated and the decision-makers' perspective unduly clouded by judicial paternalism. The practice of paternalism of the courts in respect of Jehovah's Witness children who refuse blood transfusions is not just an inconvenience to the mentally competent child. It is actually, under the PGC, an infringement of their basic rights. By denying them something that reflects their personhood, their self-identity, their self-worth, the expression of their settled belief; a basic harm is caused to them. This infringes their rights under the PGC and is impermissible.

37 *F (Mother) v F (Father)* (n 15).

The corollary also exists whereby there is a grave risk that allowing a mentally competent child to refuse the transfusion will result in his or her death and so cause basic harm to that child. There is, however, a welfare right involved with enforced transfusion that is, arguably, hierarchically stronger than the need to protect the child's life. Just as in the case of a mentally competent adult, where giving any form of treatment requires consent or refusal, so too in the case of a mentally competent child, in line with the PGC, the requirement to be true to the child's consent or refusal, based upon their purposiveness and voluntariness, will trump the child's need to be safeguarded. This, of course, involves a grave decision for the courts. This is where a test for legal capacity must be rigorously applied and where *Gillick* and its developments/dis-applications are proven to be insufficient by imposing impossible thresholds and giving insufficient weight to the opinions of mentally competent apparent agents (adolescents).

Age, maturity and the PGC

Can the PGC sustain an argument that the legal capacity of a child is determined by the age of the child? At a principled level, *no*, because the PGC does not derogate on the basis of age. Beyleveld and Brownsword assert, however, that there are distinctions to be adopted in terms of children:

> Children approaching adulthood are a different kind of case. They are on the cusp of... [apparent] agency. 'They are very possible agents. They are very possibly subjects of consent with communicative competence. In line with the thinking in *Gillick*, extra care needs to be taken in dealing with those who are about to enter the consenting community.[38]

Beyleveld and Brownsword explain that age is no determinant of decision-making ability and they argue for case-by-case consideration, where individualised judgments are essential.[39] The difference between setting an age limit for an action such as voting and not setting an age limit for a personal decision is that the former impacts on other people's rights in a way that the latter does not.[40]

Thus, the current law, which sets age limits for determining legal capacity, does not comply with the PGC. For example, in *Re E*, set out above, there was surely

38 Deryck Beyleveld and Roger Brownsord, *Consent in the* Law, (Hart, 2007) p 97. In exercising a Gewirthian perspective, precautionary reasoning recognises that a child moves from pre-apparent agency to apparent agency. From the point of view of the PGC, in the case of *Birmingham Children's NHS Trust v B & C* (n 21), the fact that the judge has allowed the administration of blood transfusion is to be welcomed. The baby's welfare (and the saving of his or her life) must outweigh the Jehovah's Witnesses' religious belief, as a consequence of the protection that must be given to the baby under Beyleveld and Pattinson's precautionary theory. See chapter 2 in relation to precautionary reasoning.

39 ibid. p 111.

40 ibid. p 112.

little difference between E's decision to refuse the transfusion prior to age 18 and the same decision when he was almost 16. The question there should have been the legal capacity of E to make the decision, instead of using his age to prevent him from exercising his rights. Beyleveld and Brownsword, however, set a cautionary note to this largesse in so far as they consistently refer to the need to ensure that the child has specific mental competence to make the relevant medical decision, particularly in the case of complex or unusual medical treatments.[41]

To exemplify the difficulty that exists in making a finite link between age and legal capacity, let us look, first of all, at how cognitive abilities of children are assessed and have been assessed. The primary barometer of this assessment, for many years, was Piaget's states of cognitive development, but there is an acceptance nowadays that he underestimated the abilities of children.[42] There is no definitive standpoint at which the cognitive processes of a child suddenly become adult-like. This development of cognitive ability is a developmental one and there is no line of demarcation in the sand: age is not a finite determinant of mental competence. Other factors apply as well as age, including the knowledge, views, personal circumstances, physical and emotional views, cultural development, and any form of decision-making by the child that encompasses some or all of these variables. The PGC would hold that such variables need to be brought into the equation in the sense of vindicating the expression of generic rights and ensuring that there is consideration of the unique circumstances that apply to the decisions made by the child, that are based upon their purposiveness and voluntariness. This means that in English law, there should, on a principled basis, be a required shift from the generic question of the age of the child to a more right-based consideration of the individual circumstances of each case and of the individual and his or her autonomy. The focus in this deliberation still, however, must rest upon whether a child has legal capacity to make requisite decisions. If so, then the PGC will find that the courts should permit the child's decision. If not, the court's most appropriate response is to act in the best interests of the child.

The current approach in relation to 16–17-year-old children under the FLRA is compliant with the PGC (due to the fact that the test for legal capacity resembles the MCA two-stage test, which was supported in chapter 4), as long as the overruling approach in case law is removed. The approach used in the courts in respect of children under 16 is much more complex in term of its compliance with the PGC. As has been explained, for the most part, courts overrule the wishes of the mentally competent child, infringing the PGC. The PGC operates, however, within a social context with parallel social realities. One of these realities is the idea that maturity can be a prerequisite factor in decision-making. Case law that depended on *Gillick*, of necessity, had to consider the maturity of the child as a constituent of their legal capacity, as Lord Scarman stated that '[i]t is not enough that [a minor] should understand the nature of the advice which is being given:

41 ibid. p 113.

42 See, for example, W Huitt and J Hummel, 'Piaget's theory of cognitive development' (2003) *Educational Psychology Interactive*, 1–5.

she must also have a sufficient maturity to understand what is involved'.[43] Developments in case law following *Gillick* over-emphasised this maturity to the detriment of giving effect to the exercise of the will-rights of the child. A balanced and proportionate approach to maturity is not, however, outside the ken of the PGC. An agent's actions must pursue a particular purpose and these actions need to be voluntary. Although there is no requirement within the PGC for actions to be mature or otherwise, obviously, evolving maturity is required to instigate purposeful action in a voluntary manner. Of course, as in the case of *Gillick* and the manner of its developments/dis-application in case law, arbitrating upon that maturity is always going to be problematic as it can be a subjective measure.

Where there is evidence that a mentally competent child has been unduly influenced, then the court will also act in the best interests of the child, but will need to ensure that the burden of proof of undue influence is not overly generous and that evidence that the child has been unduly influenced does not necessarily negate the decision of the child. There is a somewhat uneasy alliance between the two, as evidenced in *Re T* in the previous chapter.

Summary of arguments presented in question 2

In English law, a conflict will exist between the need to allow for the child's autonomous decision and the need to safeguard the child's interests, if such decisions are felt not to be in the best interests of the child. This will be particularly relevant where a child makes solemn and life-limiting decisions. The courts will be guided by precedents where the tendency has been to overrule the wishes of the child. Current law means that there are, arguably, mentally competent children who are not being allowed to act in accordance with their generic rights. To suit the paternalistic agenda of the courts, mentally competent children are being denied affirmation of their legal capacity. This breaches the PGC and a solution is required. This is to be found in the answer to question 3 below.

Question 3: Are there alternative PGC-compliant approaches to the current law?

Position in Gewirthia

In Gewirthia, as long as agents are mentally competent, Gewirthians have no difficulties in accepting any decisions that are made, as long as these decisions respect the values of the PGC.[44] Gewirthians will fully accept the right of such Jehovah's Witnesses to refuse blood transfusions, even at the risk to life and health because, under the PGC, agents exercising their will-rights have the right to waive the benefit to their generic rights, including their right to life. In Gewirthia, there

43 *Gillick* (n 5) p 18.

44 Deryck Beyleveld and Roger Brownsword, 'Principle, Proceduralism, and Precaution in a Community of Rights' (2006) 19(2) *Ratio Juris*, 141–168.

would be no need to apply the MCA to children because Gewirthia would have its own test. Gewirthians would allow for children to be facilitated and supported in making their decisions, so as to ensure the expression of their generic rights. This would involve an empowering process whereby the decision-making of mentally competent children was given such supported by purposeful facilitation. In this case, judges in Gewirthia would evaluate each child as an individual against the context of the facts of each case. The child's wishes could be denied when children fail Gewirthia's test for legal capacity. The court could retain the power to veto the minor's decision-making when legal incapacity is concluded. But, at all times, the courts would be guided by the desire to ensure that the decisions reached by or for the children are in line with their generic rights.

Alternative approaches in non-Gewirthian English law

(a) Ensure that the child's voice is heard through 'empowerment' and 'supported decision-making'

Cave assesses the MCA's attempt to 'balance safeguarding of vulnerable people and their empowerment to make decisions for themselves'.[45] She argues that new measures are needed to support the understanding and implementation of the empowering ethos of this Act. The main problem with the implementation of the MCA is that some people who could make supported decisions have to be subject to decisions made about them by others.[46] Cave contends that the variance of the threshold in the case law above (question 1) is a breach of minors' human rights. She calls for the rejection of judicial paternalism and suggests, instead, that the law on legal capacity ought to be more focused on 'empowerment'.[47] Thus, case law should move 'capacity as the expression of autonomy to…the achievement of autonomy'.[48] Ultimately, the law, according to Cave, should be concerned with empowering the person who comes under the remit of the MCA to make decisions for themselves through facilitating, enabling and supporting the decision-making process.[49] Some groups are excluded from the provision of the Act. This is particularly relevant in the context of vulnerable adults, including adults with psychosocial disorders, or in the context of this specific chapter, children.[50]

The PGC can support Cave's call to promote supported and enabled decision-making, in accordance with the human rights of children.[51] Adolescents are accepted as apparent agents and have the required freedom and well-being.

45 Cave, 'Determining Capacity to Make Medical Treatment Decisions Problems Implementing the Mental Capacity Act 2005' (n 3) p 86.
46 ibid.
47 ibid.
48 ibid. p 104.
49 ibid.
50 ibid.
51 ibid. p 86.

Everything should to be done to ensure that these children are empowered to express and act in accordance with their generic rights. Accepting that children who could make decisions or supported decisions have to be subject to the decisions of others is not in line with the PGC. This denies their access to their generic rights.

In view of the historical intransigence of the courts and their pattern of overruling the wishes of the child, a procedure will have to be put in place whereby the child's decision-making is empowered and whereby the level of understanding of accepting or refusing treatment is not set at so high a threshold as to be unattainable. At a very practical level, this will require the appointment of people who liaise with the child, who thrash out the implications of the child's decision in a non-judgmental and non-directive way, but one that ensures that the child has all the required available information and that the decisions reached reflect appropriate understanding of the consent or refusal. There is a requirement to ensure that those who are involved in the assessment of legal capacity have what Cave calls 'a parallel duty to facilitate and empower capacity'.[52] This empowering of the child's decision-making should, of course, be a facilitative one but, at another level, there is a very real danger that the process of facilitation could, once again, smuggle in adult paternalism: 'I know the right decision. Let me help you come to that decision'. The PGC has the potential (in its indirect application in English law) to provide a strong empowerment tool whereby an individual's generic rights are put to the forefront. This would support the negation of the paternalism of other approaches and introduce an even greater focus on mental competence as being a determinate factor in decision-making for children.

It is recognised that some children may be able to make some decisions on their own and not others. Their ability to make these decisions could vary over time depending on their characteristics of agency and their level of mental competence. Support should be given to those who have difficulty making decisions in line with the level and scope of support that they require. On a practical level, this supported decision-making could be overseen by a child-focused decision support service, which could have specific responsibility for providing guidance, requisite information and for overseeing decision-making arrangements in respect of children.

(b) Alterative approach in respect of children aged 16–17: no significant change

No significant change is required to the procedures used to assess the legal capacity of children aged 16–17, due to the fact that legal capacity, in this instance, is measured by the FLRA which, effectively, mirrors the MCA, and is compliant with the PGC. The same reservations as made about adults in respect of the MCA in chapter 4 apply in this context also. In particular, the tendency of the courts to overrule the wishes of children within this age group should no longer apply.

52 Emma Cave, 'Goodbye Gillick? Identifying and resolving problems with the concept of child competence' (2014) 34(1) *Legal Studies*, 103–122, p 121.

(c) Acceptance of Cave's proposal that legal capacity of children under 16 be determined by the adoption of the MCA's capacity test in conjunction with common law

The argument could be made that, instead of relying on *Gillick* (under 16), that the MCA legal capacity test under sections 2–3 should be extended to children under the age of 16, thus 'embracing one concept of capacity for all, [where] the law would operate in a manner which is more coherent, consistent and comprehendible both to those applying and those subject to it.[53] At a procedural level, however, the process of applying the MCA to these children may be difficult.[54] Cave and Stavrinides' call for the development of the ambit of a more limited jurisprudence by which the legal capacity of minors could be assessed at common law:

> More radical reform might seek to address the problems inherent with the vague *Gillick* competence test, whilst protecting minors' best interests. This could be achieved by extending the presumption of capacity to minors, but developing a new common law test to apply in conjunction with the Mental Capacity Act test in order to identify those who lack capacity on the basis of immaturity or undue influence in order that a decision can be made in their best interests.[55]

To address this, Cave makes a number of nuanced suggestions in respect of determining the legal capacity of a child, but I will focus on her idea of applying the MCA in conjunction with a common law test for legal incapacity to children under 16.[56] It is not within the remit of this chapter to dissect Cave's proposal in detail, but, rather, to accept and build upon it to ensure that procedures that are recommended respect the generic rights of both mentally competent and incompetent children and are compliant with the PGC.[57] Cave proposes that an additional common law test for legal incapacity would develop over time and could begin to reflect even more a growing societal wish to base decisions around the rights of children. This rights-based approach is in line with the PGC. It is crucial that any test to prove legal capacity should not be based upon impossible thresholds, as in the current law. Cave's call to develop this new approach would give a greater expression to the will-rights of mentally competent children and also respect patients/children who only have interest-rights. The procedural operation of this approach will be outlined in (f).

53 Note that most provisions of the MCA do apply to 16–17-year-old children.
54 Cave, 'Goodbye Gillick? Identifying and resolving problems with the concept of child competence' (n 52) p 119 and p 122.
55 Cave and Stavrinides (n 1) p 6.
56 See Cave, 'Goodbye Gillick? Identifying and resolving problems with the concept of child competence' (n 52) pp 120–121.
57 For the sake of clarification, the second stage of the MCA test, as articulated in chapter 4, states that the patient lacks legal capacity if they cannot understand relevant information, retain such information, weigh the information up in coming to a decision and communicate it.

In summary, therefore, in English law, the MCA capacity test can work in conjunction with common law, where an evolving test for legal incapacity is developed. Procedurally, the difficulty to date in ensuring that the child's voice is heard has been the tendency of the courts to overrule the decision of the child, even when he or she has mental competence.

(d) The issue of societal competence

There is a need to extend the understanding of legal capacity to encompass the societal competencies that are required by an agent to act competently. Bielby suggests that there is a sliding scale in terms of agency when dealing with adults with intellectual disabilities.[58] They will have a particular type of what he calls 'societal competence' (i.e. ability to act appropriately within society) that is in line with their intellectual disability and, in accordance with precautionary reasoning, adults with intellectual disabilities can make particular decisions.[59] The same argument can be drawn here. There is a parallel between intellectual ability, which can encompass maturity, and societal competence. A child with a particular competence/intellectual ability can have a societal competence that allows him to make a decision that is proportionate to the child's maturity, that is valid in a social world. The PGC would allow for this interaction between maturity, societal competence and decision-making as long as these inter-locking paradigms embrace the values of the PGC. In the event that they do not do so, then arguments for maturity in respect of decisions cannot be permissible. Individuals who might be able to act competently with reasonable assistance should be given that assistance before they are treated as incompetent.

Let us take, for example, Ann, who is a Jehovah's Witness child of 16 who refuses a blood transfusion. She shows the societal competence that is in line with the intellectual ability that is evident in the maturity of her reflections and that shows that she has an understanding of the decision. This is permissible under the PGC. Now also consider Lucy. Lucy has a mild intellectual disability and her ability to make decisions that are appropriate for the social world is in line with her intellectual ability. She doesn't want a blood transfusion and the courts rule that her decision-making is compromised by her lack of legal capacity. However, no attempt was made to facilitate or to empower Lucy or to arbitrate for her. This is not fully in line with the PGC because, while the PGC accepts that, as people have diminishing agency, in line with increasing intellectual disability, this does not mean that they have no agency at all and this does not mean that they have no right to formulate their own decisions. Thus, the PGC would hold that Lucy's

58 Phillip Bielby, 'Competence and Vulnerability in Biomedical Research' (Springer, 2008). Also note that the term 'societally competent agent' was first used by Deryck Beyleveld and Shaun D Pattinson in an unpublished paper from 1998 entitled 'Proportionality under Precaution: Justifying Duties to Apparent Non-Agents' and first used in print in Deryck Beyleveld and Roger Brownsword, *Human Dignity in Bioethics and* Biolaw (OUP, 2004) p 129.

59 ibid. (Bielby) pp 9–38.

generic rights are compromised by not empowering and enabling her decision-making. This is not to say that the right decision is not made, because Jowitt shows that rights are inseparable from duties and mentally incompetent children, in this case, may not fully understand that their rights in society derive from their duties.[60] For the child lacking mental competence, he or she may not be able, under the PGC, to make these life-limiting decisions, but, at the very least, the child should be supported in the decision-making process. The language of competence should now extend beyond mere consideration of mental competence and include the type of competencies that children need to possess when living in their social world.

(e) The additional consideration of self-fulfilment

This chapter has shown how the current approach to the determination of legal capacity of children does not really work in practice and is not compliant with the PGC. An adoption of the method suggested by Cave, as a way of maximising the attention that is given to the voice of the child, has been advocated. This approach, however, might not, in itself, suffice to combat the paternalism that seems to be inbuilt into judicial reasoning, when it comes to children. What is required is to put what the child wants, in accordance with that child's belief-structure and deepest-held wishes at centre stage. Gewirth has proposed a mechanism by which life-affirming aspirations that define the self can be brought into the equation, and this process involves giving recognition to what he called 'self-fulfillment'.[61] Gewirth, in outlining his views on self-fulfilment, provides a conceptual link between it and morality, a morality that has to be based on universal human rights. Essentially, for him, the quest for self-fulfilment equates to the aspiration to have a life well lived. Self-fulfilment involves the fulfilling of the aspirations and the capacities of the agent, subject to moral criteria (the PGC). This quest for self-fulfilment, however, is not a 'me' quest, an egotistical or egoistical odyssey.[62] Rather, other people's rights are factored into self-fulfilment and this 'personalist morality'.[63] Self-fulfilment, according to Gewirth, 'consists in counsels or precepts for living a good life, a life that best fulfils one's intellectual, aesthetic, and other capacities in ways that contribute to one's development and dignity'.[64]

According to Gewirth, self-fulfilment, 'consists in carrying in fruition one's deepest desires or worthiest capacities', which is bound up with morality and includes an important social dimension whereby society must reflect the character of self-fulfilment.[65] He divides it into two forms: aspirational and capacity self-

60 Joshua Jowitt, 'Monkey See, Monkey Sue? Gewirth's Principle of Generic Consistency and the Rights of Non-Human Agents' (2016) XVI *Trinity College Law Review*, 71–96.
61 Alan Gewirth, *Self-Fullfillment* (Princeton University Press, 1998).
62 ibid. p 85.
63 ibid. p 54.
64 ibid.
65 ibid.

fulfilment. The former relates to the ability of a person to achieve purpose in accordance with an objective understanding about the facts in relation to these desires.[66] Capacity self-fulfilment, which is the most relevant here, takes account of people's choices—those, according to Gewirth, 'they make and those they ought to make, where this "ought" has among its criteria people's deepest desires and strivings'.[67] For a Jehovah's Witness, their capacity self-fulfilment includes the choice they ought to make and, in many cases, for conservative Jehovah's Witnesses, this choice must include a refusal of blood transfusions. To allow for the capacity self-fulfilment of a Jehovah's Witness child means allowing for the expression of that child's deepest desires and strivings, which may include the need to refuse a transfusion, if they are mentally competent. The idea of self-fulfilment is not based upon some type of personal gratification that promotes the exclusive self-interest of any agent. Rather, at its most simple level, it is a valid aspiration of an apparent agent who seeks to live a life of purpose and voluntariness. This personalist morality applies, in particular, but is not confined to, those who hold religious beliefs, such as a Jehovah's Witness. For them, the manifestation of that belief is part of their self-fulfilment. The law must recognise that this belief, and the aspiration to manifest it, has validity, and should be upheld, as long as this manifestation is derived from the aspirations of an apparent agent who has the required mental and societal competence which allows him to exercise his will-rights and from actions that are within the PGC's zone of moral permissibility.

Thus, a Gewirthian perspective is very much needed in synthesising Cave's development of the common law element with the MCA in order to ensure that the determining of legal capacity serve the freedom and well-being of the patient and respect the values of dignity and autonomy that are conceived within the PGC's concept of self-fulfilment.[68] Coming to this synthesis may require not only judicial action, but action at the level of community, where all come to an agreement as to how capacity can be constructed within the context of giving effect to mentally competent and incompetent patients' rights. It is recommended that consideration be also given to the maturity of the child to enable him to articulate his capacity-self-fulfilment, free from the influence that others might impose upon him, where he would demonstrate an ability to comprehend and apply the information that would be relevant to the decision that he makes.

(f) Procedural operation of Cave's suggested use of the MCA's capacity test and a common law's development approach to legal incapacity, which is underpinned by a recognition of societal competencies and self-fulfilment: a concentric circle of factors

How would Cave's call for the common law test for legal incapacity, working in conjunction with the MCA, apply in practice and how compliant would its associated protocols be with the PGC? Over time, according to this approach, society

66 ibid. p 16.
67 ibid.
68 Gewirth (n 61) p 3.

would develop a test for legal incapacity that reflects a continuing focus on respecting the wishes of patients and fulfilling a rights-based agenda. It is likely that such a test would include elements such as the particular circumstances of the child, the cognitive abilities, the gender, the age and experiences of the child, the knowledge and understanding of the child, the parental and familial context, and other variables, which will include a consideration of cultural pluralism, as to be discussed in chapter 7. These variables will add to the composite picture of the child, but should not be used as an excuse to smuggle in paternalism or as a way of providing impossible thresholds that a child could never reach. The specific prescription of relevant variables will only develop over time. I submit the following by way of explanation: (i) from a pragmatic/societal point of view, there are differences between an adult's ability to express autonomy and self-determination than a child's ability; (ii) it is more difficult for a child to attain capacity-fulfilment because history has shown that children's deepest held beliefs are likely to be undermined by adults or overridden in the courts, leaving their ability to achieve their earnest strivings more difficult.

In relation to (i), a child is in a process of continual genesis. There are factors that impact directly and indirectly upon the process of maturation, including the development of cognitive abilities. The factors in the child's societal contexts constitute parts of that movement from pre-apparent agency to apparent agency. A pre-apparent agent cannot, by definition, be either societally or specific-task competent. In contrast, an apparent agent could be (with regard to the tasks normally required in a particular society) societally competent/incompetent and (with regard to a specific task) mentally competent/incompetent. There is no current presumption of legal capacity for a child who is under 16, whereas that presumption exists for an adult under the MCA or for a child of 16–17 under the FLRA. Thus, for the child under 16, the pivotal forces that impact upon the formation of mental competence are a necessary part in the arbitration of that mental competence, which underpins legal capacity. The ability of a child under 16 to be societally competent is not a prerequisite for the legal capacity to make relevant decisions, but the decision of the societally competent child to decide X or Y should, under the approach suggested, be given greater weight than the decision of a societally incompetent child to do X or Y. For example, the decision of a Jehovah's Witness child who demonstrates an ability to weigh up competing variables and not be swayed by others' arguments would be more likely to be accepted than that of a Jehovah's Witness child who does not show such societal competence.

In relation to (ii), developing societal competence is linked to capacity-fulfilment. As the child becomes sufficiently mentally competent to examine issues clearly, this brings him closer to be able to articulate his capacity-fulfilment. It is not enough for the Jehovah's Witness child under 16 to assert a belief or a faith. He must be able to communicate that belief in a societally competent manner. Of course, that will bring into play the old chestnut that can also apply to adults: does or should the lack of communicative skill/language ability to express the most deeply held religious belief negate the validity of that desire or belief? Principally, probably not, but pragmatically the courts and/or medical personnel need to be able to gauge a child's decision by judging whether he has communicated his argument in a societally competent manner. This is in line with Beyleveld and Browsnword's idea that, for children, individualised judgments are required.[69] Adding this dimension, for children under 16, provides another level of extra care that ensures they are protected, even if they are protected and safeguarded from their own decisions.

The factors that I have delineated as encompassing societal competence are relevant due to the fact that moving from being a pre-apparent agent to being an apparent agent involves engagement with other agents in social contexts and the use of evolving societal competences in that process. Factors, such as the ones I have suggested, should not be wholly prescriptive and could develop, in line with the jurisdiction of the court. For some children, some factors will be more important than others. This is why there can be no prescription and why such factors can only be gauged on a case-by-case basis. For example, a child of a parent addicted to drugs will conceivably be more affected by the problems associated with drug use than a child who is not brought up in that environment. This is where the nature/nurture divide becomes, perhaps, not a tangential, but a relevant factor in determining which factors are relevant in assessing societal competence, which is, in turn, a factor in the construction of mental competence. Thus, the combination of the cognitive abilities and societal experiences is relevant to self-fulfilment. We cannot negate the social nurturing that is involved in the formation of the apparent mentally competent agent. Therefore, the developing common law will factor in some of these variables on a case-by-case basis.

The additional common law aspect develops the idea of assessing the child in his unique context with his unique abilities and experiences.[70] This reflects the PGC's determination of an agent as being akin to what Kant called a rational being with a will.[71] The synthesis of the MCA's legal capacity test, which focuses on the rational aspect of humanhood, with the common law test for legal incapacity, whose primary focus is on the individual, will jointly provide compliance with the PGC.

Notwithstanding the recommendations made about inclusion of common law dimensions in the determining of legal capacity, the PGC, in fact, does not require a common law consideration. They are simply a way in which the PGC can be indirectly applied in English law. It is likely that common law, under this new way of assessing the legal incapacity of children under 16, would begin to better reflect the emerging pattern in society of acting to support the rights of patients and it is only over time that such a test, which would be rights-based, would evolve. It is submitted that the PGC could provide a guiding light in the development of this test, as it would ensure that the rights of the child were upheld and that the

69 Beyleveld and Brownsword, *Consent in the Law* (n 38) p 111.

70 See Cave, 'Goodbye Gillick? Identifying and resolving problems with the concept of child competence' (n 52) pp 120–121.

71 See chapter 2.

mentally competent child had the ability to waive the benefits to his generic rights and so ensure that decisions reached are based upon a rights-formulation and not on judicial paternalism.

What is proposed in relation to the manner in which the legal capacity of children under 16 can be determined is not a linear chronology. An understanding of the MCA is situated within an evolving common law which gives recognition to variables within a child's life that impact upon the formation of his mental competence, but that are applied on a case-by-case basis and are underpinned by the recognition that is given to self-fulfilment. It is not a process of A+B+C. It is more a *concentric circle* where all factors are part of the same thing. Through the empowering of the child, self-fulfilment can be achieved and that happens within a societal context, where societal competencies are required. It is not so much a question for the child of 'I think, therefore, I am' as much as it is a question of 'I think, therefore, I can become' and the process of becoming involves the interlinking of mental competence and social variables, all underlined by the child's need to express his generic rights, leading to capacity-fulfilment.

So many arguments that are made in respect of children focus upon a very narrow perspective of legal capacity. We need to broaden the consideration of *how* decisions are formed by children and their capacity to make these decisions to also consider *why* such decisions are formed by them. This *why* relates to the self-fulfilment, to the decision that is taken to fulfil the child's purpose. Without that consideration, there will be insufficient attention given to the child's viewpoints and there will be still a danger that paternalism will come into play. Self-fulfilment should be considered as the outcome of autonomy. A decision is not just about legal capacity and autonomy is not the end goal. It is only part of the pathway towards the goal of self-fulfilment. It is the end game that also must be in sight and that element is currently missing within Cave's suggestion.[72] Ensuring that the desires that are at the core of the child's sense of self-identity are given prominence would help to mitigate against paternalism coming into play in the courts. Common law, as it develops, can provide the procedural mechanism for the consideration of self-fulfilment as a criterion of central importance in evaluating the decision-making of the child. Indeed, Gerwith says that self-fulfilment may only be reached in the quest for other purposes.[73] Through the dialogical process that is involved in common law formation, greater understanding of the importance of allowing for the expression of the rights of the child to strive towards the goal of self-fulfilment may begin to emerge. The religious beliefs of the Jehovah's Witness child, including the rejection of blood transfusions as a tenet of that belief, may, indeed, be validly considered as part of an individual child's capacity-fulfilment.

72 Cave, 'Goodbye Gillick? Identifying and resolving problems with the concept of child competence' (n 52) pp 120–121.
73 Gewirth (n 61) p 3.

(g) Revisions to the best interests test

In addition to the recommendation that a change should be made to the current practice of relying on *Gillick*, a further recommendation is made as to an amendment in the law. Due to the fact that decisions should primarily be based upon legal capacity, the best interests test should only apply in situations where the child is actually legally incapacitated, instead of coming into effect where such legal incapacity is questionable, as in the current law. The recommendations here replicate Cave and Stavrinides' proposal that '[m]inors' best interests would be protected through the rigorous test for capacity rather than application of the best interests test.[74] This focus on legal capacity, which tracks mental competence, is in line with the PGC's rights-based approach, that negates the paternalism implicit in decisions made simply on the basis of best interests.

Conclusion

This book examines a number of cases that have been chosen specifically because the intersection between law, religion, autonomy, and medical practice was complex, complicated, convoluted. No quick fix could exist; no easy solutions are easily available in these hard cases. Jehovah's Witnesses and the issue of refusal of blood transfusions by children is one of the hardest cases of all. It is one that would place great demands and responsibilities on the shoulders of the judge. There is no doubt about the gravity of the decisions that are to be made. There is some evidence that the agenda of paternalism is a force behind and within the judgments that are made. The opinions of others are, perhaps, more important than the opinions of the child. This discounting of the rights of the mentally competent child to act in accordance with their beliefs has the potential to result in an implicit denial of their self-determination.

This chapter and the following two chapters relate primarily to children and, in many ways, to the way in which religious belief or religious upbringing can influence a child. Does this religious upbringing negate the child's autonomy, the child's ability to make (medical) decisions? Religious belief can have a very significant impact upon a child. This is due to a number of factors, including the child's social interactions, the influence of the particular Church's teachings, the way in which parents relate to their children and the manner in which they 'hand on the faith'. Consequently, religious upbringing may have an impact upon the child's decision-making. Where the PGC has found that the rights of the mentally competent child to exercise his will-rights are breached in cases pertaining to this issue, then these judgments are seen not to comply with the framework. When the mentally competent child capably makes a decision, then the PGC supports the decision. Obviously, when it comes to children under 16, the judgment of the legal capacity of the child must be undertaken with care, as the consequences of some of the decisions made have the potential to be very grave. These findings

74 Cave and Stravinides (n 1) p 54.

support the mentally competent child's right to act in accordance with religious belief, even if such belief gives rise to actions which can have severe consequences.

Age, however, should not be the primary criterion of determining legal capacity. There is an additional underlying dimension that must be considered along with the tests for legal incapacity suggested by Cave, a consideration of the requirement that all actions should be in line with the child's self-fulfilment. A specific focus on self-fulfilment as part of the amended approach to determining legal capacity of children under 16 (building on Cave's suggestions) will ensure that the child's rights are protected and that his generic conditions of agency are promoted. The two elements of using the MCA's legal capacity test, in conjunction with common law, are a primary requirement within this process, because without a confirmation of legal capacity, robustly evidenced, then a child's transient and non-settled wishes and desires could easily be taken as a finite expression of purpose and given undue credence. This added dimension brings together principle and procedure; the principle that the child's voice must be heard, in line with their generic rights and in accordance with their deepest desires and strivings. The operation of the common law test in conjunction with the MCA, underpinned by the quest for self-fulfilment, provides the procedural mechanism to implement this PGC-compliant principle and, so, the whole process offers a good faith attempt at allowing for the exercise of the generic rights of the child.

Consideration of the implementation of this approach would ensure that McFarlane's aim is reached and that 'mental competence is not linked to the blunt instrument of "age", "intelligence" and "understanding"'.[75] What would be put in place would be 'a move from paternalism and protectionism to a rights-based evaluation of each child as an individual against the context of the facts of each case'.[76]

References

Adhar, Rex and Leigh, Ian, *Religious Freedom in the Liberal State* (2nd ed, OUP, 2013).

Beyleveld, Deryck and Brownsword, Roger, *Consent in the Law* (Hart, 2007).

Beyleveld, Deryck and Brownsword, Roger, 'Principle, Proceduralism, and Precaution in a Community of Rights' (2006) 19(2) *Ratio Juris*, 141–168.

Beyleveld, Deryck and Brownsword, Roger, *Human Dignity in Bioethics and Biolaw* (OUP, 2004).

Beyleveld, Deryck and Pattinson, Shaun D, 'Proportionality under Precaution: Justifying Duties to Apparent Non-Agents' (Unpublished, 1998).

Bielby, Phillip *Competence and Vulnerability in Biomedical Research* (Springer, 2008).

Cave, Emma, 'Determining Capacity to Make Medical Treatment Decisions: Problems Implementing the Mental Capacity Act 2005' (2015) 36(1) *Statute Law Review*, 86–106.

Cave, Emma, 'Goodbye Gillick? Identifying and resolving problems with the concept of child competence' (2014) 34(1) *Legal Studies*, 103–122.

75 Andrew McFarlane 'Mental capacity: one standard for all ages' [2011] 41 *Fam L* 479, p 484.

76 ibid.

Cave, Emma and Stavrinides, Zenon, *Medical Practitioners, Adolescents and Informed Consent* (University of Leeds, 2013), available at: http://www.law.leeds.ac.uk/assets/files/research/cfig/Medical-Practitioners-Adolescents-and-Informed-Consent-Final-Report-2013.pdf (accessed 27 January 2017).

Gewirth, Alan, *Self-Fullfillment* (Princeton University Press, 1998).

Grubb, Andrew 'Commentary on Re L (Medical Treatment-Gillick Competency)' (1999) 7 *Medical Law Review*, 58–61.

Huitt, W and Hummel, J, 'Piaget's theory of cognitive development', (2003) *Educational Psychology Interactive*, 1–5.

Jackson, Emily, *Medical Law: Text, Cases and Materials* (3rd ed, OUP, 2013).

Jowitt, Joshua, 'Monkey See, Monkey Sue? Gewirth's Principle of Generic Consistency and the Rights of Non-Human Agents (2016) XVI *Trinity College Law Review*, 71–96.

McFarlane, Andrew, 'Mental capacity: one standard for all ages' [2011] 41 *Fam L* 479.

Ó Néill, Clayton, 'Jehovah's Witnesses and Blood Transfusions: An Analysis of the Legal Protections Afforded to Adults and Children in English European Human Rights Contexts' (2017) 24(4) *European Journal of Health Law*, 368–389.

Pattinson, Shaun D, *Medical Law and Ethics* (5th ed, Sweet & Maxwell, 2017).

Ziebart, David, 'Jehovah's Witnesses- Medical Care, Minors and the Religious Rite/Right' (2007) 19(1) *The Denning Law Journal*, 233.

6 Ritual male circumcision and the manifestation of religious belief in English medical law

Introduction

The previous two chapters dealt with an issue that often makes headlines in the news, but is, nonetheless, confined to a very small sector of the population. An issue that has a much broader reach, particularly in a global landscape, is that of circumcision and this issue provides the focus of this chapter and the following chapter.

Non-therapeutic male circumcision is a medical procedure that is commonly performed on children throughout the world, usually for religious and cultural reasons. It is associated with two Abrahamic religions—Judaism and Islam. It is part of the cultural and religious heritage of those religions. This chapter explores English law's differential response to genital cutting and the intersection between law and religious practice as it pertains to ritual male circumcision. Deliberations are confined to English law within the context of the European Convention on Human Rights (ECHR) and its jurisprudence. The particular effectiveness and adequacy of the current English law in respect of circumcision is assessed accordingly.

In order to determine the appropriateness of protection given to the manifestation of Abrahamic religious belief, the chapter applies the methodological framework and, as such, poses three questions.

Firstly, in dealing the approach of English law, the chapter considers relevant case law, human rights jurisprudence, and the relevance of the 'best interests' test. Ritual male circumcision is situated within the context of the European Court and the impact of the European Convention and its jurisprudence on English law. Secondly, it is suggested that English law's approach to ritual male circumcision is inappropriate because the current law is in breach of the PGC as it constitutes 'basic' harm. Thirdly, a new statute is proposed as an alternative. It would be would only allow for a child to be circumcised if has the legal capacity to make the irreversible decision.

The differing perceptions of the courts and of society between the circumcision of young boys and the female genital mutilation (FGM) of girls, as brought to the fore in the case of *Re B and G*,[1] will be dealt with in the next chapter.

1 *Re B and G (No 2)* [2015] EWFC 3.

What is non-therapeutic circumcision?

Non-therapeutic circumcision is one of the oldest surgical procedures in existence.[2] Circumcision is almost impossible to be reversed and, therefore, has a significant effect on the child. There is little evidence to suggest that it is of considerable medical benefit to the patient.[3] It is true that circumcision can sometimes be beneficial in protecting against certain infections. However, these infections could be safeguarded by non-irreversible measures.[4] Even though circumcision has often little benefit medically, it is, without question, part of Jewish and Muslim religious belief and cultural heritage.

Carrying out a male circumcision is not 'risk free'. Some short-term risks include bleeding and infection following the procedure.[5] It is also possible to have long-term problems. These include pain on erection as well as psychological problems.[6] According to Anna Freud 'any surgical interference with the child's body may serve as a focal point for the activation, reactivation, grouping, and rationalisation of ideas of being attacked, overwhelmed and (or) castrated.'[7] Similarly, Cansever, following a study of twelve boys who underwent circumcision, found that:

> [C]ircumcision is perceived by the child as an aggressive attack upon his body, which, damaged, mutilated, and in some cases destroyed him. The feeling of 'I am now castrated' seems to prevail in the psychic world of the child. As a result he feels inadequate, helpless and functions less efficiently.[8]

It is also not a pain free procedure. There are some who argue that it is wrong for a boy to be circumcised without having his own say in matters affecting his bodily integrity.[9] How prevalent is this practice? In the UK the number of people who are circumcised is much less than, for example, the United States. It is estimated by Williams and Kapila that most of the procedures are carried out on young children[10] and that approximately 5 to 6 per cent of British men are

2 N Williams and L Kapila 'Complications of Circumcision' (1993) 80 *British Journal of Surgery*, 1231–1316.
3 British Medical Association, *The Law and Ethics of Male Circumcision: Guidelines for Doctors*, 12 November 2007, fn 1.
4 See JM Hutson, 'Circumcision: A Surgeon's Perspective' (2003) 30 *Journal of Medical Ethics*, 238–240.
5 Williams & Kapila, 'Complications of Circumcision' (n 2) pp 1231–1326.
6 Shane E Peterson, 'Assaulted and Mutilated. A Personal account of Circumcision trauma' in GC Denniston, FM Hodges, MF Milos (eds), *Understanding Circumcision* (Kluwer Academic, 2001) p 271.
7 Anna Freud, 'The Role of Bodily Illness in the Mental Life of Children' in Psychoanalytic Study of Children (International University Press, 1952) p 75.
8 G Cansever, 'Psychological effects of circumcision' (1965) 38 *B J Med Psychol*, pp 321–331.
9 E.g. Steven Svoboda, 'Circumcision of male infants as a human rights violation', (2013) 39 *J Med Ethics*, 469–474.
10 N Williams and L Kapila 'Why are children referred for circumcision?' (1993) 306 *BMJ*, p 28.

circumcised.[11] Those who are circumcised are usually to be found in the Muslim and Jewish community.

Importance of ritual male circumcision in Abrahamic religions

Why is circumcision important to Jewish people? In Judaism, circumcision is a religious ritual and has traditionally been carried out on a baby eight days after his birth by a *Mohel*. This is a Jewish person who is trained to circumcise children. It is believed that, in order to be a true Jew, it is important to be circumcised. This is because of the fact that it is proclaimed in Genesis[12] that all men should be circumcised. As well as this, in Leviticus it written that '…in the eighth day the flesh of his foreskin shall be circumcised.'[13] Glass points out that '[c]ircumcision represents the covenant between God and Abraham, and Abraham's descendants, according to the Torah, the five books of Moses'.[14] It is further stated in Genesis that:

> This is My covenant that you shall keep between Me and You and your descendants after you: every male among you shall be circumcised. You shall circumcise the flesh of the foreskin… At the age of eight days every male among you shall be circumcised throughout your generations… an uncircumcised male… that soul shall be cut off from its people, he has invalidated My covenant.[15]

This piece of scripture demonstrates that, for those of the Jewish faith, there is more than an expectation that Jews should be circumcised. If you are not circumcised you may suffer the penalty of *kareit* and be 'cut off from its people'.[16] Glass says that '[t]here is therefore no debate within Judaism about the necessity for circumcision in Jewish law.[17] There is no need to seek justification based on health or other grounds; circumcision is a commandment (a mitzvah) from God and, as such, no intervention would persuade religious Jews to stop performing this ritual'.[18] Glass also says '[t]hat circumcision is so central to Judaism is demonstrated by the fact that even the most unobservant Jews insist on circumcising their male children'.[19] Glass asserts that it is every father's obligation to have his son circumcised and, if the child is not circumcised, according to Glass, 'God will punish the child by shortening his life'.[20] For Jews, therefore,

11 Williams & Kapila, 'Complications of Circumcision' (n 2) p 1231–1326.
12 *Genesis*, Chapter 17, verses 10–14.
13 *Leviticus*, Chapter 12.
14 JM Glass, 'Religious Circumcision: a Jewish view' (1999) 23 *BJU International* 17–21, p 17.
15 *Genesis* 17:10–14.
16 ibid.
17 Glass (n 14) p 17.
18 ibid.
19 ibid.
20 ibid. p 18.

circumcision is not a practice that is open to refusal, it is not a social habit, embedded in changing societal norms; rather it is a central and traditional tenet of religious adherence and an overt and important sign of religious affiliation.

Circumcision, as previously stated, is also practised by the Islamic community. This circumcision occurs between the ages of four and 13. Circumcision is not explicitly mentioned in the Quran but is, nevertheless, very important to Muslims.[21] Muhammad informed his followers that the male population should be circumcised after seven days of life. In Islam circumcision is one of the five elements of personal hygiene that must be followed.[22] The others are the shaving of pubic hair, trimming of moustaches, nail paring, and removing under-arm hair. Price feels that 'there is no reason why the decision cannot be left to the boy himself when he is old enough to form his own independent view as to his belief-systems and his own body'.[23] It is further contended by Price that belief in circumcision is connected to the historical belief that Abraham was circumcised.

The practice of circumcision within these two Abrahamic religions is heavily connected to the religious principles underpinning these religions. More than that, it is connected to a sense of identity, of affiliation or, to misrepresent Shylock, it is the 'badge of all our tribe'. Consequentially, a strong argument can be made that the practice of circumcision cannot be simply dismissed by non-Jewish or Muslim medical practitioners or courts.

This is an era that rightly seeks to protect the child from any form of harm. For some, male circumcision is seen to be a physical harm that is meted out to a voiceless, powerless child and is an affront to his bodily integrity. For others, this practice of circumcision is not about a meaningless physical act: it is about an integral expression of religious belief, a tribal branding that has unique and important religious associations that are considered by parents to be important to their child. In line with this perspective, male circumcision is a ritual, a rite of passage that proclaims belonging to a religious faith. For most children that sense of belonging is important; it involves forming attachments and connections to a faith system that has (usually) been handed down from one generation to another. For Jews, in particular, it connects the circumcised child back to ancestral practice and the Torah itself. Ritualistic practices have an importance in society that must be, at least, respected. This is sometimes a difficult task due to the competing voices of parents, society, religion, secularism, and, of course, the child himself.

It can be summarised that male ritual circumcision is an important aspect of Jewish and Islamic cultural and religious tradition.

21 ibid.

22 See AR Gatrad et al, 'Religious Circumcision and the Human Rights Act' (2002) 86 (2) *Arch Dis Child*, 76–78, p 76.

23 Christopher Price, 'Male Circumcision: A Legal Affront', Submission to the Law Commission of England and Wales in Response to Consultation Paper Number 139-Consent in the Criminal Law, December 1998 at 6.1, available at: http://www.cirp.org/library/legal/price-uklc/#mus (accessed 27 January 2017).

Medical guidelines on ritual male circumcision

What is the main point of reference for legal advisors and the medical profession when dealing with the issue of circumcision? The British Medical Association (BMA) has published their guidelines for doctors on circumcision under English law.[24] These guidelines set out the circumstances that must exist in order for circumcision to be carried out. They consider a number of key areas and principles including consent and refusal. The guidelines state that all children who have legal capacity ought to have a role in the decision-making process and that their views should be considered.[25] The following can give consent for the treatment of a child: a 16–17-year-old,[26] a child with 'sufficient understanding and intelligence',[27] or any person with parental responsibility or the court.[28] The Association also notes that a balancing act must be carried out in relation to the child's refusal and the harm caused by not undertaking the circumcision.[29] They note that surgery is often not carried out until the child has the maturity and the relevant understanding about making a decision. In situations where the child cannot decide, the choice is usually made by the parents.[30] As a result, the choices that parents can make are limited by the fact that the surgery must not be contrary to the best interests of the child.[31]

Is there general and consistent use of these guidelines? Under the 1997 UK General Medical Council (GMC) guidelines, permission from both parents should be given 'whenever possible' when a child undergoes a ritual male circumcision.[32] This has been reaffirmed by the BMA who have said that medical practitioners ought to 'make every effort to contact the other parent in order to seek consent'.[33] Robinson et al's study concluded that there was inconsistency in doctor's searching for parental consent from two parents: this may have been linked to lack of knowledge of 'the legal rules pertaining to their parents'.[34] As will be later

24 British Medical Association (n 3). Also see Clayton Ó Néill, 'Religious and Cultural Beliefs: The Potential for Patient safety to be Compromised' in John Tingle, Clayton Ó Neill and Morgan Shimwell (eds), *Global Patient Safety Law Policy and Practice* (Routledge, 2019).
25 ibid. 4.2.1.
26 Family Law Reform Act 1989, s 105 (1).
27 *Gillick v West Norfolf and Wisbech AHA* [1986] AC 112.
28 See Shaun D Pattinson, *Medical Law and Ethics* (5th ed, Sweet & Maxwell, 2017) p 166.
29 ibid.
30 ibid.
31 ibid. 4.2.2.
32 General Medical Council, *Guidance for doctors who are asked to circumcise male children* (GMC, 1997).
33 British Medical Association, *Medical Ethics Today* (BMJ Books, 2004) p 151.
34 Robinson et al, 'Consent for Non-Therapeutic Male Circumcision on Religious Grounds' (2009) 91 (2) *Ann R Coll Surg Engl* 152–154, p 152. They examined 62 boys between the ages of 1 and 14 who were circumcised for non-therapeutic reasons. They found that in only 6.4 per cent was the written consent of both parents given. Also, in none of the 62 cases, was any consent given by the patient (child). As well as this, in the majority of cases (58 out of 62) there was written consent made by one parent, the father in 34 (55 per cent) and the mother in 24 (45 per cent). They

pointed out, this approach was agreed with in *Re J* where, at the Court of Appeal, it was said that '[t]he decision to circumcise a child on a ground other than medical necessity is a very important one; the operation is irreversible, and should only be carried out where the parents together approve of it'.[35] Therefore, it is quite surprising that medical practitioners are making a poor effort to gain consent from both of the child's parents.[36]

What mechanism can be used to define such limits and to set thresholds/ criteria that protect the child's rights? Or is such a mechanism possible at all? First, all action in respect of circumcision must be compliant with human rights law and, secondly, should be underpinned by the specific guidance provided by the BMA. An additional and complementary parameter that sets specific thresholds and criteria of action is the application of the proposed framework.

Question 1: How have English law and the ECtHR dealt with the issue of ritual male circumcision?

The legal position in respect of male circumcision in European human rights law

There is no specific protection or rejection of circumcision in any international dictate or statute. Currently there is no legislation on ritual male circumcision. There are, however, different interpretations of how existing legislation could be used either in defence of circumcision or to refute its legality. In other words, lack of legal prescription about legal circumcision one way or another leads to a type of legal free-for-all, where differing views could possibly bring diverse results in differing courts. According to Fox and Thomson, this 'leaves open the question of whether circumcision is lawful surgery or "proper medical treatment".'[37] Boyle et al have argued that ritual male circumcision breaches the United Nations Convention on the Rights of the Child and the Convention Against Torture.[38] Edge states that circumcision could be considered to be a breach of the ECHR and consequently the Human Rights Act 1998 (HRA) in English Law because the provisions on assault (as evident in the Offences Against the Person Act and the Children and Young Persons Act 1933) could be extended to include circumcision.[39] Others have argued that circumcision is a breach of Article 3 of the

concluded that there is, consequently, 'non-conformity with recommended practice and the common law'.

35 *Re J (Specific Issue Orders: Child's Religious Upbringing and Circumcision)* [1999] 2 FLR 678.

36 Robinson et al (n 34) p 154.

37 Marie Fox and Michael Thomson, 'A Covenant of the status quo' (2005) 31 *J Med Ethics*, 463–469, p 466.

38 Boyle et al, 'Circumcision of healthy boys: criminal assault?' (2000) 7 *Journal of Law and Medicine*, p 301.

39 Human Rights Act 1998, s 8.

Convention. The argument has been put forward by Feldman that, if someone were to be guilty of breaching Article 3 for inhuman treatment without there being degrading treatment, then circumcision could be a violation of the Convention.[40] However, Edge suggests that the 'uncertainties, together with a reluctance by the Court and Commission to deal with applications under Article 3, make it more likely that circumcision will be resolved by reference to some other Convention right, probably Article 8'.[41] Gatrad et al point to the fact that the potential application for Article 3 ECHR is obvious in view of the fact that circumcision and its related pain have not been sought by the child.[42] However, they also argue that it is unlikely that Article 3 ECHR is breached in ritual male circumcision due to the high threshold test that exists.[43]

Case law of the ECtHR provides evidence to the fact that agreement does not exist as to whether or not circumcision goes beyond a threshold of 'harm'. Human rights law tries to set out a minimum threshold. For example, a minimum threshold exists under Article 3 ECHR. In order for Article 3 to be violated, the conduct must involve a minimum level of severity. The more vulnerable the victim is, the more likely that the threshold will be met.[44] The calculation of the minimum threshold is relative and consideration is given to the facts of the case. This includes the treatment duration, sex, mental or physical effects, as well as the victim's health.[45] Due to the vulnerability of children, the threshold for torture, inhuman, or degrading treatment is lowered. Article 3's threshold also involves considering the ability of the victim to complain or the effect of the particular treatment.[46] In order for treatment to be considered as 'torture' it must be particularly severe. Treatment that causes extreme physical/mental suffering, but not enough to be considered as torture, is regarded as inhumane treatment.[47] Article 3 ECHR has a negative obligation on the State to abstain from exposing anyone to treatment who meets the threshold for torture, inhumane or degrading treatment.[48] The State also has a positive duty to necessitate that public authorities take steps to prevent breaches of Article 3. This means that laws must exist that protect vulnerable people from being ill-treated and the State must protect people from harm being inflicted on them by others.[49]

40 David Feldman, *Civil Liberties and Human Rights in England and Wales* (OUP 1991) pp 159–160.
41 Peter W Edge, 'Male Circumcision after the Human Rights Act 1998' (2000) 5 *J Civil Liberties*, pp 320–337.
42 Gatrad et al (n 22) p 77.
43 ibid. p 77.
44 *Price v United Kingdom* [1988] 55 DR 224.
45 See *Ireland v United Kingdom* [1978] 2 EHRR 25, at [162]; *Selmouni v France* [1988] EHRLR 510, at [160].
46 *Herczegfalvy v. Austria* [1992] 15 EHRR 437, at [82]; *Aerts v. Belgium* [1998] 29 EHRR 50, at [66].
47 See Equality and Human Rights Commission, 'Article 3: Freedom from torture and inhumane and degrading treatment or punishment' (2012) *Human Rights Review*, 69–134, pp 74–75.
48 ibid.
49 ibid.

Articles 8/9 ECHR and the Convention on the Rights of the Child

Given that Article 9 protects freedom of thought, conscience, and, crucially religion, the argument could be made that this Article can be used to justify the circumcision of a child for religious reasons. Feldman, however, argues that the religious freedoms ascribed to parents cannot provide a justification to interfere with the child's right to bodily integrity.[50] Feldman raises points that merit consideration: bodily integrity is something that must be protected, especially in the context of a child/infant who has no say in this matter. Once again, difficulties apply in the balancing of rights and in the defining of 'threshold'.

The specific issue of circumcision is not addressed in the Convention on the Rights of the Child. However, it can be inferred that circumcision is an undercurrent, unspecified theme in Article 8 (1) that says that 'States Parties undertake to respect the right of the child to preserve his or her identity'. This could imply that a child should not be circumcised as it attacks the child's 'identity'. It could, however, be argued paradoxically that Article 8 gives implicit permission to have their child circumcised because circumcision brings with it a type of tribal branding and identity formation that is an integral part of some religious traditions. Edge infers that Article 9 rights are not without limit and he believes that the rights about circumcision are more appropriately connected to Article 8 ECHR:

> Family life carries with it the idea of parental authority over children, for instance in relation to medical treatment, which can clash with a child's individual autonomy rights. The Convention organs may well be reluctant to require, as opposed to allow, the State to make decisions for the family.[51]

It is recognised that the provisions within Article 8 must be balanced with Article 9 ECHR. It is very hard for a human rights law to protect a child against everything, every possibility, and every danger. Perhaps, the hardest thing of all that human rights law must do is to protect the child against its own parents or their wishes. Human rights law must walk a very difficult tightrope where the rights of the child must be weighted against other prevailing rights. The fusion of Articles 8 and 9 provides a protection for religious expression and potentially a case could rely on these articles to defend the practice of ritual male circumcision. It is probable that such a conflict could exist between the protections given under Articles 8/9 and those given under Article 3. A judge could find it difficult to balance the freedom of parents to have their infants circumcised as potentially protected under Articles 8 and 9 with the possibility that ritual circumcision could be defined as inhuman or degrading treatment under Article 3. Later sections of this chapter will suggest that the use of the framework will be a support to the judiciary in the resolution process.

50 Feldman (n 40) p 159.

51 Peter W Edge, 'Male Circumcision after the Human Rights Act 1998' (2000) 5 *Journal of Civil Liberties*, 320, available at: http://www.cirp.org/library/legal/edge1/ (accessed 27 January 2017).

In the event that a case is taken to the ECtHR involving ritual male circumcision, it is likely that a judgment would be made based upon the resolution of the conflict that will exist between the protections that are given to religious expression under Articles 8 and 9 of the Convention and that of Article 3 which outlaws inhuman and degrading treatment. It is likely that in such an event, given the socio-religious nature of the practice of ritual circumcision and its associated sensitivities, both ethnic and religious, that the courts will give a wide margin of appreciation to the practice in their judgment. The likelihood of this position being adopted derives in part from *Lautsi and Others v Italy* that allowed for the presence of a crucifix in Italian state classrooms primarily based upon the application of a wide margin of appreciation.[52] Following this case, the ECtHR may be reluctant to interfere with the sovereignty of individual states and their treatment of issues that are based upon religious expression.

ECtHR case law on circumcision: application of Article 3 ECHR and breach of human rights?

In *The Greek Case,* the European Commission of Human Rights espoused a general definitional method that differentiated between three prohibited acts, i.e. 'torture', 'inhuman' and 'degrading treatment'. The method of regarding the acts as separate breaches with different features, while later refined, is still the standard method of the ECtHR. Within this way of dealing with Article 3, torture has been signalled out having a special stigma. This makes it different from other types of ill treatment. In this case, it was held that, instead of focusing on the nature and severity of the act undertaken, the purpose for which the act was carried out was the defining feature of torture where torture was the 'purposive use of inhuman treatment'. However, following developments in the jurisprudence, this purposive method has been marginalised in support of a threshold that is based upon a sliding scale of severity between the acts.

This threshold was developed in *Ireland v UK.* In distinguishing between torture, inhuman, and degrading treatment, the Commission held that a distinction was needed as a result of the 'special stigma' attached to torture.[53] It was held that in order for torture to exist, the actual treatment must result in 'serious and cruel suffering'. As a consequence, the Commission referred to a 'measuring stick' in order to assess whether the act can be classified as torture. This is a subjective decision that is reflective of how painful and how much suffering was caused by the act in question. This threshold was restated in subsequent decisions.[54]

The Court has decided not to set out a list of acts that can automatically be regarded as severe enough to be determinate of torture in order to continue to adopt a flexible approach and also due to the recognition that the ECHR should be interpreted 'in light of present-day conditions'. As such, the Court does not

52 *Lautsi and Others v Italy* App. No. 30814/06, 2011 Eur. Ct. H.R. (G.C.).
53 *Ireland v UK* (n 45).
54 Also see *Aydin v Turkey* (application nos 28393/95,29494/95 and 30219/96).

need to follow previous cases and can re-evaluate the jurisprudence and make decisions on acts that were formerly not looked upon as constituting torture.[55] Essentially, inhuman treatment can be regarded as involving acts that do not cross the threshold of torture but are severe enough to be regarded as inhuman.[56] This broad way of dealing with inhuman treatment was illustrated in *Campbell and Cosans v UK*,[57] which concerned corporal punishment of school boys (that did not actually occur). It was held that 'provided it is sufficiently real and immediate a mere threat of conduct prohibited by Article 3 may itself be in conflict with the provision. Thus, to threaten the individual with torture might in some circumstances constitute at least "inhuman treatment"'.[58]

Clear reasoning is delivered in *Ireland v UK*: if an act fulfils the threshold set for deciding whether an act quantifies as torture, inhuman, or degrading treatment or punishment, it is unjustifiable. To come within the sphere of Article 3, as stated, a 'minimum level of severity' must be met.[59] In assessing the 'entry level' threshold of severity, the Court can consider the duration, physical effects, mental effects of the treatment, as well as the victim's sex, age, and health status. Does ritual male circumcision go beyond Article 3's threshold of harm? It is difficult to benchmark circumcision against what is included in this Article because it is problematic to define circumcision as 'torture, inhumane or degrading treatment.' To some degree, such definitions are relatively subjective when the individual's agency is not factored into the equation. In a later stage in the chapter, it will be shown how the methodological framework can be used to suggest that circumcision does breach Article 3 because it causes 'basic harm' to a child. The threshold for harm in Article 3 is set so high that any harm indicator will hardly resonate unless it is in the gravest format. There is an argument that would suggest that any harm at all that is meted out to a child impinges upon the rights of a child to bodily integrity. It can also be argued that these rights are stronger and more intransigent than the rights of parents who want to have their child circumcised. There is a problem here in negotiating these rights and this Article does not define with sufficient clarity the thresholds of harm that can apply.

Is the practice of ritual male circumcision, therefore, a violation of human rights? Svoboda asserts that male circumcision, or what he calls 'this needless and harmful trauma,' violates core human rights documents.[60] Svoboda contends that circumcision constitutes a violation of physical integrity and, thus, implicitly contravenes the Universal Declaration of Human Rights (or, indeed, the ECHR). He argues that infant male circumcision fits this definition in so far as the procedure can cause severe pain and it is intentionally inflicted. Equally, he finds that infant male circumcision fits the statutory definition for child abuse and could also fit the

55 ibid.
56 Malcolm Evans and Rod Morgan, *Preventing Torture* (Clarendon Press, 1998) p 93. See *The Greek Case* 12 (1969) YECHR, p 186.
57 *Campbell and Cosans v UK* (Application No 7511/76; 7743/76).
58 ibid.
59 *Ireland v UK* (n 45).
60 Svoboda (n 9).

international definition of torture.[61] Svodoba's arguments are thought provoking in the extreme; he talks of an American and International context, and, primarily, of the practice of circumcising young infants for social and habitual reasons rather than for religious reasons. Nonetheless, his contentions have relevance for English law and for religious-based circumcision: the ECHR specifically protects an individual against torture in an unqualified way. Articles of the ECHR can be used to support Svoboda's argument that circumcision is a human rights violation and 'fit the international definition of torture'.[62] Ritual male circumcision can be seen to be an affront to Article 3's provision that '[n]o one shall be subjected to torture or to inhuman or degrading treatment or punishment'. The physical integrity of the infant/young child, which is protected under an interpretation of this Article, is compromised by circumcision. Article 5 ECHR provides that everyone has the right to liberty and security of person, and circumcision can be viewed as compromising the security and liberty of persons in so far as the child has no legal capacity to give informed, free consent to a practice that is intrusive, invasive and constitutes basic harm under the PGC.

There is, therefore, no definitive consensus between academic writers and human rights case law about whether or not circumcision breaches human rights laws. Perhaps, some of this uncertainty arises from the fact that the harm that is meted out to the boy, as a consequence of this medical procedure, has not been measured against other variables in an arguably objective manner.

Circumcision and the law of England

The discussion above concerning the ECHR has a direct impact on English law under the HRA. The differing international views about the legality or otherwise of male circumcision are also be seen at a more local level in the English courts system. The current stance of English law is that parents are legally permitted to have their children circumcised.[63]

There is, however, no universal agreement about the lawfulness of circumcision. The Law Commission said that law reform to 'put the lawfulness of ritual male circumcision beyond any doubt' would be useful.[64] Hinchley notes that the 'crux of this debate revolves around the primacy of parental religious conviction versus the primacy of the human rights of the child, the preservation of its bodily integrity, and its right of self-determination.'[65] How does or should the law balance the rights of the child with the rights of parents to raise their child with particular religious beliefs and convictions?

The position of the law has been summarised by Wall J in *Re J*:[66]

61 ibid.
62 ibid. p 473.
63 See Caroline Bridge, 'Religion, Culture and the Body of the Child' in Andrew Bainham et al (eds), *Body Lore and Laws* (Hart, 2002) p 279.
64 Law Commission Consultation Paper 139, *Consent in the Criminal Law* (1995) fn 9.
65 Geoff Hinchley, 'Is infant male circumcision an abuse of the rights of a child? Yes' (2007) 335 *BMJ*, 1180.
66 *Re J* (n 35).

> English law, as I understand it to be, is as follows: (1) that as an exercise of joint parental responsibility, male ritual circumcision is lawful, however (2) where there is a disagreement between those who have parental responsibility for the child as to whether or not he should be circumcised, the issue is one within the court's jurisdiction under s 8 of the 1989 [Children] Act; and (3) the court must decide the question by the application of s 1 of the 1989 Act [the welfare test] to the facts of the individual case.[67]

The legal status of male circumcision is complex due to the fact that no statute exists that makes a direct statement about of the legal status of this medical procedure. The background to *Re J*[68] sets out the legal and medical context that provided the framework for the judgment by Wall J. The Law Commission[69] has supported that following statement of Lord Templeman in *R v Brown*:

> Even when violence is intentionally afflicted and results in actual bodily harm, wounding or serious bodily harm the accused is entitled to be acquitted if the injury was a foreseeable incident of a lawful activity in which the person injured was participating. Surgery involves intentional violence resulting in actual or sometimes serious bodily harm but surgery is a lawful activity. Other activities carried on with consent by or on behalf of the injured person have been accepted as lawful notwithstanding that they involve actual bodily harm or may cause serious bodily harm. *Ritual circumcision*, tattooing, ear-piercing and violent sports including boxing are lawful activities.[70]

These words, at the House of Lords, have been very influential in informing the presumption that ritual male circumcision is legal. The Law Commission have argued that ritual male circumcision, tattooing and ear-piercing are all exceptions to the general rule that a person cannot be inflicted with bodily harm.[71] The Law Commission may have put too much of a focus on the words of Lord Templeman and may have failed to include any controls, even in relation to safety and hygiene aspects of male circumcision.[72] Even though Lord Templeman lists ritual male circumcision as a lawful infliction of bodily harm, 'he is the only one to do so'.[73] Circumcision was not properly argued in *R v Brown*,[74] as this case concerned consensual sadomasochistic sexual acts. Price argues that Lord Templeman's mentioning of circumcision was actually in *obiter* because listing a number of acts which could be seen to be lawful was not essential to the question at hand.[75]

67 ibid. 358.
68 ibid.
69 Law Commission, *Consent in the Criminal Law* (n 64).
70 *R v Brown* [1992] UKHL 7, 231 (emphasis added).
71 Price (n 23) para 9.1.
72 ibid. para 11.
73 ibid.
74 *R v Brown* (n 70).
75 Price (n 23).

The above cases illustrate a number of similar points. Essentially, there is broad legal agreement, following Lord Templeman in *R v Brown*, that the practice of ritual male circumcision is a legal one. According to the current approach, unless there is evidence of valid and persuasive conflict, then the practice of non-therapeutic (ritual) circumcision is allowable. Of course, therapeutic circumcision, based upon identified medical need is in a different category. Where conflict exists in the case of ritual circumcision, the best interests test is applied and its conclusion to date has been that it is in the child's best interests to postpone circumcision until the child has the legal capacity to make such a grave decision.

This legal discourse is compelling in the sense that it highlights the fact that the undercurrent of the acceptance of circumcision as a valid medical procedure has only very thin legal grounding, given that it is a procedure that is carried out widely and to a relatively large number of boys.

The 'best interests' test in relation to ritual male circumcision

A mechanism has existed in the courts to try to ensure that the rights of the child are identified, maintained, and protected. When weighing the course of action to be taken in respect of a child, a best interest test is applied in the courts. The best interests principle is outlined in respect of children in the Children Act 1989, which states that any act done or decision made on behalf of a child who lacks legal capacity must be in their best interests. A determination of the best interests is based upon the whole child—consideration of their age and emotional development, the nature of the proposed treatment and its possible consequences to the child, the conceived impact on the child of the imposition of treatment that goes against their wishes and the possible effect on the child if treatment is not provided. The best interests test is a multi-layered, complex mechanism. The issue of best interests of the child is not simple in the context of religious belief and medical law. It is not just a matter of acting with the good of the child in mind. Because who defines that good? Who defines those best interests? Children, to a large degree, are dependent upon others to advocate for their rights. They are, or can be, relatively voiceless when decisions are made about them and their medical care. Parents are the people who usually make decisions about this medical care. Sometimes the decisions that they make are subject to challenge in the courts. In these cases, the legal system usually has one main priority—ensuring that the best interests of the child are served by whatever decisions are made or actions taken. In medical contexts the best interests test was devised to meet this requirement as apparent in the Children Act 1989.[76]

76 A list of factors has been introduced under the Children Act 1989 that must be considered when deciding what is in the best interests of the child concerned. Section 1 (3) of the 1989 Act states that courts should pay attention to: (a) the ascertainable wishes and feelings of the child concerned (considered in the light of his age and understanding); (b) his physical, emotional and educational needs; (c) the likely effect on him of any change in his circumstances; (d) his age, sex, background and any characteristics of his which the court considers relevant; (e) any harm which he has suffered or is at risk of suffering; (f) how capable each of his parents, and any other

Many examples of the use of best interests can be seen in current and previous case law. The use of the best interests test has been subject to a measure of query.[77] The issue of subjectivity and determining whether something is right or wrong is, according to Archard, undoubtedly an issue if the views of the child are considered to be paramount to all other factors.[78] Archard's point that we should not give absolute weight to the adult's right to choose when the choice is radically contrary to the individual's best interests and involves the pursuit of something significantly harmful of status of the child merits significant consideration in the context of how a child is conceptualised from a rights perspective.[79]

The main criticism of the application of the best interests test, according to Herring, is that it is unpredictable, too generalised, and takes a narrow view of best interests.[80] He points to the fact that 'best interests' often relies on a view of normal behaviour that is not always applicable in contentious cases.[81] Herring refers to the current emphasis on autonomy and supports the view that autonomy is not limitless; the child fits into a broader society and usually has the care of parents.[82] This care, he finds, is central to human thriving.[83] For parents with strong beliefs about circumcision as an integral part of the religious upbringing of their son, the relational values that they ascribe to and inculcate their child with should be factored into the discourse around the welfare of the child because any decision making process, if it is to be of value, must listen to all perspectives. Failing to understand that ritual circumcision is an integral part of belief means failing to engage fully in the reciprocal process. Equally, therefore, those who support circumcision need to recognise that arguments against it can have validity.

The best interests test potentially provides ammunition for the judge either to defer too readily to medical opinion as being authoritative or, less obviously, put in his or her unrecognised world values to where the best interests of the child lie. The best interests test, in itself, doesn't tell you what values are to be attached to religious belief. Another mechanism is needed to answer that question. At present, the test places little, if any, focus on the mental competence of the patient to make a decision and for it to be fully effective, the best interests test needs to include additional recognition of and focus on the mental competence of the patient to made a decision. Giving greater weight to this competence in this test would allow the voice of the patient to be heard more loudly.

person in relation to whom the court considers the question to be relevant, is of meeting his needs; (g) the range of powers available to the court under this Act in the proceedings in question.

77 See Rob Heywood, 'Parents and Medical Professionals: Conflict, Cooperation, and Best Interests' (2012) 20(1) *Medical Law Review*, 29–44.

78 David Archard, 'Children, adults, best interests and rights' (2013) 13(1) *Medical Law International*, 55–74.

79 ibid. p 73.

80 ibid. p 40

81 ibid. p 53.

82 ibid.

83 ibid.

Legal controversy surrounding circumcision: the implications of Re J,[84] Re S *and* SS (Malaysia)

A number of cases are now discussed in which the circumcision of a child was disputed. The analysis of these cases provide clarification as to the current stance of the law pertaining to this subject and, so, helps to answer the first methodological question of this book. These cases have been chosen to illustrate the fact that, in the main, there is consistency as to how the courts approach ritual male circumcision and the judgments that they make.

Objections to the circumcision of a child have been made in the courts. These objections usually involve disagreement about circumcision on the grounds of differing religious beliefs or practice on the part of the parents of the child. In the case of *Re J*, a mother (non-practising Christian) made an objection to the circumcision of her child. This objection was contrary to the Islamic religious views of the father who wanted his child to be circumcised. In this case the best interests test was applied, and it was concluded that the child should not be circumcised.

Due to the fact that the child did not have the ability to give informed consent to the circumcision[85] Wall J applied the best interests tests. It was Wall J's contention that the issue was one 'for society, not the health professionals'.[86] The Court referred to Section 1 (3) of the Children Act 1989 in their use of the 'best interests' test. On the whole, it was held that it was in the best interests of the child not to be circumcised and that it would be unsuitable to make such an irreversible decision without the child's consent.[87] Adhar and Leigh state that:

> It was in J's best interests that circumcision be prohibited. Being raised in a predominantly secular environment by his mother, circumcision would achieve little for J: it was a painful, irreversible operation, not medically necessary and the benefits to J, such as strengthening the bond with his father, did not outweigh this.[88]

The Court of Appeal agreed with Wall J. The Court of Appeal concluded that the child should not be circumcised because he was not likely to be raised as a Muslim and that, instead, he had 'a mixed heritage and an essentially secular lifestyle'.[89] This meant that it was very unlikely that the child would have so much of a connection to Islam as to justify his circumcision for cultural and religious reasons. Butler-Sloss LJ's note of caution at the Court of Appeal alerts the community to the fact that decisions around circumcision are important and even grave:

84 *Re J* (n 35)
85 ibid. p 356.
86 ibid. p 361.
87 ibid. p 365.
88 Rex Adhar and Ian Leigh, *Religious Freedom in the Liberal State* (2nd ed, OUP, 2013) p 335.
89 *Re J (Child's Religious Upbringing and Circumcision)* [2000] 1 FLR 571 at [4] where Thorpe LJ quoted the Official Solicitor in *Re J* (n 34) at 349.

> The decision to circumcise a child on a ground other than medical necessity is a very important one; the operation is irreversible, and should only be carried out where the parents together approve of it, or in the absence of parental agreement, where a court decides that the operation is in the best interest of the child.[90]

This cautionary statement has relevance for the whole discussion around circumcision—society should be reticent about accepting as a given the fact that a child can be ritually circumcised without question or query. Ritual male circumcision was also raised in *Re S (Children)*.[91] This case concerned an eight-year-old child who was raised under his father's Jain faith. Following their separation, his mother (a Muslim) wanted the boy to be circumcised. The best interests test was also used in this case. It was ruled that the child's mother had no authority to permit the circumcision of the young boy. The decision was upheld by the Court of Appeal.[92]

Baron J's concluded in *Re S*[93] that the decision should not be made until the child is *Gillick*-competent.[94] In English law, a child is someone under the age of 18. However, consent can be given by a child who is 16–17 or a child who is *Gillick*-competent. What is the relationship between the parents and children in this context? Under s 3 (1) of the Children Act 1989 the responsibilities of parents involve 'all the rights, duties, powers, responsibilities and authority which by law a parent has in relation to the child and his property'. The legal capacity to consent on behalf of the child to medical treatment, such as male circumcision, is included. Usually it is enough for one parent to consent to treatment. However, in the case of circumcision, approval must be given by both parents.

In *Gillick*, Lord Scarman said that a child under the age of sixteen would be capable of legally consenting if the child has 'sufficient understanding and intelligence to enable him or her to understand fully what is proposed.[95] In *Re S*, Baron J said that children under the age of ten were 'too young to seek to favour one of their religions of origin in favour of the other'.[96] Research put forward by Alderson and Montgomery shows that very young children who have experienced, for example, illness, can make decisions that affect themselves.[97] In the context of circumcision, it can be difficult to determine what the best interests are for the child, given that this procedure is usually carried out on very young children who may be at a very early communicative stage. However, Fox and Thomson argue

90 ibid. at [32].
91 *Re S* [2004] EWHC 1282, upheld by the Court of Appeal: [2004] EWCA Civ 1257.
92 See Pattinson (n 28) p 174.
93 *Re S* (n 91).
94 ibid. (Baron J).
95 *Gillick* (n 27) at 189.
96 *Re S* (Baron J) (n 91) at 256.
97 Priscilla Alderton and Jonathan Montgomery, *Health Care Choices: making decisions with children* (Institute for Public Policy Research, 1996).

that 'some older minors will be sufficiently mature to be entrusted with this decision themselves'.[98]

This test concerns the understanding and intelligence that a child under 16 has.[99] Hinchley contends that:

> The unpalatable truth is that logic and the rights of the child play little part in determining the acceptability of male genital mutilation in our society. The profession needs to recognise this and champion the argument on behalf of boys that was so successful for girls.[100]

This issue of circumcision is directly related to how society views the concept of harm.

More recently, circumcision has been discussed in *SS (Malaysia) v Secretary of State*.[101] This case concerned a six-year-old child who was raised as a Catholic by her Catholic Malaysian parents. During a period when the appellant (child's mother) and her son were in the UK, her husband converted to Islam. Consequently, she claimed asylum in the UK and claimed that if she went back to Malaysia, she would be arrested, treated badly by her husband. She claimed their returning to Malaysia would mean that the child would have to be circumcised. She argued that it would be a breach of Article 8 of the Convention if she were not able to teach her son about her own religion.[102] She also contended that her rights under Article 9 ECHR would be breached. The appeal was dismissed by the Court of Appeal. Why did the court come to this conclusion?

Moore-Bick LJ accepted that there is an expectation that Muslim boys are to be circumcised and that the child would be circumcised due to the father's culture and religion.[103] It was his contention that '[a]lthough invasive in nature and not commanding universal approval, it is regarded as an acceptable practice among communities of all kinds, provided it is carried out under appropriate conditions.'[104] He refused to agree that it could be compared to other religious practices such as female genital mutilation because male circumcision does not have such an attack on the physical integrity of the child.[105]

Moore-Bick LJ said that 'it is difficult to see how C's circumcision would involve any infringement of the appellant's Convention rights'.[106] Moore-Bick LJ contended that it was unnecessary to come to a conclusion whether the

98 Marie Fox and Michael Thomson, 'Older Minors and Circumcision' (2008) 9(4) *Medical Law International*, 283–310, p 292.
99 Hinchley (n 64), p 1180.
100 ibid. p 1181.
101 *SS (Malaysia) v Secretary of State* [2013] EWCA Civ 888.
102 ibid. at [2].
103 ibid. at [13]
104 ibid. at [15].
105 K v *Secretary of State for the Home Department, Fornah v Secretary of State for the Home Department* [2006] UKHL 46 considered (see [93] (Baroness Hale)).
106 *SS (Malaysia)* (n 101) at [14].

circumcision of the child could breach his Article 3/8 Convention rights because '[t]he tribunal's findings make it clear that in this case C would have the positive emotional support of his father and that he would be conforming to the broad expectations of the culture and society in which he would grow up'.[107] In line with the previous discussion of human rights law and, in particular, in accepting Svoboda's claim that ritual male circumcision constitutes inhuman treatment and so breaches human rights law, there is a strong possibility that the judge, in this case, accepted too readily that ritual male circumcision does not, in any way, constitute a breach of Convention rights. There is also an even stronger indication that the judge trivialised the physical harm meted out to the child in the carrying out of this procedure.

What have these cases told us about the current law? They promote the use of best interests test and suggest waiting until the child is *Gillick* competent before he can make a decision. This approach essentially finds that ritual male circumcision is not in the best interests of the child. Notwithstanding this, *R v Brown* suggests that circumcision is an allowable legal procedure. A disparity exists between the findings of the courts in *Re J* and *Re S* and evidence that the ritual circumcision of boys is routinely practised in the UK. English puts forward the conundrum that exists: one presumption accepts that religion is a private matter and has no place in the courts.[108] In parallel to this, however, another presumption accepts that the child's best interests are linked to practices within the religious faiths practised by the parents of the child. Can these two competing factors meet? At the very least, English recommends that '[i]f circumcision is one of the sharp demands placed on the child by religious faith, it should be scrutinised with the same rigour as any other practice which affects the interests of the child'.[109] Such scrutiny, unfortunately, does not apply to the many thousands of circumcisions that happen on a continual basis each year in England.

Question 2: Why is this approach sufficient or insufficient in the context of the PGC?

There is consistency in the current approach of English law: ritual male circumcision is a permissible practice and it is only when disagreement exists in the courts that the practice is disallowed until the child is *Gillick* competent. Case law does not give any significant attention to the human rights implications (e.g. Articles 3, 8 and 9 ECHR) of this irreversible practice. In line with the framework, the sufficiency of this approach is now assessed in the context of the PGC.

107 ibid. at [15].
108 Rosalind English, 'UK court ducks position on circumcision' available at: http://ukhumanrightsblog.com/2013/07/20/uk-court-ducks-position-on-circumcision/ (accessed 27 January 2017).
109 ibid.

Precautionary reasoning and the hierarchy of rights

Beyleveld and Pattinson's theory of precautionary reasoning, outlined in chapter 2, is pertinent in this context.[110] Precautionary reasoning applies, in particular, when circumcision involves infants.[111] Under precautionary reasoning, we do not know whether an infant is an agent, but the very possibility that he could be or is an agent means that he has interest-rights. An infant (who is to be circumcised) appears to be a partial apparent agent and therefore has interest-rights. The protection of his bodily integrity as a basic right under the PGC is called for. He is not able to say circumcision is 'the badge of all my tribe'.[112] He can't say 'I want to be circumcised and I don't care about any harm that is meted out to me'.

According to precautionary reasoning, there is a criterion of avoidance of more probable harm. How does this work in practice? A is a father and B is a baby (A's son). A wants B to be circumcised. Both display evidence that they have purposes that they wish to pursue. Although, in the case of the baby, there is no evidence of his ability to form a relationship between himself and his own purpose. B, in all probability, will display the traits and characteristics of apparent agency as he grows older, but A is already displaying the generic conditions of agency. In this situation, the PGC asks us to fulfil our duties to those who are more probable agents, rather than to those who are in a state of becoming. In this case, A is an apparent agent, whereas B is apparently only a partial agent approaching apparent agency. This means that if the level and likelihood of harm to both is equal, A's will-rights should take priority over B's interest-rights. The level of harm is to be measured by the criterion of degrees of needfulness for action, as explained in chapter 2.

In the context of circumcision, the generic conditions of agency with the most importance is bodily integrity and this can override the generic right to private and family life which has, therefore, a lower importance in terms of needfulness for action. The level of harm that is inflicted upon a baby who is circumcised is a basic harm because of the irreversibility and physical harm caused by this procedure. His basic right to physical integrity must be given paramountcy. The level of harm inflicted upon the parents by refusing permission to have their child circumcised is an additive harm because it inhibits the manifestation of their religious belief, but is not so consequential as to constitute grievous transgression of that religious belief, such as might be involved in the requirement for practising Catholics to conscientiously object to abortion, which, for them, can be a 'mortal sin'. The harm inflicted upon, for example, a Jewish parent whose wish to have his child circumcised is refused, arises from the fact that he is not able to fully manifest his religious belief, but adherence to this aspect of belief does not, however, constitute grave derogation of the tenets of his faith. More probable harm, therefore,

110 See Deryck Beyleveld & Shaun D Pattinson, 'Precautionary Reason as a Link to Moral Action' in Michael Boylan, *Medical Ethics* (Prentice-Hall, 2000) pp 39–53.

111 ibid.

112 William Shakespeare, *The Merchant of Venice*, (Act 1, Scene 3) available at: http://shakespeare.mit.edu/merchant/merchant.1.3.html (accessed 27 January 2017).

is caused to the child by virtue of the infliction of basic harm to him, by virtue of the carrying out of an irreversible procedure, than is caused to the parents' additive right in acting in accordance with their religious belief. Thus, the infliction of basic harm to the child trumps the infliction of additive harm to the parents and so, in accordance with the PGC, the child, at this stage, cannot be circumcised. The mentally competent male child has will-rights and can waive the benefits to his generic rights. Therefore, at that stage, he can make a decision whether or not he can be circumcised. Therefore, it is appropriate to wait until the child has legal capacity to make the decision before he is circumcised.

To revert to the case law dealing with ritual male circumcision, Wall J in *Re J* made an appropriate conclusion that the child could not be legally circumcised until he was *Gillick* competent. At least in theory, this was a sensible decision (notwithstanding some of the difficulties that exits with the *Gillick* test). Wall J's use of the best interests test was appropriate, due to the fact that the child lacked legal capacity. He was correct not to allow for the child to be circumcised because, from the point of view of the PGC, basic harm would have been inflicted on the child, who clearly lacked the mental competence to make this serious decision.

Under the current approach, inappropriate weight is given to the will-rights of mentally competent patients. The same arguments in relation to the Mental Capacity Act 2005's (MCA) two-stage test for legal capacity and the test on best interests for legally incapacitated adults and/or children, as presented in the chapter dealing with Jehovah's Witnesses who refuse blood transfusions, are applicable here. Arising from these arguments, if a patient lacks the mental competence to make the specific decision whether or not he can be circumcised, then the circumcision ought to be disallowed. The banning of ritual circumcisions in cases involving mentally incompetence (or, indeed, legal incapacity), is justified by the basic harm inflicted upon the vulnerable patient. Just as advocated for Jehovah's Witnesses, the law on the legal capacity of children needed needs to be amended in order to provide a more PGC-compliant response that is not overly paternalistic or involves setting the *Gillick* competence bar too high. For example, the overruling of the courts or parents in the case of legally capacitated children (e.g. *Re R*[113] and *Re W*[114]) does not reflect the values of the PGC as this approach gives insufficient weight to the will-rights of the agents (mentally competent children). An affront to physical integrity is considered by the PGC to be a basic harm. Equally, in *SS (Malaysia)*[115] returning the child to Malaysia, where he would undergo circumcision, would result in an invasion of his physical integrity to the extent that it would constitute basic harm. This is impermissible under the PGC and, therefore, Moore-Bick LJ's decision is inappropriate.

113 *Re R* [1991] 4 ALL ER 177.
114 *Re W* [1992] 3 WLR 758.
115 *SS (Malysia)* (n 101).

Consent and best interests

The issue of consent is also relevant. For consent to be valid, this consent must be voluntary. It is obvious that a young baby cannot give voluntary consent because that baby lacks the mental competence to do so. An older boy may be able to give consent, but his acquiescence may also derive from parental pressure and so denude him of the power to make an independent decision. Unless a decision is arrived at in a voluntary way without acquiescence to the undue influence excerpted by third parties, which in the case of boys may comprise of well-meaning parents, then consent to treatment is not fully valid. The lack of opportunity for, or ability of a baby, to make this sort of independent choice negates his ability to act with voluntariness and purposefulness and so infringes the PGC.

The same arguments made in respect of best interests and Jehovah's Witnesses who refuse treatment can be replicated here. In *Re J* and *Re S*, the best interests test was used in order to refuse permission for the carrying out of circumcision and the children had to wait until they were *Gillick* competent to make the decision. Once again, these cases show an example of how ritual male circumcision is at variance with the PGC, namely due to the infringement of the mentally incompetent child's basic rights under Gewirth's hierarchy. The bigger issue here is not, however, how the best interests test was applied, and the justification of the judges' decision based on it. The bigger issue related to the determination of legal capacity. It was convenient in both cases that the children had no legal capacity and so the best interests test could be used. This left a resolution that suited the court. However, there is some doubt in both cases as to whether these children actually did lack legal capacity. Perhaps, they were apparent mentally competent agents and so could have made their own decision. For example, if it could be shown that S were mentally competent, then there would be no need for the best interests test to be used, as he, as a mentally competent apparent agent, could decide whether or not he wanted to be inflicted by basic harm/be circumcised (waive the benefit to his generic rights). Thus, the best interests test should not be invoked in situations where it is simply applied in order to come to a 'simple' resolution. Because of the doubts that have been articulated hitherto about the law surrounding legal capacity and children, there are problems with the application of the best interests tests. Under this current approach and its covert paternalism, the best interests test could quite likely be used when a child is actually mentally competent.

Circumcision, the PGC and the ECHR

It is suggested that Moore-Bick LJ was incorrect in arguing that circumcision did not breach the child's Convention rights because, as indicated in chapter 2, human rights law must be guided by the PGC and must potentially change to reflect its principles.[116] Thus, it is apparent that Article 9 ECHR protects the will-rights of agents in a universally acceptable way. However, the protection of

116 See, for example, Deryck Beyleveld and Roger Brownsord, *Consent in the* Law (Hart, 2007) p 50.

interest rights, particularly of infants, is insufficient in this instance. The interpretation of Article 9's limitations does not recognise sufficiently the interest-rights of infants. Article 9(2) puts some halt to religious expression in order to protect 'public order, health or morals, or for the protection of the rights and freedoms of others'. These rights and freedoms need to be appropriately interpreted as safeguarding the interest-rights of infants in the context of circumcision. If the European Court were to be guided by the suggested methodological framework, it is likely that they would err on the side of protecting the basic interest-rights of infants and so find against the practice of non-therapeutic circumcision of infants. It is conceivable that, in order to be compliant with the PGC, human rights law should also make reference to the circumcision of infants as being a derogation of their rights.

The issue in these cases is not about whether or not the parents are in dispute. Instead, the focus is on the issue of mental competence/legal capacity of the child to make the relevant decision. For parents to act a way that is PGC-compliant means that they cannot simply circumcise the child without giving him a say in the decision, due to the infliction of basic harm and lack of the task-specific mental competence. At one level, therefore, aspects of current case law are sufficient. However, this case law reflects isolated cases where circumcision is disputed and, in these cases, it has been found that the best interests of the child are served by waiting until the child has legal capacity to make a decision. There is an anomaly here: if case law determines that the best interests are served by adopting a wait-for-choice-of-circumcision approach, what does this say about the fact that ritual circumcision is a routine procedure in common and daily use within society? There is a danger that permitting ritual circumcision in non-contested cases does not actually serve the best interests of children. The legal approach, which is currently confined only to cases of contention, does not sufficiently address the need to ensure that the rights of children not be inflicted with basic harm until they have sufficient mental competence to make that decision are not currently being protected. Another approach is needed to provide that additional protection.

Question 3: Is there an alternative approach that will provide greater compliance with the framework?

It is clear that the legislative context of circumcision is flawed in English law. Currently, ritual male circumcision is allowed even though it causes basic harm to a mentally incompetent child. There is inadequate statute governing ritual circumcision. In the context of change in the common law, the courts can't override the Children Act 1989 and this Act requires them to maximise the welfare of the child. Therefore, the judge cannot go beyond the Children Act and so judicial action is constrained. There is no specific legislation but maybe judges could have done more in the judgments that they have made to respect the right to protect the child from basic harm. For significant change to occur, legislative action is required instead of amendments in the common law that will never be sufficient enough to represent an indirect application of the PGC.

A principled approach to this difficulty is the enaction of legislation that would make ritual male circumcision of legally incapacitated children illegal. Change at societal level is also required where there is some interaction with religious leaders whereby the practice of ritual male circumcision is looked at with the realisation that it could take generations to change existing practice. Therefore, a pragmatic element needs to apply which could involve, initially, changing elements of the approach taken to circumcision in the common law (including change to the best interests test, the MCA and the test for determining the legal capacity of minors).

The existing law does not prohibit circumcision and in situations of dispute, the courts use the best interests test in order to wait until the child has legal capacity. This represents a contradiction in the law because why is it in the best interests of the child not be circumcised until determined to have legal capacity in these circumstances and, on the other hand, to be automatically circumcised without consideration of mental competence?

Approach in Gewirthia

The community in Gewirthia is not wholly identical, but is united by acceptance of the PGC and its values. Legislation in Gewirthia is based upon PGC principles and respect for the rights of all agents.[117] It outlaws circumcision of a mentally incompetent child on the basis that this infringes their generic rights. It allows for the circumcision of mentally competent children who express a desire to have this procedure, in line with their will-rights

Alternative approaches in a non-Gewirthian English context

To date, this chapter has focused on this issue of conflict between dissenting parents and their wish to have or not to have their child circumcised. But the framework goes beyond the arena of dissention and proposes that the practice of circumcision, involving as it does, basic and irreversible harm to an infant or a young child, should be prohibited until such a time as the child has mental competence (and, consequently, legal capacity) to make a decision of this gravity for himself. The adoption of this stance would require significant amendment to existing legal practices. The limitation that basic harm occurs to potentially mentally incompetent children on a daily basis is unlikely to be changed without significant alteration in the law in the form of an Act of Parliament. Change in the common law will help in changes of dispute, but without legislative change, there will be little fundamental change in the practice. The most effective way of doing this would be the introduction of this new Act, which specifically deals with the prohibition of circumcision until such time as a child has the legal capacity (which tracks mental competence) to make decisions in this regard and so exercise his will-rights in accordance with the PGC. The Act should, consequently, be legal

117 See Deryck Beyleveld and Roger Brownsword, 'Principle, Proceduralism, and Precaution in a Community of Rights' (2006) 19(2) *Ratio Juris*, 141–168, p 143.

capacity-focused, rather than providing a blanket prohibition to ritual circumcision. In this way, the right to manifest religious belief, as underpinned by Article 9 ECHR, will be protected as long as such expression is gauged to have been made when the child has sufficient mental competence (i.e. legal capacity).

It is proposed that the current legal status should be changed and that ritual male circumcision should be considered to be illegal until the child is deemed to be mentally competent to make this decision (i.e. has legal capacity). It is recognised that this stance has broad societal implications, particularly within Jewish and Islamic communities where this practice is an important embedded cornerstone of religious belief. There are dangers, too, in rendering this practice illegal in so far as such a change in the law could result in the carrying out of this procedure in a hidden backstreet manner, free from medical safeguards and with potential injurious consequences. However, to comply with the PGC and to ensure that harm is prevented, such an option must be considered.

At a principled level, the new Act of Parliament on ritual male circumcision could be called the Circumcision Act. Unlike a development in the common law, a dedicated statute would allow for a principled approach to legal change. Following the principle of parliamentary sovereignty, enacting a new Act would give a measure of legal certainty to the issue of ritual male circumcision and add a necessary measure of prescription: judges could only interpret the legislation and not challenge the validity of the Act.

Under the Act, the child will not be circumcised until he has legal capacity. This capacity will be determined in the same manner as that articulated in the previous (Jehovah's Witnesses and Blood Transfusions) chapter i.e. the vetoing of children's decision by the courts/parents (e.g. *Re R*[118] and *Re W*[119]) and the application of the inappropriate test of *Gillick* should not be accepted or applied unilaterally. Instead, the Mental Capacity Act 2005, in conjunction with developments in common law, aligned to evidence of societal competence and underpinned by Gewirth's concept of self-fulfilment will apply.[120] If the child's satisfies the terms of this new approach to legal capacity, and, consequently, has the relevant mental competence, he can be circumcised, if he so wishes, in accordance with his will-rights.

Of course, the application of this Act will not be simple and it will be subject to many contexts and variables that will challenge both the spirit and the content of the Act. The terms that the Act could achieve can be summarised in the following indicative and non-prescriptive suggested guidelines:

Circumcision is defined as surgery that involves the removal, or partial removal of foreskin covering the glands of the penis being removed. Recognition is given to the importance of circumcision as a manifestation of religious belief or identity

118 *Re R* (n 113).

119 *Re W* (n 114).

120 See Emma Cave, 'Goodbye Gillick? Identifying and resolving problems with the concept of child competence' (2014) 34(1) *Journal of Legal Studies*, 103–122 and Alan Gewirth, *Self-Fulfillment* (Princeton University Press, 1998). The application of this test has been explained in chapter 5.

and a person with capacity can legally be circumcised in accordance with ritual procedures that are in line with specific healthcare standards. A minor must not be circumcised until he has capacity to make such a decision and has voluntarily consented to the procedure that he understands fully, due to the information that has been disclosed and comprehended. Legal capacity shall be determined in light of the new test summarised above (see chapter 5 for more detail) and the wishes of such a patient with legal capacity shall not be overruled by parents/guardians or the courts. However, anyone who carries out a circumcision or assists in the procedure when a child is regarded as lacking capacity shall be liable to prosecution. Circumcision for therapeutic contexts is permissible where procedures are carried out in accordance with good practice medical guidelines. Failure to comply with the terms of the Act will result in such consequences as deemed appropriate by the relevant authorities.

While this chapter does not support the practice of ritual circumcision of legally incapacitated children and recommends a change in English law, it is important to reiterate that this proposed ban applies only to circumcision at a specific time. It is not argued that circumcision should never take place, only that it can only be undertaken when a child is properly considered to have legal capacity. There is no compelling justification under the PGC for allowing this irreversible procedure to take place before a child is able to make the decision. This is in line with current English law in cases of legal dispute.

Additional approaches at European level could include the use by the ECtHR of Article 3 ECHR to indicate that ritual circumcision explicitly violates the child's Convention rights when this procedure is undertaken when they lack the legal capacity to accept or refuse the procedure. In relation to the balancing of rights, in this case, the breach of the child's basic rights would override parental additive rights. There is a need for proper use and interpretation of a human rights framework (such as the HRA/ECHR) that is reflective of PGC principles.

In line with the chapter on Jehovah's Witnesses (children) and blood transfusions, the courts' overly paternalist approach is deemed to be insufficient. What should be determinate is legal capacity that tracks mental competence. A properly applied best interests test that requires that we wait until the child becomes legally capacitated is advocated. In England into the future, the Act will have to be contextualised within the societal landscape of the time, which may prove challenging. English law will need to be human rights law centred and reflective of Article 3, as an absolute right, and so comply with the PGC. In tandem with Article 9's protections afforded to manifesting belief and the clear association between ritual male circumcision and the expression of one's Jewish or Islamic faith, the Act should include provisions relating to religion, identity, and recognition that circumcision is part of the manifestation of that identity. Thus, this has the potential to add in, in the context of male circumcision, an additional element of maturity which, while not specifically required by the PGC, would provide society with a rigorous determinant that would help to ensure that the child was based upon mature reflection and that reflects the child's general values and does not just constitute an elusive idea of the moment. Such legislation would need to expressly restrict circumcision to those instances where there is certainty that the procedure gives effect to the child's religious beliefs.

What would happen in the future if this Act were in force and what challenges could there be to the application of the Act and how might judges interpret the Act? Prosecuting parents who arranged for their child's circumcision would be a breach of the Act because the child must have legal capacity to make the decision to be circumcised or not before acting before any ritual procedure is carried out. Obviously, the case would be different in therapeutic contexts, where there would be a proven need for the child to undertake a medically necessary procedure. Cases involving young babies are those involving apparent partial agents who lack the ability to make the decision. In line with precautionary reasoning, such babies would have interest rights and could not waive the benefits to their generic rights. Additionally, these babies would not satisfy the two-stage test of the revised MCA, which would now apply to all citizens, including children.

It is likely that judges would interpret the legislation in a PGC-compliant manner. This could include invoking Article 3 ECHR in cases where legally incapacitated children have been circumcised. Challenges to the Act could include arguments based on Articles 8 and 9 and the assertion that the respective rights to respect for private and family life and the right to manifest religious belief, which are protected under these Articles, could be violated. It is contended that a stronger and powerful argument exists to the effect that circumcising a child who does not have the legal capacity to make a valid decision breaches Article 3, as an absolute right and constitutes inhuman treatment that cannot be permitted without proper consent. Additional challenges might focus upon the perception that this procedure is an important tenet of the Jewish faith and is sensitive to the parents' actions as meeting the requirements of their faith. The Act recognises the importance of ritual circumcision in relation to the manifestation of religious belief. However, the terms of the Act very carefully balance religious manifestation and the need to protect the child from injurious harm because it explicitly provides for permissible ritual circumcision once the child has legal capacity. It is surely appropriate for parents to wait until their child can meaningfully agree to a procedure that will have irreversible physical consequences for him. A baby is not in a position to decide himself whether or not he wants this procedure, which is irreversible. Parents who facilitate the circumcision of their child may be found into the future to have failed to protect their child from this harm and also to have failed to comply with the law of the land.

Conclusion

The law tries to arbitrate between the rigidity of these two viewpoints when contention arises. Usually, it comes to conclusions that balance these competing rights and also protect the child's voiceless rights. It is concluded that, in cases of dispute, a male child should not be circumcised until he has the legal capacity to make the decision due to the level of irreversible harm being imposed upon him.

This chapter has moved beyond the issue of dissention in terms of circumcision and has attempted to address the more general question of the legality of circumcising young infants/children before they have the legal capacity (including the necessary mental competence) to make irreversible decisions. The framework was used to interrogate this practice and comes to the conclusion that the practice of circumcising young boys constitutes basic harm and, under the criterion of degrees for needfulness of action, cannot be permissible. Their basic right to physical integrity must be given paramountcy. The mentally competent male child has will-rights and can waive the benefits to his generic rights. Therefore, at that stage, he can make a decision whether or not he can be circumcised. Therefore, it is appropriate to wait until the child has the legal capacity to make the decision.

Overall, therefore, it is determined that the practice of ritual circumcision of infants and young boys is at variance with the framework. A new Act is called for where a boy cannot be circumcised, for religious reasons, until has legal capacity, in line with the approach suggested in chapter 5. The courts recognise the child's decision when such a decision is linked to an expressed self-identification by the child, as requiring this procedure to explicitly fulfil a religious affiliation requirement.

We have to accept, however, that this radical change might not, in fact, be accepted at societal, religious, or parliamentary level due, in the main to the fact that it is an embedded and historical part of religious manifestation of a considerable amount of people living in the UK who espouse either Jewish or Muslim beliefs. This does not mean that we cannot decry the practice and call for legislative change, but it does mean that the potential for such change is limited. In view of this reality, the pragmatic approaches here are more likely to be accepted and are more likely to be implemented. While they fall short of stopping the practice of circumcision, they, nonetheless, constitute a good faith attempt at applying the PGC in cases of conflict.

References

Adhar, Rex and Leigh, Ian *Religious Freedom in the Liberal State* (2nd ed, OUP, 2013).

Alderton, Priscilla and Montgomery, Jonathan, *Health Care Choices: making decisions with children* (Institute for Public Policy Research, 1996).

Archard, David, 'Children, adults, best interests and rights' (2013) 13(1) *Medical Law International*, 55–74.

Beyleveld, Deryck and Brownsword, Roger, *Consent in the Law* (Hart, 2007).

Beyleveld, Deryck and Brownsword, Roger, 'Principle, Proceduralism, and Precaution in a Community of Rights' (2006) 19(2) *Ratio Juris*, 141–168.

Beyleveld, Deryck and Pattinson, Shaun D, 'Precautionary Reason as a Link to Moral Action' in Michael Boylan, *Medical Ethics* (Prentice-Hall, 2000).

Boyle et al, 'Circumcision of healthy boys: criminal assault?' (2000) 7 *Journal of Law and Medicine*.

Bridge, Caroline, 'Religion, Culture and the Body of the Child' in A Bainham et al (eds), *Body Lore and Laws* (Hart, 2002).

British Medical Association, 'The Law and Ethics of Male Circumcision: Guidelines for Doctors', 12 November 2007.

British Medical Association, *Medical Ethics Today* (BMJ Books, 2004).

Cansever, Gocke, 'Psychological effects of circumcision' (1965) 38*B J Med Psychol*, 321–331.

Cave, Emma, 'Goodbye Gillick? Identifying and resolving problems with the concept of child competence' (2014) 34(1) *Journal of Medical Ethics*, 103–122.

Edge, Peter W, 'Male Circumcision after the Human Rights Act 1998' (2000) 5 *J Civil Liberties*, 320–337.

English, Rosalind, 'UK court ducks position on circumcision', available at: http://ukhumanrightsblog.com/2013/07/20/uk-court-ducks-position-on-circumcision/ (accessed 27 January 2017).

Equality and Human Rights Commission, 'Article 3: Freedom from torture and inhumane and degrading treatment or punishment' (2012) *Human Rights Review*, 69–134.

Evans, Malcolm and Morgan, Rod, *Preventing Torture* (Clarendon Press, 1998).

Feldman, David, *Civil Liberties and Human Rights in England and Wales* (OUP, 1991)

Freud, Anna, 'The Role of Bodily Illness in the Mental Life of Children', in *Psychoanalytic Study of Children* (International University Press, 1952).

Fox, Marie and Thomson, Michael, 'A Covenant of the status quo' (2005) 31 *J Med Ethics*, 463–469.

Fox, Marie and Thomson, Michael, 'Older Minors and Circumcision' (2008) *Medical Law International*, 283–310.

Gatrad, AR et al, 'Religious Circumcision and the Human Rights Act' (2002) 86(2) *Arch Dis Child*, 76–78.

General Medical Council, *Guidance for doctors who are asked to circumcise male children* (GMC, 1997).

Glass, JM, 'Religious Circumcision: a Jewish view' (1999) 23 *BJU International*, 17–21.

Gewirth, Alan, *Self-Fulfillment*, (Princeton University Press, 1998).

Heywood, Rob, 'Parents and Medical Professionals: Conflict, Cooperation, and Best Interests, (2012) 20(1) *Medical Law Review*, 29–44.

Hinchley, Geoff, '*Is infant male circumcision an abuse of the rights of a child? Yes*' (2007) 335 BMJ, 1180.

Hutson, JM, 'Circumcision: A Surgeon's Perspective' (2003) 30 *Journal of Medical Ethics*, 238–240.

Law Commission Consultation Paper 139, *Consent in the Criminal Law* (1995).

Ó Néill, Clayton, 'Religious and Cultural Beliefs: The Potential for Patient safety to be Compromised' in John Tingle, Clayton Ó Neill, and Morgan Shimwell (eds), *Global Patient Safety Law Policy and Practice* (Routledge, 2019).

Pattinson, Shaun D, *Medical Law and Ethics* (5th ed, Sweet & Maxwell, 2017).

Peterson, SE, 'Assaulted and Mutilated. A Personal account of Circumcision trauma' in GC Denniston, FM Hodges, and MF Milos (eds), *Understanding Circumcision* (Kluwer Academic, 2001).

Price, Christopher, 'Male Circumcision: A Legal Affront', Submission to the Law Commission of England and Wales in Response to Consultation Paper Number 139- Consent in the Criminal Law, December 1998 at 6.1, available at: http://www.cirp.org/library/legal/price-uklc/#mus (accessed 27 January 2017).

Robinson, R et al, 'Consent for Non-Therapeutic Male Circumcision on Religious Grounds' (2009) 91(2) *Ann R Coll Surg Engl*, 152–154.

Shakespeare, William, *The Merchant of Venice*, available at: http://shakespeare.mit.edu/merchant/merchant.1.3.html (accessed 27 January 2017).

Svoboda, Steven, 'Circumcision of male infants as a human rights violation' (2013) 39 *J Med Ethics*, 469–474.

Williams, N and Kapila, L, 'Complications of Circumcision' (1993) 80 *British Journal of Surgery*, 1231–1316.

Williams, N, Chell, J, and Kapila, L, 'Why are children referred for circumcision?' (1993) 306 *BMJ*.

7 Illegal circumcision: Female Genital Mutilation

Introduction

The chapter considers Female Genital Mutilation (FGM) and concludes that, notwithstanding the fact that aspects of the Female Genital Mutilation Act 2003 are not fully in line with the PGC, due to practical and societal realities, this Act represents a good faith attempt at applying the PGC. There is a general tendency in Western countries to have a blanket ban on FGM. As such, the position in English law is very clear: it is always prohibited under the Female Genital Mutilation Act 2003. Under this Act, the carrying out of a FGM can result in a fine or the imprisonment of the person carrying out the procedure. FGM is defined by the World Health Organisation (WHO) as comprising 'all procedures that involve partial or total removal of the external female genitalia, or other injury to the female genital organs for non-medical reasons'.[1] This practice is prevalent in a variety of countries, ranging from Ghana to India to Liberia. An estimated 137,000 women and girls are reported to be living with the effects of FGM in England and Wales.[2] The WHO attest to that fact that FGM assigns women to an inferior place within society and results in reduction in women's sexual desire. They point to a number of influential organisations who view FGM as being universally unacceptable and an infringement of the physical and the psycho-sexual integrity of women.[3]

Rationale for inclusion of FGM in this book

This book deals with adequacy of the legal protection that is afforded to the manifestation of religious belief in medical law. Is there a place in this book for consideration of a procedure that, at one extreme, is seen as a religious obligation

1 World Health Organisation, 'Female Genital Mutilation' available at http://www.who.int/mediacentre/factsheets/fs241/en/ (accessed 27 January 2017).
2 Macfarlane et al, *Female Genital Mutilation in England and Wales: Updated statistical estimates of the numbers of affected women living in England and Wales and girls at risk Interim report on provisional estimates*, (City University London, 2014) available at: http://www.city.ac.uk/__data/assets/pdf_file/0020/266033/FGM-statistics-report-21.07.14-no-embargo.pdf (accessed 27 January 2017).
3 ibid.

and an integral part of cultural and ethnic identity that ensures a rite of passage into womanhood and, at the other extreme, is viewed as being a ritualised form of child abuse and a violation of women and human rights themselves?

Many feel that FMG relates, fundamentally, to ethnicity rather than religion.[4] FMG can be conceived as being about a conceptualisation of the place of women within society, a conceptualisation that is not affiliated to religious viewpoints, but is, rather, linked to gender order hierarchical positioning. A consideration of the other ethnic factors that are aligned with FGM is not within the remit of this book, whose focus is on the manifestation of FGM as a quasi-religious belief. The analysis of FGM will focus on its compliance with the PGC and will also involve comparison between this practice and that of ritual male circumcision, particularly in terms of harm or potential harm.

For many, the place of FGM as a religious manifestation is untenable because the link between religion and FGM is not definite. There is no consensus amongst Islamic scholars that any religious scripts advocate this practice and '[t]here is no major Islamic citations that makes female genital mutilation a religious requirement. Neither the Quran nor the "hadith" includes a direct call for FMG'.[5] The Human Rights Watch point to the flawed link between religion and female genital mutilation and show how religious leaders need to play a role in disassociating FGM from religion.[6] The WHO demonstrates that this practice has no health benefits and is a violation of human rights and is rooted in gender equality issues.[7] This report indicates that the religious obligation factor in the practice of FGM is only one factor within a number of contributing elements—the story, beliefs, values, and codes of conduct of society that must be taken together to form 'overwhelming and conscious motivation' for the continuance of its practice within religious or other sub-groups.[8] FGM has, however, been linked in public perception to Islam because of the perceived emphasis this religion places on chastity and modesty, but only a small minority of followers of Islam encourage the carrying out of this procedure. Notwithstanding the efforts made in the global context on the part of some leaders within Islam to decry this practice,[9] there remains significant potential for even stronger leadership at political, community, educational, and religious level.

Thus, FGM is not part of the mainstream of any of the Abrahamic religions, but people who think that it is important and that it is required can articulate religious

4 ibid.
5 ibid. p 230.
6 Human Rights Watch 'Q and A on Female Genital Mutilation' (June 16, 2010) available at: http://www.hrw.org/news/2010/06/10/qa-female-genital-mutilation (accessed 27 January 2017).
7 World Health Organisation, 'Female Genital Mutilation' (n 1).
8 World Health Organisation, 'Female Genital Mutilation – Programmes to Date: What Works and What Doesn't – A Review' (World Health Organisation, 1999).
9 Mike Pflanz, 'Religious leaders join the fight to end female circumcision in Somalia' (Unicef Somalia, 2011) available at: https://www.unicef.org/somalia/reallives_10195.html (accessed 03 June 2018).

grounds for it. FGM is, thus, linked to religion because those who promote it can give it religious undertones. Therefore, the fact that this practice is linked, at the very least, in public consciousness with some (marginalised) followers of Islam, in particular, gives a rationale for its inclusion in this book.[10]

Support for people to manifest religious belief, within limits, is provided for under Article 9 of the European Convention on Human Rights (ECHR), which does not have to accept any formal, regimental religion. It can accept very minority expressions of belief, but can propose countervailing arguments and limitations. Article 9's deliberate vagueness and lack of specificity in terms of religion leaves it up to an individual to self-determine the religious base. Human rights law supports this self-definition. If something is self-identified as religious in nature, the way that the law regulates it is not by saying 'you're wrong about that'; it is about saying 'yes, but…there is this countervailing interest which would trump it for whatever reason'. Clearly Article 9(2) ECHR provides a mechanism for that rather than denying that the claim is religious in nature. As such, while FGM is not a tenet of mainstream of Islam and many within that religion would eschew this practice, it can still fall within the ambit of Article 9's understanding of religion or belief.

Risks associated with FGM

The risks associated with FGM are severe and significant and include those listed by the WHO: cysts, severe pain, urine retention, a greater chance of being infertile, reduced sexual enjoyment, psychological problems, and infections.[11] Rymer and Comfort describe the trauma associated with this procedure. Traditionally, a person who performs a female genital mutilation is not surgically trained, as may be the case with some male circumcision.[12] Often, the girl is under no anaesthetic and has to be held down by her family and friends. It is quite possible for haemorrhage to occur[13] and there is also a risk of sepsis.[14] Female Genital Mutilation can have long term complications: scarring may result and the opening for menstrual blood may be limited. As such, surgery will be needed to resolve the problems. It very often causes psychological effects: women who have had undergone female genital mutilation according to Rymer and Momoh, 'often have low self-esteem and feel denied of their sexuality. They often suffer from flashbacks and

10 Machie and leJeune attest to the fact that a purely religious interpretation and understanding of FGM is inadequate due to the fact that FGM is not universally practised within the broad Muslim population, but, rather, is often in evidence in marginal subgroups of that population. Gerry Mackie and John LeJeune, 'Social Dynamics of Abandonment of Harmful Practices: A New Look at the Theory', (2008, Innocenti Working Paper, UNICEF Innocenti Research Centre) available at: http://pages.ucsd.edu/~gmackie/documents/UNICEF.pdf (accessed 27 January 2017).

11 World Health Organisation, 'Female Genital Mutilation' (n 1).

12 Janice Rymer and Comfort Momoh, 'Managing the Reality of FGM in the UK' in Comfort Momoh (ed), *Female Genital Mutilation*, (Radcliffe Publishing, 2005) p 22.

13 ibid. p 23.

14 ibid.

anxiety'.[15] They say that '[i]t is inevitable that having undergone FGM a woman's genital region will be associated with pain and trauma'.[16]

There are differing ways of carrying out this procedure: clitoridectomy, excising, infibulation, and other procedures.[17] Varying religious groups within geographically-specific areas of Islamic practice have differing views towards FGM, ranging from seeing types of FMG as being obligatory, optional, or preferred.[18] These procedures range in severity of physical invasion. They all, however, constitute grave physical invasion and they have at their root a desire to limit female sexual enjoyment.[19] This is a crucial difference between male circumcision and female genital mutilation, where, in the former, no such intent exists.

Dissent and discourse

FGM is not without its supporters, however, and LaBarbera revisits the anti-FGM discourse and provides some meaningful discussion around this topic.[20] Her argument centres around the fact that FGM is criminalised and found to be unacceptable on the basis that, amongst its negative consequences, the sexual stimulation of women is reduced.[21] She draws parallels between attitudes to breast implantation and FGM in terms of depicting how the former reduces sexual arousal in the woman and, yet, is socially acceptable. This comparative analysis, according to LaBarbera, shows how Western society does not fully accept women's autonomy and diversity. She refers to Kenyatta's research in the 1930s which found what she calls 'ritual female genital cutting' was linked to tribal psychology and to religious belief.[22] She calls for an understanding of difference in such a way that an understanding of FGM would lead to socio-cultural integration, rather than being a call to arms that in some way reflects racial discrimination.[23] Her central argument that the criminalisation of FGM is dangerous in so far as it places this practice in the same subterranean context as back street abortions does provoke some questions that are difficult to answer.[24] It is true

15 ibid. p 25.
16 ibid. p 24.
17 See, for example, Nahid Toubia, 'Female Genital Mutilation' in Julie Peters and Andrea Wolper, *Women's Rights, Human Rights: International Female Perspectives* (Routledge, 1995) p 226.
18 Ibrahim Lethome Asmani & Maryam Sheikh Abdi, *Delinking Female Genital Mutilation/Cutting from Islam*, (United States Agency for International Development, 2008) 6 available at: https://www.unfpa.org/sites/default/files/pub-pdf/De-linking%20FGM%20from%20Islam%20final%20report.pdf (accessed 27 January 2017).
19 See, for example, World Health Organisation, 'Female Genital Mutilation' (n 1).
20 Maria Caterina LaBarbera, 'Revisiting the anti-Female Genital Mutilation Discourse' (2009) 9 *Diritto & Questioni Pubbliche*, 485–507 available at: http://www.dirittoequestionipubbliche.org/page/2009_n9/05_studi-03_MC_LaBarbera.pdf (accessed 27 January, 2017).
21 ibid. p 488.
22 ibid. p 492. Also see Jomo Kentatta, *Facing Mount Kenya. The Traditional Life of the Giyuku* (Secker and Warburg, 1938).
23 LaBarbera (n 20) p 487.
24 ibid. pp 500–503.

that Western society can approve significant medical procedures, such as genital alternation of inter-sex children, transgender surgery, 'designer' vaginopasty, and subject these procedures to socially acceptable norms, whereas FGM, which belongs to a less-white cultural ethnicity is a social pariah. It is equally true that the main criticism of FGM, from the point of view of the law and morality, is that this procedure is used on children using physical force. Where does the autonomous decision of a mentally competent adult woman to have this procedure belong within this debate and does a blanket ban deny this woman her autonomy?

Question 1 How have English law and the ECtHR dealt with the issue of FGM?

FGM was first outlawed under the Prohibition of Female Circumcision Act 1985. The current Female Genital Mutilation Act 2003 contains a blanket ban of FGM and renders this practice illegal for all, where the reference to 'girls' is taken to specifically include 'women'. According to s 1 (1) 'it is a is a criminal offence to excise, infibulate or otherwise mutilate the whole or any part of a girl's labia majora, labia minora or clitoris'. Section 1 (2) states that 'no offence is committed by an approved person who performs – (a) surgical operation on a girl which is necessary for her physical or mental health, or (b) a surgical operation on a girl who is in any stage of labour, or has just given birth, for purposes connected with the labour or birth. Importantly, s 1 (5) says that '[f]or the purpose of determining whether an operation is necessary for the mental health of a girl it is immaterial whether she or any other person believes that the operation is required as a matter of custom or ritual'.

This Act has been subject to interrogation in the courts. For example, a recent prosecution of a medical doctor under Section 1 of the Female Genital Mutilation Act 2003 conveys a strong message that this practice is erroneous, illegal, and an affront to women.[25] The ECtHR has not dealt with this issue and it has not come before the courts. Coleman outlines an interesting and potentially contentious compromise that was proposed between the need to ensure the cultural Americanisation of immigrant Somali population and the desire to respect their indigenous cultural practices.[26] An American hospital (Harborview Medical Center) suggested that they would perform a 'simple symbolic cut with no tissue removal or subsequent scarring' on a young girl. This action would have been seen to satisfy some members of the immigrant community who wanted FGM for their daughters.[27] This compromise was never put in place due to a successful counter-campaign. The framework proposed here would not have accepted this compromise because even this symbolic cut compromises the bodily integrity of girls

25 See BBC News, 'FMG: UK's first female genital mutilation prosecutions announced' (21 March 2014) available at: http://www.bbc.com/news/uk-26681364 (accessed 27 January 2017).

26 Doriane Lambelet Coleman, 'The Seattle Compromise: Multicultural Sensitivity and Americanization' (1998) 47 *Duke Law Review*, 717–778.

27 ibid.

and causes basic harm. The important part of this compromise, however, is that it raises questions about multi-cultural sensitivity and the fact that 'the tradition cannot be eradicated simply by telling the newer immigrants that it is illegal or contrary to American [or English] culture'.[28] La Barbera also analysed this proposed compromise and conceived this symbolic circumcision as being presented as a transitional measure that had the potential to succeed in a participated abolition of the practice in future generations of migrants. She was disappointed in the outcome '[y]et, an incredible outcry aroused against the misunderstood proposal'.[29]

In summary, a blanket ban exists in relation to the practice of FGM. There is no distinction made on the basis of age or mental competence.

FGM and ritual male circumcision: a case of double standards in English law, a reflection on Re B and G

The important case of *Re B and G*[30] is the first judgment in the UK courts that deals specifically with the issue of FGM. This is noteworthy, given that evidence exists that this practice is prevalent in some communities.[31] This lacuna in prosecuting may derive from a type of 'cultural relativism', where local authorities are reluctant to engage in legal action concerning 'cultural practices'.[32] *Re B and G* concerned two Muslim children, a boy (B) and a girl (G). The proceedings were implemented due to the fact that G was abandoned in the street and the children were put into foster care.[33] The most significant issue in the case was whether G had been subjected to FGM and, if this were the case, how it impacted upon her and her brother's future.[34]

In relation to the alleged FGM, Sir James Munby listened to a number of experts in order to determine whether or not G was subjected to FGM and, if so, what type of FGM was involved. However, the experts were inconsistent in their determinations. This lack of consistency meant that the judge could not categorically determine whether or not G was subjected to FGM. As a consequence, he had no alternative but to hold that she was not so inflicted and that the parents were not guilty of subjecting their child to FGM and contravening the 2003 Act. Notwithstanding the fact that there was no definite evidence that G was subjected to FGM or to the future risk of it,[35] given the significance of the opportunity to address this issue, the judge questioned whether if G were, in fact subjected to

28 ibid. p 745.
29 LaBarbera (n 20) p 486.
30 *Re B and G (No 2)* [2015] EWFC 3.
31 World Health Organisation, 'Female Genital Mutilation' (n 1).
32 See Sandra Danial, 'Cultural Relativism vs. Universalism: Female Genital Mutilation, Pragmatic Remedies' (2013) 2(1) *The Journal of Historical Studies*, 1–10.
33 *Re B and G* (n 30) at [1].
34 ibid. at [4].
35 ibid. at [51] and [52].

FGM, would this result in 'serious harm' under s 31 Children Act 1989. According to s 31:

> A court may only make a care order or supervision order if it is satisfied:
> (a) that the child concerned is suffering, or is likely to suffer, significant harm; and
> (b) that the harm, or likelihood of harm, is attributable to:
>
> (i) the care given to the child, or likely to be given to him if the order were not made, not being what it would be reasonable to expect a parent to give to him; or
> (ii) the child's being beyond parental control.

Serious harm under s 31 involves, therefore, evidence of reasonable harm being inflicted and some determination on the assessment of parenting. Sir James Munby also made reference to the definition of 'mutilation'. According to the *Oxford English Dictionary*, it is defined as 'the action of mutilating a person or animal; the severing or maiming of a limb or bodily organ' and 'mutilate" defined as '[t]o deprive (a person or animal) of the use of a limb or bodily organ, by dismemberment or otherwise; to cut off or destroy (a limb or organ); to wound severely, inflict violent or disfiguring injury on'.[36] The judge held that such mutilation was aligned to 'serious harm' and that FGM is 'totally unacceptable' and 'intolerable'. He referred to Lady Hale in *Re B (Care Proceedings: Appeal)*,[37] who concluded that FGM constitutes 'significant harm'.[38] He explained that any type of FGM cannot be regarded as 'trivial or unimportant, having regard not merely to its purely physical characteristics but also to its associated trauma and potential emotional or psychological consequences'.[39] In relation to the second element of the s 31 test, Sir James Munby said that:

> The fact that it may be a 'cultural' practice does not make FGM reasonable; indeed, the proposition is specifically negatived by section 1(5) of the 2003 Act. And, as I have already pointed out, FGM has no religious justification. So, he submits, it can never be reasonable parenting to inflict *any* form of FGM on a child. I agree.[40]

Thus, he concluded that FGM involves serious harm. He also concluded that a significant difference exists between ritual male circumcision and FGM: 'FGM in any form will suffice to establish "threshold" in accordance with section 31 of the Children Act 1989; male circumcision without more will not'.[41] He was less willing to accept that the ritual male circumcision of B would meet the requirements to s 31.

36 ibid. at [12].
37 *Re B (Care Proceedings: Appeal)* [2013] UKSC 33, [2013] 2 FLR 1075 at [185].
38 *Re B and G* (n 30) at [67].
39 ibid.
40 ibid. at [71].
41 ibid. at [73]

Sir James Munby held that it would 'never be reasonable parenting to inflict any form of FGM' but that ritual male circumcision can be accepted by both society and the law. As such, English law is prepared to accept it as it represents 'reasonable' parenting, unlike FGM. In justifying this position, the judge explained that many circumcisions are undertaken for religious, social, cultural and hygiene reasons.[42] He also made reference to the fact that belief exists that it can reduce the risk of HIV transmission or penile cancer.[43] He referred to the case law on circumcision (*Re J*[44] and *Re S*[45]) and said that '[t]here is nothing in the case-law to suggest that male circumcision is, of itself, such as to justify care proceedings'.[46]

The court, in this instance, set out in some detail the reasons why FGM was considered to constitute 'significant harm'. The judge contrasted this to ritual male circumcision. For the first time in the courts, however, there was a clear indication that male circumcision could represent significant harm, even though Sir James Munby provides subsequent justification for permitting the practice of ritual male circumcision.[47]

To summarise the difference between FGM and circumcision, he said that:

> It is at this point in the analysis, as it seems to me, that the clear distinction between FGM and male circumcision appears. Whereas it can never be reasonable parenting to inflict *any* form of FGM on a child, the position is quite different with male circumcision. Society and the law, including family law, are prepared to tolerate non-therapeutic male circumcision performed for religious or even for purely cultural or conventional reasons, while no longer being willing to tolerate FGM in any of its forms. There are, after all, at least two important distinctions between the two. FGM has no basis in any religion; male circumcision is often performed for religious reasons. FGM has no medical justification and confers no health benefits; male circumcision is seen by some (although opinions are divided) as providing hygienic or prophylactic benefits. Be that as it may, 'reasonable' parenting is treated as permitting male circumcision.[48]

On a number of occasions in the judgment, the judge has negated any connection between FGM and religious practice. As has been determined, a tenuous link does exist that cannot be categorically denied. In addition to this, the judgment involved some trivialisation about B's ritual male circumcision. As has been argued in the previous chapter dealing with ritual male circumcision, the infliction of any basic harm on interest rights (in the case of young babies) is too much harm.

42 ibid. at [61].
43 ibid. at [61].
44 *Re J (Specific Issue Orders: Child's Religious Upbringing and Circumcision)* [1999] 2 FLR 678.
45 *Re S* [2004] EWHC 1282, upheld by the Court of Appeal: [2004] EWCA Civ 1257.
46 *Re B and G* (n 30).
47 ibid.
48 ibid. at [72].

Equally, for someone who lacks legal capacity, the same will apply. The non-findings of the FGM or non-FGM of G cause one to wonder if expert witnesses, local authorities, and even the courts themselves succumb, in some way, to trepidation in the face of cultural/quasi-religious practices that are an embedded part of some community practice. It is worrying that the court, through its expert witnesses, was unable to conclude definitively if FGM had taken place. This points to the future need to ensure that expert witnesses have consistent practices in place that are underpinned by a shared understanding of the various types of FGM.

The fact that the court found that if FGM had been in place, there would be no automatic annulling of parental rights or forced adoption of the affected child raises many questions for society that are beyond the scope of this monograph. Suffice to mention that Article 8 ECHR's protection of the right to respect for family and private life surely does not allow parents to instigate FGM on children in contravention of the children's human rights. If FGM is a cultural practice that has an arguably skewed connection to a manifestation of Islamic belief, then it still cannot be accepted legally or societally just on the basis of respect for cultural practice/family and private life. This is where the PGC would offer a powerful tool in the mediation of such cases because it declares quite categorically and unambiguously that children have rights and, in many instances, such children cannot waive the benefits to their generic rights. It cannot be permissible to inflict them with basic (significant) harm.

Question 2: Why is this approach to FGM under English law sufficient or insufficient in the context of the PGC?

There are two conflicting and paradoxical responses to the question of the sufficiency of current law as it relates to FGM and its compliance to the PGC. The first reading of current law, from the perspective of the PGC, indicates that the blanket ban of FGM, as exists under the 2003 Act, is at variance with the PGC. In theory, the PGC could not support the blanket ban because such a ban does not respect the will-rights of mentally competent women. In the case of the PGC, actions are permissible as long as they do not contravene the rights of others. Disallowing the FGM of girls who are not deemed to be mentally competent under objective measures is sufficient under the PGC. However, the current law does not differentiate between mentally competent and mentally incompetent 'girls'. If mentally competent women willingly consent to FGM, the PGC, when directly applied, would hold that their right to manifest this belief or cultural practice is a vindication of their will-rights and should be allowed.

The second reading of the current law, however, indicates that this insufficiency is not as determinate as in other instances and this derives from the way in which society could potentially use different forms of legislation that might allow FGM. The blanket ban under the Female Genital Mutilation Act 2003 is reflective of significant and merited concern about this practice and will have to be enforced even where specific cultural practices could be shifting towards acceptance of this practice.[49]

49 Kasmira Gander, 'FGM case reported in England every 109 minutes, as WHO says worldwide case rise above 200 million', available at: http://www.independent.co.uk/

FGM involves procedures that veer from being of little harm to those that are catastrophically harmful.[50] These practices occur in society where there are no clean-cut delineations between these levels of proportionate harm, and it would be almost impossible to arbitrate between the nuances of distinction in this practice. It has been argued here that the physical harm inflicted because of this intervention is more injurious than the level of physical intervention itself. In terms of weighting the (dubious?) rights of parents to have their daughters 'circumcised' against the potential harm inflicted upon the girl, the level of harm is so injurious that it overrides any cultural or quasi-religious value associated with the procedure. The type of safeguards that are required in English law in terms of FGM will, of necessity, be reflective of the social mores and arguably democratic principles that provide for or negate the enculturation of particular practices within this society. The cultural values that promote FGM in England are likely to be at variance with the social code of practice. This may be different from the cultural values that apply in other countries. The documented rise of FGM in England is noteworthy and of concern.[51] The Health and Social Care Information Centre have shown, for example, that 2,421 cases of FGM were reported in England between April and September 2015.[52] From a practical point of view and in line with this second form of assessment, notwithstanding the fact that the 2003 Act does not allow for the exercise of will-rights, it still is a good faith attempt to indirectly apply the PGC because distinctions between practices that cause harm could not be drawn in practice.

Cultural pluralism, gender, FGM and the PGC

Gewirth marks out a zone of morally permissible social relations at all levels of social organisations. By specifying what must be done to comply with this moral behaviour, and what must not be done, the PGC, essentially, delineates a set of positive and negative imperatives that provide a guide to moral action.[53] The fact that the PGC and its zone of moral permissibility celebrates what Dobson calls

life-style/health-and-families/health-news/fgm-cases-in-england-reported-every-109-minutes-a6854911.html (*The Independent*) (accessed 27 January 2017).

50 For example, in considering the differences between FGM and ritual male circumcision, FORWARD state that: 'If male circumcision was carried out in the same way as FGM then most of the penis would be cut off. The most important difference between male circumcision and FGM is the reasons behind the practices… while FGM is practiced to control women's sexual behaviour: to make sure that they remain virgins before marriage and faithful during marriage'. See Foundation for Women's Health, Research and Development (FORWARD), *Female Genital Mutilation: Frequently Asked Questions: A Campaigner's Guide for Young People*, (2012) available at: https://www.gov.uk/government/uploads/system/uploads/attachment_data/file/332732/FGMfaqFORWARD.pdf (accessed 27 January 2017).

51 ibid.

52 ibid.

53 See Lynn Dobson, *Supranational Citizenship*, (Manchester University Press, 2006) p 144.

'freedom of and in action' leading to an acceptance of richness, diversity and pluralism within society.[54] This society is marked by a large diversity of cultures that can be segregated in terms of race, class, gender, ethnicity, religion, ideology, and other partly interpenetrating variables. Gewirth argues that '[c] ulture signifies a way of life as it is understood, symbolized and evaluated by the group that lives it'[55] and this culture comprises of 'a set of group practices and of related beliefs and it includes both mores and positive moralities'.[56] According to him:

> ...the PGC requires emphatic recognition that individuals as members of various suppressed groups have equal rights to freedom and well-being. These rights include acceptance, toleration, and support for diverse cultures so long as these do not transgress the PGC's requirements.[57]

The PGC, thus, encourages and upholds the diverse practices of cultural pluralism, the 'differences between human beings with regard to values and ways of life',[58] and this would, of course, include acceptance of religious pluralism, but the crucial aspect of this acceptance is that the values within this cultural pluralism must accord with those of the PGC.

Thus, while the PGC encourages discursive autonomy and freedom in purposiveness and promotes the negotiation of different discourses of values, such discourse still needs to be framed within a context where the values of the PGC, values that promote autonomy and do not allow for derogation on the basis of gender or race, are in force. The PGC sets the outer limits of the legitimacy of the various practices of cultural pluralism. It imposes boundaries upon purposiveness and one of those boundaries comes into play when the proposed action contravenes what is required by the PGC. While the moral relationships that agents construct can subsist alongside other relationships, based upon other values, it is the PGC that determines the zone of moral permissibility. The practice of FGM would not be perceived as valid within this zone for the previously articulated harm-related reasons.

While the PGC promotes freedom and well-being and the discourse of autonomy, aligned to that, the search for this freedom must be situated with a framework of moral and ethical meaning through which agents can express their own individual identity in a manner that does not assign a lower moral status to those of a different gender. FGM and gender are irrevocably interlinked, and international research points to the fact that this practice is related to assigning a lower

54 ibid.

55 Alan Gewirth, 'Is Cultural Pluralism Relevant to Moral Knowledge?' in Christopher W Gowans (ed), *Moral Disagreements Classic and Contemporary Readings* (Routledge, 2000) p 181. Originally published as Alan Gewirth, 'Is Cultural Pluralism Relevant to Moral Knowledge?' (1994) 11 *Social Philosophy and Policy*, 22–42.

56 ibid. p 184.

57 Alan Gewirth, *Self-Fulfillment* (Princeton University Press, 1998) p 156.

58 Dobson (n 53) p 190.

status to women.[59] This contravenes the PGC where all apparent agents are afforded the same status. This means that, in theory, the PGC cannot accept FGM because significant evidence exists that it does not afford equality of status to women and, so, is not compliant with the PGC. Thus, the practice of FGM is constrained by the limits and boundaries that the PGC imposes upon action that is not compliant with the idea that value is given to all apparent agents.

While Gewirth does not actually write about FGM himself, he gives a definitive answer as to whether practices that are perceived to have a foundation in religious belief, but may, in fact, derive from non-religious sources of cultural practices, are compliant with the PGC.[60] He assesses the compliance with the PGC of the Hindu religious practice of sutee, whereby the widow throws herself onto the burning pyre of her dead husband, as follows:

> Even if one gives the most benign interpretation of the widow's willingness to commit suicide with this justification, there remains the question of whether her conduct is free or voluntary in the sense that she not only controls her behavior by her unforced choice but has knowledge of relevant circumstances, and is to this extent rational. If one views the religious belief in question as having been instilled through a long process of enculturation provided for their critical (including empirical) assessment, the sutee and similar practices are egregious violations of the rights to freedom and well-being.[61]

This same argument can apply to FGM. This (seeming) religious belief has been instilled through what is acknowledged as being a process of, perhaps enforced, enculturation. Therefore, in the same way as the sutee was found to be a violation of the generic rights, then FGM is also an 'egregious violation of the rights to freedom and well-being'.

Why is it permissible for the PGC to differentiate between FGM in English law and female genital cosmetic surgery?

A line is drawn in practice between FGM, which is illegal/illegitimate and cosmetic genital surgery, which is legal/legitimate. The latter practice involves anatomical change, where surgical modification's main purpose is twofold: to improve appearance and, in some cases, to improve sexual function. The growth in practice has derived from greater awareness of the availability of such procedures and, perhaps, increased search for some form of perfect self-image where the genitalia correspond to perceptions of normality. There is some disagreement, however, among some academics as to whether this latter type of

59 See, for example, World Health Organisation, 'Female Genital Mutilation' (n 1) and World Health Organisation, 'Female Genital Mutilation – Programmes to Date: What Works and What Doesn't – A Review' (World Health Organisation, 1999).

60 Gewirth, 'Is Cultural Pluralism Relevant to Moral Knowledge?' (n 55) p 188.

61 ibid.

surgery should also be banned. Sheldon and Wilkinson, for example, wonder, if FGM is banned, why such procedures, which involve parallel but not wholly different physical modifications, would not also be banned.[62] Kelly and Foster also outline, using fictional cases, the arguments for and against banning such cosmetic surgery. They conclude that 'there are no medical or ethical objections to FGP [female genital piercing] that are remotely comparable with the objections to FGM or FGCS [female genital cosmetic surgery], and it should not be regulated by criminal law'.[63] What is the stance of the PGC in this regard? A Gewirthian society would not ban cosmetic genital surgery because such procedures are requested by women, in line with their generic rights. In non-Gewirthian England, these procedures would continue to be lawful because mentally competent apparent agents can exercise their will-rights and act with voluntariness and purpose. There is little evidence that such procedures derive from undue influence or societal pressures that would give rise to lack of voluntariness or consent. This is the crucial difference between this procedure and FGM, where, in the case of the latter, there is much evidence to suggest that consent is often not freely given and cultural influences are such that they represent undue influence with significant physical, irreversible consequences.[64]

It is, therefore, argued that significant practical societal problems that might adversely impact upon young girls would exist if any change were made to the Act. Therefore, the Act, as it stands, is likely to be sufficient as an indirect application of the PGC.

If these arguments are applied to the recent *Re B and G* case, it is clear that Sir James Munby was correct to state that FGM is impermissible in English law (even though it was found that the girl was not actually subjected to the practice). In this non-Gewirthian society, G could never be subjected to FGM. Even if G were much older and mentally competent to make the decision, under an indirect application of the PGC (i.e. the 2003 Act), the procedure would still be illegal.

Question 3: Is there an alternative approach that will provide greater compliance with the framework?

The PGC is opposed to gender discrimination and gendered expectations because it involves denial of equal generic rights to those who share the same moral status. Dobson points to the way in which agents can come from diverse, but intersecting cultural and ethical contexts. One of these contexts is that of gender, but a Gewirthian viewpoint would not allow for any type of derogation on the basis of

62 Sally Sheldon and Stephen Wilkinson, 'Female genital mutilation and cosmetic surgery: regulating non-therapeutic body modification' (1998) 12 (4) *Bioethics*, 263–285.

63 Brenda Kelly and Charles Foster, 'Should female genetic cosmetic surgery and genital piercings be regarded ethically and legally as female genital mutilation?' (2012) 119 *British Journal of Obstetrics and Gynaecology*, 389–392.

64 See Carla Makhlouf Obermeyer, 'The Consequences of Female Circumcision for Health and Sexuality: An Update on the Evidence' (2005) 7(5), *Culture, Health & Sexuality*, 443–461.

gender.[65] Such an action would not be in keeping with the PGC's commitment to assigning equality for those with similar moral status.

While it could be argued that the current legal position outlawing FGM is a contravention of the PGC, given societal and cultural factors as well as the potential of this practice to induce great harm, the current legal position is a good faith attempt at applying the PGC in non-Gewirthian society and should not be changed.

Position of FGM in Gewirthia

The working of the legal and social system in Gewirthia is predicated upon acceptance that all agents have generic rights. In many ways, they can do as they will, and social and legal structures must support this will as long as they are mentally competent do so and do not interfere with the generic rights of others. Gewirthian society is not constrained by the practical limitations that exist in English society whereby the social order may inhibit the exercise of will-rights due to other existing factors.[66] In Gewirthia, mentally competent women can exercise their will-rights to undergo FGM as long as doing so does not interfere with the rights of others. They can waive the benefit of their right to bodily integrity and, thus, FGM will not be deemed to be illegal. The legality of its practice will simply be mental competence/legal capacity focused. This would still mean, for example, in *Re B and G* (if shown that FGM had actually occurred), G's rights would have been breached, given her lack of legal capacity to consent to the procedure.

Position of FGM in non-Gewirthia

When comparing Gewirthia and future English law that acts as an indirect application of the PGC, a number of commonalities and contrasting variables exist. The community in Gewirthia consists of a society focused on mutual respect for the values and rights of each other, with procedural processes in operation whose justification is based upon their adherence to PGC values. With that acceptance in place and the related procedural applications towards resolution of conflict in operation, legislation in Gewirthia is based upon PGC principles and respect for the rights of all agents. Gerwirthia outlaws FGM of young girls on the basis that this infringes their generic rights. However, if the girl/woman has legal capacity to make the decision, it would not be unlawful for her to undergo the procedure.

The difference between English law and Gewirthia is the fact that English law must always be situated within a societal landscape and, in some way, be reflective of the multiplicity of cultures, ethnicities, warring factions, and religions of that society. Gewirthia is highly unlikely to be a monocultural society because, while acceptance of the PGC would be universal, it would celebrate diversity in its expression of morally optional cultural values and structures. The greater the range of such diversity, the greater protection given to the exercise of rights to the

65 Dobson (n 53) p 145.

66 See Deryck Beyleveld and Roger Brownsword, 'Principle, Proceduralism, and Precaution in a Community of Rights' (2006) 19(2) *Ratio Juris*, 141–168.

generic conditions. The loss of a culture is at least an additive harm to those who want to expand their understanding and cultural experience, and the removal of cultural options will often involve nonsubtractive and even basic harm. Cultures and religions only pose problems when they constrain choices and the right of all to an open future with maximal exercise of their generic rights. The internalisation of the PGC as the supreme norm could have societal implications in the context of the PGC. For this reason, English law will not be able to change the 2003 Act because of the grave potential for misuse and consequent basic harm.

Let us consider the issue of consent from the point of view of FGM. A woman of 26 requests an FGM procedure. This is currently illegal. She consents to this, but is this consent voluntary or does it derive from pressure that can be quantified as undue influence? To formulate an answer to this problem necessitates looking at the social context, including the religious context, from which such voluntariness of action might derive. Arising from social concerns, in non-Gewirthia (English law) no apparent consent is valid if it can be shown that the woman has acquiesced the FGM procedure as a consequence of any form of coercion imposed by those who require this procedure of her. The WHO is concerned that most of the women who have had an FGM procedure live within lesser educated families and in particular ethnic communities.[67] According to the United Nations Population Fund (UNPF), the most significant factor in the prevalence of FGM is ethnicity:

> Members of certain ethnic groups often adhere to the same social norms, including whether or not to practice FGM, regardless of where they live. The FGM prevalence among ethnic Somalis living in Kenya, for example, at 98 per cent, is the same as in Somalia, and far higher than the Kenyan national average of 27 per cent.[68]

U v The Centre for Reproductive Medicine[69] demonstrates that undue influence, exerted by a medical advisor in relation to the removal of consent to posthumous storage and use of sperm, is quite difficult to establish as long as the patient is intelligent, in good health, and educated. In the case of FGM and the often economically educationally-impoverished context in which it is promoted, undue influence might be more easily proven in the courts. In such cases, it is possible that the courts would rule that the actions of the woman in consenting are not voluntary and this lack of voluntariness would render such consent invalid.

The current law imposes a blanket ban on FGM. It is clear, following public debate on the issues, that consensus exists that FGM should not be permitted. In deciding upon the 2003 Act, Parliament clearly followed the deliberative and democratic process in order to come to this decision. A number of approaches

67 World Health Organisation, 'Female Genital Mutilation' (n 1) p 4.

68 United Nations Population Fund, 'Female genital mutilation (FGM) frequently asked questions' (2015) available at: http://www.unfpa.org/resources/female-genital-mutilation-fgm-frequently-asked-questions#women_affected (accessed 27 January 2017).

69 *U v The Centre for Reproductive Medicine* [2002] EWCA Civ 565.

could now be adopted which would represent indirect applications of the PGC. The first and, perhaps, most obvious approach would suggest that this blanket ban should be cast aside and FGM be prohibited until women have legal capacity. This proposal might be legitimate if we lived in Gewirthia and all adhered to the principles and practices of the PGC. However, we do not live in Gewirthia and allowing for the FGM of mentally competent girls/women would not ultimately be feasible in the context of other compelling societal factors, such as evidence of significant undue influence, evidence as victims working as perpetrators, evidence of injurious harm that is tantamount to torture and falls within the remit of Article 3 ECHR.

It is important to bear in mind that culture is not fixed and is always shifting and adapting. However, it is important when implementing laws that cultural sensitivities are addressed. The Foundation for Women's Health, Research and Development's report of FGM also address the issue of girls/women consenting to FGM by relating such consent to cultural issues:

> As cultural and societal pressures to practice FGM are so strong, it is difficult to judge whether a woman is truly giving consent. There is almost always the question of whether she is undergoing FGM because she wants to, or because she feels like she has to. This leads to the question: is it possible to separate the two? Similarly, because FGM is a taboo subject that is not openly discussed; it is difficult to ensure that a girl or a woman knows all the facts and has all the information about FGM before giving her permission to undergo the procedure.[70]

Even though cultural arguments might exist to support FGM, the basic harm caused to the child is indisputable.

A second option would be to redefine 'girl' within the current Act and to make the procedure in some way age-specific. However, this book has emphasised the need for the law to be mental competence-based, rather than age-based, as age is not a determinant of mental competence or legal capacity. Option three is to continue the blanket ban. It is admitted that such an option does not fully address the right of mental competent women to have access to medical procedures, in line with their will-rights, and so might be perceived to contravene the PGC. Nevertheless, the practical difficulties of disallowing the blanket ban are significant and the societal factors are too strong to recommend that this ban be lifted. For many of the women who are subjected to FGM, their lives are far from Gewirthia and their decisions are often controlled by others. To remove the blanket ban without evidence of freely made decisions, lack of coercion, lack of undue influence is too fraught with the potential for misuse to be advocated. Therefore, the continuance of the blanket ban is justified and the PGC can support this justification as it is a good faith attempt at applying the PGC: this is the best attempt that can be made to ensure that vulnerable girls/women do not suffer basic harm.

70 Foundation for Women's Health, Research and Development (FORWARD) (n 50).

To return to the 26-year-old consenting woman who requests an FGM procedure. The inherent dangers associated with permitting FGM on a case by case basis or on a legal capacity-focused basis mean that granting this permission would not serve as a 'proper' indirect application of the PGC. Given the nature of FGM, it is more appropriate for the law to act with caution and to adopt their current stance.

The current legal approach is, therefore, deemed appropriate and, as such, no further action is required. It is accepted, however, that this position might be viewed as refusing to understand the cultural practices, in particular, of significant numbers of immigrant populations. There is also a need for society at large to engage at a deeper level with the cultural forces and traditional values (quasi-religious or otherwise) that underpin this practice.

Conclusion

This chapter, ultimately, argues that the retention of the existing absolute ban on FGM in the Female Genital Mutilation Act 2003 be retained because the level of (basic) harm in FGM is so injurious that it overrides any cultural or quasi-religious value (additive harm) associated with the procedure. Thus, FGM is an illegitimate procedure that is correctly prohibited under English law and the subjection of girls to FGM is at variance with the PGC. A clear difference exists between the permissibility of FGM in Gewirthia and in England. The fact that the potential for harm is so grave and the social and cultural issues associated with FGM so suppressive, the current outright ban is the most appropriate way of indirectly applying the PGC in English law. Principled pragmatism recognises the fact that we don't live in Gewirthia. The principled approach would be to permit women who have legal capacity to be subjected to FGM, but pragmatically, it is necessary for the law to remain as is.

It is worrying that there have not been more cases in the courts to date dealing with FGM. Society, in general should reject the cultural relativism that has prevented prosecutors taking cases of FGM to the courts. FGM concerns broader issues of objectification and suppression of women in society that have, in the opinion of this author, no place in England. The level of invasion from the least invasive to the most invasive FGM procedure is linked to the demeaning of personhood. Ultimately, the barbaric practice of FGM should not be shrouded in some sort of religious belief that has little textual foundation: religion or cultural justification should not be used as an excuse for a practice that is not and should never be lawful.

References

Asmani, Ibrahim Lethome, and Abdi, Maryam Sheikh, *Delinking Female Genital Mutilation/Cutting from Islam* (United States Agency for International Development, 2008) available at: https://www.unfpa.org/sites/default/files/pub-pdf/De-linking%20FGM%20from%20Islam%20final%20report.pdf (accessed 27 January 2017).

BBC News, 'FMG: UK's first female genital mutilation prosecutions announced' (21 March 2014) available at: http://www.bbc.com/news/uk-26681364 (accessed 27 January 2017).

Beyleveld, Deryck and Brownsword, Roger, 'Principle, Proceduralism, and Precaution in a Community of Rights (2006) 19(2) *Ratio Juris*, 141–168.

Coleman, Doriane Lambelet, 'The Seattle Compromise: Multicultural Sensitivity and Americanization' (1998) 47 *Duke Law Review*, 717–778.

Danial, Sandra,'Cultural Relativism vs. Universalism: Female Genital Mutilation, Pragmatic Remedies' (2013) 2(1) *The Journal of Historical Studies*, 1–10.

Dobson, Lynn, *Supranational Citizenship* (Manchester University Press, 2006).

Foundation for Women's Health, Research and Development (FORWARD), 'Female Genital Mutilation: Frequently Asked Questions: A Campaigner's Guide for Young People' (2012) available at: https://www.gov.uk/government/uploads/system/uploads/attachment_data/file/332732/FGMfaqFORWARD.pdf (accessed 27 January 2017).

Gander, Kasmira, 'FGM case reported in England every 109 minutes, as WHO says worldwide case rise above 200 million' available at: http://www.independent.co.uk/life-style/health-and-families/health-news/fgm-cases-in-england-reported-every-109-minutes-a6854911.html (*The Independent*) (accessed 27 January 2017).

Gewirth, Alan, *Self-Fulfillment* (Princeton University Press, 1998).

Gewirth, Alan, 'Is Cultural Pluralism Relevant to Moral Knowledge?' in Christopher W Gowans (ed), *Moral Disagreements Classic and Contemporary Readings* (Routledge, 2000) Originally published as Alan Gewirth, 'Is Cultural Pluralism Relevant to Moral Knowledge?' (1994) 11 *Social Philosophy and Policy*, 22–42.

Human Rights Watch, 'Q and A on Female Genital Mutilation' (16 June 2010) available at: http://www.hrw.org/news/2010/06/10/qa-female-genital-mutilation (accessed 27 January 2017).

Kelly, Brenda and Foster, Charles, 'Should female genetic cosmetic surgery and genital piercings be regarded ethically and legally as female genital mutilation?' (2012) 119 *British Journal of Obstetrics and Gynaecology*, 389–392.

Kentatta, Jomo, *Facing Mount Kenya. The Traditional Life of the Giyuku* (Secker and Warburg, 1938).

LaBarbera, Maria Caterina, 'Revisiting the anti-Female Genital Mutilation Discourse' (2009) 9 *Diritto & Questioni Pubbliche*, 485–507 available at: http://www.dirittoequestionipubbliche.org/page/2009_n9/05_studi-03_MC_LaBarbera.pdf (accessed 27 January, 2017).

Mackie, Gerry and LeJeune, John, "Social Dynamics of Abandonment of Harmful Practices: 'A New Look at the Theory"' (2008), Innocenti Working Paper, UNICEF Innocenti Research Centre). Available at: http://pages.ucsd.edu/~gmackie/documents/UNICEF.pdf (accessed 27 January 2017).

Macfarlane, BA et al, *Female Genital Mutilation in England and Wales: Updated statistical estimates of the numbers of affected women living in England and Wales and girls at risk Interim report on provisional estimates* (City University London, 2014) available at: http://www.city.ac.uk/__data/assets/pdf_file/0020/266033/FGM-statistics-report-21.07.14-no-embargo.pdf (accessed 27 January 2017).

Obermeyer, Carla Makhlouf, 'The Consequences of Female Circumcision for Health and Sexuality: An Update on the Evidence' (2005) 7(5) *Culture, Health & Sexuality*, 443–461.

Pflanz, Mike, 'Religious leaders join the fight to end female circumcision in Somalia', (Unicef Somalia, 2011) available at: https://www.unicef.org/somalia/reallives_10195.html (accessed 3 June 2018).

Rymer, Janice and Momoh, Comfort, 'Managing the Reality of FGM in the UK' in Comfort Momoh (ed), *Female Genital Mutilation* (Radcliffe Publishing, 2005).

Sheldon, Sally and Wilkinson, Stephen, 'Female genital mutilation and cosmetic surgery: regulating non-therapeutic body modification' (1998) 12 (4) *Bioethics* 263–285.

Toubia, Nahid, 'Female Genital Mutilation' in Julie Peters and Andrea Wolper, *Women's Rights, Human Rights: International Female Perspectives* (Routledge, 1995).

United Nations Population Fund, 'Female genital mutilation (FGM) frequently asked questions' (2015) available at: http://www.unfpa.org/resources/female-genital-mutilation-fgm-frequently-asked-questions#women_affected (accessed 27 January 2017).

World Health Organisation, 'Female Genital Mutilation' available at: http://www.who.int/mediacentre/factsheets/fs241/en/ (accessed 27 January 2017).

World Health Organisation, 'Female Genital Mutilation – Programmes to Date: What Works and What Doesn't – A Review' (World Health Organisation, 1999).

8 Is appropriate protection given under English law to conscientious objection to abortion?

Introduction

This book, in general, explores whether or not the Abrahamic religious beliefs of patients and healthcare professionals are given appropriate protection in English medical law. So far, a focus has been placed on patients and the conflict that exists between their religious beliefs and medical procedures that involve them and/or their family members. This chapter looks beyond that familial domain and focuses on healthcare professionals who refuse to carry out particular procedures due to their own deeply held religious beliefs. This chapter focuses on the conscientious objection provision in the Abortion Act 1967, because it is the principal example of legislative protection given to healthcare professionals to act in accordance with religious belief on an issue of recognised sensitivity.

Differing interpretations of conscience and conscientious objection are explored within the context of a human rights regime. It is contended that the right to conscientiously object to abortion on the grounds of religious belief is underpinned by Article 9 of the European Convention on Human Rights (ECHR) and this chapter recommends that legal deliberations, actions, and judgments made in respect of conscientious objection should take additional account of a human rights framework, which represents an indirect application of the PGC. This chapter considers, in particular, the recent decision of the Supreme Court (SC) in *Greater Glasgow Health Board v Doogan and Others* (*Doogan*).[1]

The question of conscientious objection does not operate independently of context and that context is created from the particular setting, the particular protagonists, the particular societal and religious influences, and the particular urgency caused by acting in accordance with conscience or, alternatively, disallowing this action because no alternatives exist.

In order to assess the appropriateness of English law/the position under European human rights jurisprudence, the three methodological questions articulated in chapter 2 are asked in this specific context. The Abortion Act's conscientious objection provision is defended as one that can be supported as an indirect application of the PGC.

1 *Glasgow Health Board v Doogan and Others* [2014] UKSC 68.

This chapter provides a Gewirthian evaluation of conscientious objection by reference to the Abortion Act's particular provision. Part of that evaluation includes a Gewirthian steer on the types of religious belief that are suitable candidates for the right to conscientiously object. It is argued that the right to conscientiously object should be restricted to abortion/end-of-life scenarios.

However, it is also argued that the failure to sufficiently address the human rights aspect in *Doogan* constitutes basic harm and consequently violates the PGC. As such, a new approach to the manner in which Strasbourg and domestic courts deal with conscientious objection is proposed. This would require procedures to be PGC-compliant and give greater consideration to both the concept of conscience and its human rights implications.

Conscience: a multi-hued tapestry

Conscientious objection in medicine is quite self-explanatory. It involves a medical practitioner abstaining from a particular procedure as a result of his or her beliefs. Conscientious objection has its roots in religion and, in particular, Christianity as well as in the notion of pacifism. This form of objection originated in the refusal by military personnel to kill combatants due to a soldier's moral or religious objections. This objection has spread into the medical arena, in the context of controversial medical procedures.

Diverse interpretations of conscience have existed and continue to exist throughout history. Although no uniformity of perspective exists, a number of similar factors appear in differing conceptions of conscience. These include conscience being about some form of self-knowing and involving self-assessment.[2] Conscience can be perceived to involve a regulation of moral action and can be a motivating force in actions that are committed. Interestingly, as well as being perceived as a form of inner-dialogue, conscience can also be defined in terms of acting in accordance with a sense of duty.[3] In other words, we are duty bound to act in accordance with our conscience.

Morton and Kirkwood identify three different elements of conscience: existence, actions, and effects of conscience.[4] There are some academics who argue that conscience as a separate entity does not exist.[5] However, the majority of commentators presume its existence. Emerson and Daar describe it as 'motivation, inner voice, or intuition that tells us that something is right or wrong; ... the locus of moral knowledge ... human virtue'.[6] In relation to the issue of action, or what

2 For example, see Adam Smith, *The Theory of Moral Sentiments* (Gutenberg Publishers, 2011 (originally published in 1759)).

3 Immanuel Kant, *The Metaphysics of Morals* (CUP, 1991 (originally published in 1797)) p 161.

4 Natasha T Morton and Kenneth W Kirkwood, 'Conscience and Contentious Objection of Health Care Professionals refocusing the Issue' (2009) 21(4) *HEC Forum*, 351–364, p 353.

5 Claudia I Emerson and Abdallah S Daar, 'Defining conscience and acting conscientiously' (2007) 7(12) *The American Journal of Bioethics*, 19–21, p 20.

6 ibid.

conscience does, Morton and Kirkwood contend that 'conscience has an informing or alerting function for the individual when a potential conflict of values occurs'.[7]

Butler and Kant adopt what Brownlee calls a 'monistic' conception of conscience.[8] Wood argues that, for Kant, conscience can be looked upon as a 'motivation theory set in the context of a reflection theory'.[9] For Kant, 'every human being, as a moral being, has a conscience within him originally'.[10] For those who are not religious adherents, conscience is seen primarily as something which evolves from, but is not confined to, the influences of societal upbringing.[11] Butler postulates that conscience comes from a form of reflective reason that dominates all emotions and that directs human nature to strive to work towards virtue. Conscience, in this case, is about self-directed action in terms of self-judgment and in terms of determining the source of moral knowledge.[12] A subjectivist view of conscience, as espoused by Broad, offers an alternative approach. He sees conscience as having three dispositions, namely, cognitive, emotional, and conative.[13] Related to this view is that of Rawls who ascribes a number of rights to all citizens that are given to all citizens equally.[14] Such rights include liberty of conscience. These rights are given priority under a political conception of justice and citizens are given the means to make effective use of their freedoms. Conscience, under this important view of political society, is seen as a basic liberty and this gives, consequently, added gravitas to the idea of conscientious objection as an important right in particular contexts. Rawls accepts that liberty of conscience exists primarily to ensure that our moral and religious freedoms are protected against the moral and religious beliefs of the majority. Rawls also proposes that the law cannot consistently uphold the dictates of conscience in all cases.[15]

This subjectivist approach allows for the exercise of autonomy as a facet of conscience.[16] Somewhat distinct to that viewpoint is the cultural relativist idea of conscience, as espoused by, for example, Hill, who perceives of conscience as being merely the manifestation of whatever is the social or cultural norm that has been internalised to suit the cultural context.[17] Brownlee, in contrast, positions

7 Morton and Kirkwood (n 4) p 353.

8 Kimberley Brownlee, *Conscience and Conviction: The Case for Civil Disobedience* (OUP, 2012). For a fuller account of my reflections on Brownlee's ideas on conscience see Clayton Ó Néill, 'Review: Kimberley Brownlee, *Conscience and Conviction: The Case for Civil Disobedience*' (2015) 23(2), *Medical Law Review*, 315–319.

9 Allen Wood, *Kantian Ethics* (CUP, 2008) p 183.

10 Kant (n 3) p 160.

11 See Sigmund Freud, *Civilization and its Discontents*, Joan Riviere (trans) (Hogarth Press, 1930).

12 Joseph Butler, *Fifteen Sermons Preached at the Rolls Chapel and a Dissertation upon the Nature of Virtue* (Hackett, 1983).

13 C D Broad, 'Conscience and Conscientious Action' in John Donnelly and Leonard Lyons, *Conscience* (Alba House, 1973).

14 ibid.

15 John Rawls, *A Theory of Justice*, (HUP, 1971) 205–308, p 307.

16 ibid.

17 Thomas Hill, *Human Welfare and Moral Worth, Kantian Perspectives* (OUP, 2002) p 280.

conscience within a form of moral pluralism. She discusses how the common understanding of the term 'conscience' is problematic.[18] Its use includes the descriptive, such as in the ECHR where conscience is taken to refer to 'our freedom of thought, conscience, and religion'. Brownlee would, however, prefer to regard conscience as freedom of thought, conviction, and religion. She rejects a theistic conception of conscience as being the voice of God, and also the subjectivist idea of conscience as a type of personal inclination.[19] She advocates a non-theistic, objective conception of conscience, positioned within a pluralistic moral framework. She sets out a view of conscience as a moral property of genuine, self-conscious, moral responsibilities that make human beings more acutely aware of the moral qualities of conduct.[20]

Of most relevance to this monograph, however, are the arguments that centre upon how religious belief contributes to conscience formation and action in respect of conscience. Religious perspectives on conscience are multi-hued. According to Islam, conscience is the process whereby good and bad are decided upon. For Muslims, conscience is divided into two forms: pure and impure.[21] Jewish tradition sees conscience as being linked to autonomy and the moral independence of the individual. Jews conceive of conscience as being the human ability to make moral decisions. For Jews, autonomy and conscience are intrinsically linked.[22] The Hebrew term for conscience, *matzpun*, has only come into use since the post-Enlightenment period, indicating that conscience is not a traditional Jewish concept: conscience is not determined in the Torah. Christians do not have one perspective on conscience. Protestants vary in perspective, from those who see conscience as an inner voice, as something that tells one to do one's duty to those fundamentalist Christians whose sole source of conscience is the Bible and rigid interpretation of same. Other Christians have used Joseph Fletcher's concepts of situational ethics, which relate conscience to the four principles of pragmatism, positivism, relativism and personalism.[23] According to this perspective, decisions are made in particular situations, not in a prescriptive, one-size-fits-all manner, and conscience is linked to the response to the individual situation. There is a conflict within Catholicism between the need to be true to one's conscience, to follow one's conscience (Thomas Acquinas: '[e]ven an erring conscience binds'[24]) and the need to follow Church teachings. Cardinal Newman controversially showed

18 Brownlee (n 8).

19 ibid. p 52.

20 ibid.

21 Masqood Jafri, 'Islamic Concept of Conscience' available at: http://www.irfi.org/articles/articles_151_200/islamic_concept_of_conscience.htm (accessed 27 January 2017).

22 Fred Morgan, 'Conscience: a Jewish Perspective' available at: http://www.jcrelations.net/Conscience%3A+A+Jewish+Perspective.3107.0.html?L=3 (accessed 27 January 2017).

23 Joseph Fletcher, *Situational Ethics The New Morality* (Westminster John Know Press, 1966).

24 See Brian Davies, *Thomas Aquinas's Summa Theologica: A Guide and Commentary* (OUP, 2014) p 166.

how he gave precedence to conscience over Papal dictates in his remark: 'I shall drink—to the Pope, if you please,—still, to Conscience first, and to the Pope afterwards.'[25]

If conscientious objection is to have full validity, it must be based upon conscience, but not conscience that is an ill-considered stagnant state of judgement, but conscience that is both formed and informed. The Catechism of the Catholic Church points to the fact that conscience is not this static entity: '[c]onscience is not a funny little human capacity which tells us what to do, or not to do, into which we plug for an answer'.[26] It is something that comes about as a consequence of a formative process and it is constantly under query in sacraments such as confession where, prior to confessing, the penitent is asked to examine his or her conscience. There is an acceptance within Catholicism that conscience is somehow a moveable feast which involves the constant formation of an informed judgement: '[t]here has to be the certain judgment which implies an informed conscience'.[27] As well as the idea of the informed conscience, Catholic teaching connects conscience to reason and quite concretely states that '[c]onscience is a judgment of reason by which the human person recognises the moral quality of a concrete act'[28] and '[a] well-formed conscience is upright and truthful. It formulates its judgments according to reason, in conformity with the true good willed by the wisdom of the Creator. Everyone must avail himself of the means to form his conscience'.[29] There are many perceptions of Catholicism that could perceive it as dogmatic and intransigent in its moral stances, but this official Catechism points to a more open and questioning approach to conscience than is often understood. It can be assumed from that understanding of conscience that it is necessary for a person who conscientiously objects to have consciously examined, scrutinised, and interrogated that to which he or she is objecting.

The exercise of conscience is an integral part of the process of conscientiously objecting within the context of medicine and medical law contexts. Its use is constrained to legislation and medical guidelines. It is to that area that attention is now drawn. The dilemmas posed to doctors by the conflict posed by their right to conscientiously object, that is established under Article 9 ECHR, section 4 of the Abortion Act 1967, the medical guidelines, primarily by virtue of their Christian faith, and their need to provide for their patients were brought to light in an illuminating research carried out in Norway.[30] A limited number of GPs were

25 See Brian Patrick Green, 'Catholicism and Conscience' available at: https://www.scu.edu/ethics/focus-areas/more/religion-and-ethics/resources/catholicism-and-conscience/ (accessed 27 January 2017).

26 *Catechism of the Catholic Church*, available at: http://www.vatican.va/archive/ENG0015/_INDEX.HTM (accessed 27 January 2017), para 1795.

27 ibid. para 1800.

28 ibid. para 1796.

29 ibid. para 1798.

30 Eva Nordberg, Helg Skirbekk and Morten Magelssen, 'Conscientious objection to referrals for abortion: pragmatic solution or threat to women's rights?' (2014) 15(1) *BMC Med Ethics*, 15.

interviewed to gauge the reasons for their conscientious objection. Amongst the reasons given were the desire not to contribute to taking a life, being true to oneself, and the inability to be neutral. The research uncovered a diversity of practical, and arguably morally inconsistent, arrangements amongst GPs who conscientiously object. This diversity arose from lack of a developed legal regulation and, in the case of Protestant and non-Catholic churches, lack of guidance in bioethical situations. For the GPs who were Catholics, the clarity of their Church's objections was 'crucial in guiding and shaping the line of action chosen'.[31] For the doctors interviewed, the ability to conscientiously object and refer the patient onwards gave 'a pragmatic solution to a moral dilemma'. The researchers identified a gap in existing research: the patients' views were missing. Further research might seek to determine how patients seeking referral for abortion experience GPs' conscientious objection.[32]

It is not the role of this book to argue for or against any conception of conscience at this juncture. Suffice to say that any legal deliberation on conscientious objection must go to the root of what aspect of conscience is being threatened and interrogate to what degree any threat to conscience represents a threat to some integral part of human self. The overall context in which conscientious objection is realised is important. The more liberal ('pro-choice') the legal regime governing abortion in a particular state, the greater need for (or at least emphasis on by affected practitioners) rights of conscientious objection.[33] All medical treatment takes place within the broader context of professional ethics. Consideration of the ethics of medical treatment, as underpinned in part by the evolving Hippocratic oath, is part of any assessment of the validity of conscientious objection because the root of this objection constitutes an ethical stance, often based on religious belief. The original version of this oath has been replaced and amended and many versions of it now exist.[34] Some medical schools use the Declaration of Geneva version which has no explicit prohibition of either euthanasia or abortion but, rather, commits doctors to 'maintain the upmost respect for human life from its beginning, even under threat, and I [doctors] will not use my [their] specialist knowledge contrary to the laws of humanity'.[35] The

31 ibid. p 7.

32 Another layer of complexity to the conscientious objection question is what Sepper calls the 'symmetry argument'. Sepper argues that if, on one hand, a right to *object* to abortion based on conscience exists, then, on the other hand, a parallel and symmetrical right should exist in terms of the right to *provide* abortion in line with conscience. However, Greasley has difficulties with this symmetry argument: she says that 'being compelled to act is a more morally grave affair' than being compelled to abstain from action. See Kate Greasley, *Arguments about Abortion*, (OUP, 2017) p 261. This is yet another example of how the weighting of one right against another is a complex affair.

33 For example, the approach in England, Scotland, and Wales represents a much more liberal approach than that of Northern Ireland, where the Abortion Act 1967 does not apply.

34 Brian Hurwitz, 'Swearing to care: the resurgence in medical oaths' (1997) 315 *BMJ*, 1671 available at: http://www.bmj.com/content/315/7123/1671.full (accessed 27 January 2017).

35 World Medical Association, *Declaration of Geneva* (WMA, 1995). Also see Hurwitz (n 34).

Hippocratic oath and oaths taken to comply with good medical practice are, thus, a good faith attempt to give direction to doctors to ethically correct practice.

Question 1: How have English law and the ECtHR dealt with the issue?

Legal foundation, limits and development in English law

The right to abortion in England and Wales is set out in s 4 of the Abortion Act 1967.

Section 4 was not included in the original bill, but was part of the final iteration in order to ensure that doctors were not compelled to carry out abortions against their beliefs. It is worthwhile considering for a moment how discussion and discourse and facilitation of difference in opinion resulted in the successful passing of the Abortion Act 1967, including the conscience clause. The successful passage of the Act followed two bills that were introduced by Lord Liskin in 1965 and 1966. During the discussion of these bills, many of the likely arguments against abortion were brought to the surface in advance of the 1967 Act and discussion thereof. Such possible hurdles included the possible need for an opt-out for doctors.[36] Opinions in these discussions ranged from those who said that ‘it is quite wrong for any doctor to put his ethical considerations beyond the considerations of his patient’[37] and those who clarified that the conscience clause would give a clear right to doctors to opt-out.[38] There was some consideration of the difference between the needs of the patient and the requirement of the doctor to act on medical judgement and an attempt made to define ‘participate’ within the parameters of medical judgement: this was not successful. Notwithstanding debate and counter-debate about these issues and others, the Abortion Act 1967 (including the current s 4) passed. In many ways, the inclusion of the conscience clause was seen to be a necessary concession to the passing of the legislation.

Section 4 provides the legal foundation for the conscientious objection of medical professionals. This provision states that no person shall be under any duty, whether by contract or by any statutory or other legal requirement, to participate in any treatment authorised by this Act to which he has a conscientious objection, provided that in any legal proceedings the burden of proof of conscientious objection shall rest on the person claiming to rely on it. Subsection (2) states that nothing in s 4(1) affects any duty to participate in treatment which is necessary to save the life or to prevent grave permanent injury to the physical or mental health of a pregnant woman. Subsection (3) stipulates that in Scotland a statement on oath to the effect that one has a conscientious objection to participating in any treatment authorised by the Act is sufficient evidence for the purpose of discharging this burden of proof.

36 See Hansard HC *Deb 13 July 1967 vol 750 cc1313–85*1313.
37 Hansard 830.60, Vickers 1111.
38 Hansard (David Steel) (n 36) 1318.

Section 4 is quite categorical in stating that no person has a duty to 'participate' in an otherwise legal act of treatment to which they conscientiously object. However, the meaning of 'participate' is not clearly defined, and one's objection and refusal to participate imposes on other professionals the need to act, which has been equated to legislating morality for others:

> To the doctor who complains that he wants to practise medicine without abortions, the answer must be that he can choose to engage in private practice, and thereby arrange his affairs by agreement with his patients. If he joins the NHS, he should remember the last word of the three, 'service', and serve.[39]

The Abortion Act 1967 successfully took divergent views which implicitly include rejections based upon religious belief and allowed for the expression of these viewpoints through the conscientious objection clause.

On the matter of private practice, to which the Abortion Act 1967 applies, the court in *Barr v Matthews* stated that once a termination of pregnancy is recognised as an option, the doctor invoking the conscientious objection clause should immediately refer the patient to a colleague.[40] Kennedy and Grubb argue that general practitioners are under a contractual obligation to arrange abortion services for their patients as part of their referral duties.[41]

Obviously, there are limits to s 4's operation; a doctor must perform an abortion in cases where it is necessary to save the pregnant woman's life, or to stop permanent injury to her physical or mental health. This means that if the patient is at risk of death or of physical or mental injury, the doctor cannot rely on conscientious objection to avoid acting. Having said that, in many cases another doctor will be in a position to undertake the abortion.[42] Another limitation is that a doctor cannot use conscientious objection to refuse to advise a patient (and of course, s 4 has no limiting effect on the duties owed to people who have had an abortion.)

Further sections of this chapter demonstrate that the limitations, under the Act, are justified and that they balance the rights of healthcare professional with the patient's right to healthcare/treatment, as protected under the PGC.

Conscientious objection, religious manifestation, and ECtHR jurisprudence and the Resolution on Abortion and Conscientious Objection

Acting in accordance with religious belief include conscientiously objecting to practices that are considered to be against one's faith and, as such, are protected

39 Ian Kennedy, *Treat Me Right: Essays in Medical Law and Ethics* (Clarendon Press, 1998) p 29.
40 *Barr v Matthews* (1999) 52 BMLR 217.
41 Ian Kennedy and Andrew Grubb, *Medical Law* (3rd ed, Butterworths, 2000) pp 1446–1447.
42 Jonathan Herring, *Medical Law and Ethics* (5th ed, OUP, 2014) p 306.

under Article 9 (1) ECHR (and also given further legitimacy under the Council of Europe's Parliamentary Assembly's Resolution).[43] However, limitations of the use of conscientious objection are allowed for under Article 9(2).

It is quite evident that the right to object to participating to abortion based upon religious belief (or, indeed, conscience) is supported by Article 9. However, it is equally evident that the limitations in Article 9(2), at a very practical level, would come into play in the unlikely event that no one else could carry out the abortion. (The *Janaway*[44] and *Doogan* cases will illustrate, however, how English courts have insufficiently used Article 9 to defend conscientious objection.)

The issue of conscientious objection has been deliberated upon quite extensively in the Strasbourg court outside the field of medicine, particularly in the context of military service. In essence, this jurisprudence vindicates the legitimacy of citizens conscientiously objecting to military service. In each case, it has been held, to some degree, that the punishments to those meted out to those who conscientiously object are disproportionate to their actions in refusing to partake in military service. The ECtHR has also found that penalising persons for this refusal on the basis of conscientious objection is a breach of their rights under Article 9.[45] Resolution of the question of conscientious objection in terms of military service is to be found in making changes in the law of the particular jurisdictions and the provision of different forms of military service which do not fly in the face of the belief system underpinning conscientious objection. The need for such action is best exemplified in the Grand Chamber case of *Urcep v Turkey*[46] which involved a Jehovah's Witness who refused to partake in military service. Under Turkish legislation, he was regarded as a deserter and was sentenced to a number of terms of imprisonment. It was held in the ECtHR that these penalties could not be seen as necessary in a democratic society. Only reform in the law and the creation of alternative forms of service could be an appropriate response.

43 Conscientious objection stands alongside and usually works hand-in-hand with duties to refer the patient that are intended to safeguard her access to information and treatment. This Resolution, however, is not binding of member states because the Parliamentary Assembly acts as a consultative body within the Council of Europe and its recommendations are not, consequently, prescriptive. The adoption of this Resolution followed amendments to an original proposed Resolution. Discussion amongst the Parliamentary Assembly affirmed the right to conscientious objection, worry was articulated about the unregulated use of conscientious objection and its capacity to affect, in particular, low-income women. This Resolution affirms the place of conscientious objection in medical contexts in the Council of Europe and it also encourages member states to ensure that appropriate regulation of conscientious objection is provided. See Mark Campbell, 'Conscientious objection and the Council of Europe: The right to conscientious objection in lawful medical care. Resolution 1763 (2010). Resolution adopted by the Council of Europe's Parliamentary Assembly' (2011), 19 (3), *Medical Law Review*, 467–475.

44 *Janaway v Salford Area Health Authority* (1989) AC 537.

45 See *Thilimmeonos v Greece* (2001) 31 EHRR 411 and *Ulke v Turkey* (Application No. 39437/98).

46 *Ulke v Turkey* (n 45).

The ECtHR is consistent in its support of conscientious objection to military service or, at the very least, the provision of an alternative approach. Even though the Convention itself does not refer to conscientious objection, the Strasbourg Court has unequivocally vindicated that right, particularly in personal contexts. From the point of view of conscientious objection, military service is quite straightforward: pick up a rifle and kill someone on demand or refuse to do so. But in medical contexts, the situation is much more problematic. Sometimes a person will be doing the direct thing that violates his conscience. In other situations, he might be, for example, supplying the drug that the patient will take in order to kill himself or his actions might be even more tangential still. While much of the literature and case law recognises the importance of conscience, it sometimes fails to deal sufficiently with complex situations which involve, for example, different degrees of involvement and contribution. McGovern points to a difficulty for healthcare professionals:

> From the perspective of a doctor with a conscientious objection to abortion, referral to another practitioner is like saying, 'I can't rob the bank for you myself. But I know someone down the road who can.' In other words, referral involves becoming complicit in the abortion. It is therefore something that healthcare practitioners with an objection to abortion rightly refuse to do.[47]

Calls to reform laws and practices pertaining to conscientious objection are not confined to questions pertaining to military service. They apply, in particular, to issues arising from conscientious objection to reproductive treatments/medication and to the rights of healthcare professionals to object to participation in abortion procedures. The ECtHR has dealt with conscientious objection in the context of healthcare professionals in the French Pharmacists' case of *Pichon and Sajous v France.*[48] This case concerned two French pharmacists who argued that their Article 9 ECHR rights were breached as a consequence of their convictions for refusing to provide oral contraception to female customers. The European Court held that the case was inadmissible and concluded that their refusal did not fall within the remit of Article 9. The Court said that priority could not be given to the pharmacists' personal beliefs over professional duties 'as long as the sale of contraceptive is legal and occurs on medical prescription nowhere other than in a pharmacy'. The support of the ECtHR for conscientious objection was not as clear cut in this case primarily due to fact that there was a consideration that no professional alternatives existed for patients other than to have the contraceptives dispensed by pharmacists. The Court said that Article 9 does not necessarily

47 Kevin McGovern, 'The Victorian Abortion law-one year on' (2009) 15 (2) *Chisholm Health Ethics Bull* as cited in Fiala, Christian and Arthur, Joyce H, '"Dishonourable disobedience" – Why refusal to treat in reproductive healthcare is not conscientious objection' *Woman – Psychosomatic Gynaecology and Obstetrics* available at: http://www.sciencedirect.com/science/article/pii/S2213560X14000034 (accessed 27 January 2017).

48 *Pichon and Sanjous v France* [2001] ECHR 898.

guarantee that people could act in a way that is based upon their personal belief because the word 'practice' in Article 9 (1) does not mean every single act or type of behaviour resulting from a person's belief. In this case, the fact that the sale of contraceptives was legal and could only be dispensed in a pharmacy, meant that the applicants could not give paramountcy to their religious beliefs and that, as such, there was no breach of Article 9. Thus, recognition was given to the fact that conscientious objection cannot always be absolute.

This case is important in the overall context of conscientious objection. The fact that conscientious objection is contextualised and limited within the context of professional healthcare responsibilities is significant. There is recognition given to the rights of patients to access healthcare services. The crucial issue here is that only pharmacists can dispense this medication and no other alternatives exist. This is unlike the case of abortion where, for example, under section 4 of the Abortion Act 1967 (England, Wales, and Scotland), a doctor can refer a woman to another doctor. Unfortunately, in *Pichon* the court applied a limiting concept of religious freedom when interpreting Article 9(1). There was a failure to recognise the applicants' conscientious objections as a manifestation of their religious beliefs under the first paragraph of Article 9. Any assessment of the right to conscientiously object needs to be considered relative to the available alternatives. The issue centres around the need to ensure that conditions of employment are such that they do not preclude healthcare professionals from conscientiously objecting to procedures that are against their religious beliefs. This means that the right of people to consciously object, as protected to a degree under Article 9, should form part of the contractual obligations, subject to agreed limitations between employer and employee. This is, arguably, of more relevance to healthcare professionals than other employees because much of the immediacy of their actions can be involved in life and death/morally sensitive and contentious situations.

The case of *RR v Poland*[49] raises some important questions about the right of pregnant women to abortion in the event that foetal abnormality is suspected. The case happened in Poland, where abortion laws only allow for the most limited of possible circumstances in which an abortion might be allowed. This case concerned a pregnant woman. At the 11th or 12th week of pregnancy, the doctor could not rule out some malformation of the unborn baby. The applicant requested an abortion if this finding were verified. There followed ultrasound scans, proposals of genetic screening, agreement, and disagreement about the suspicion of either Edward's syndrome or Turner's syndrome being present in the unborn baby.[50] The applicant was moved from public to private care, subjected to rebuke by hospital personnel, and required to travel to hospital at a significant distance. At a number of stages, significant delays were encountered. For example, delays were put in place in terms of referring her for additional testing. No abortion was procured, and the woman gave birth to a child with Turner's syndrome. The woman eventually took the case to the ECtHR, which found in favour of her

49 *RR v Poland* (Application no 27617/04).
50 ibid. at [165].

in terms of evidence of infringement of her rights, primarily (and unusually) under Article 3, with some consideration of Article 8.

This case illustrates, for the first time, recognition by the ECtHR that states are obliged under the ECHR to ensure that the exercise of conscientious objection is regulated in such a way that patients are afforded access to lawful reproductive healthcare services. The Court held that states have a duty to 'organise the health services system in such a way as to ensure that an effective exercise of the freedom of conscience of health professionals in the professional context does not prevent patients from obtaining access to services to which they are entitled under the applicable legislation'.[51] In this case, although individual doctors could refuse to carry out the abortion on the grounds of conscience, the state was not absolved from its obligation to ensure that RR had access to the medical services to which she had a legal entitlement.

This very sad case brings many issues to light, including the lack of consistent protocols within the healthcare system in Poland, the supremacy of the opinion of the medical profession, and the lack of empathy with the woman contemplating the birth of a baby with serious disabilities. Cabal et al conclude that this case demonstrates that freedom of conscience cannot curtail women's rights to access reproductive healthcare.[52]

Another Polish case that deals with access to legal abortion under the Council of Europe system was that of *P and S v Poland*.[53] This case concerned a 14-year-old girl who became pregnant as a result of a rape. Supported by her mother (2nd applicant), the girl (1st applicant) sought an abortion which, under Poland's strict 1993 Act, is lawful. The Act guarantees the right to an abortion until week 12 of pregnancy when evidence exists that the pregnancy was a result of a 'criminal act'.[54] The evidence needs to be certified by a prosecutor in order for the abortion to be lawful and, in the case of *P and S v Poland*, such a statement was produced in May 2008. A number of additional steps now entered the process, including the need for the girl to seek a referral of a consultant of gynaecology, obstruction in both Lubin and Warsaw from healthcare professionals, Catholic priests, and objectors to abortion. In addition to this, the girl (a minor) was questioned without an adult or legal assistance available. Two months of procrastination were followed by the carrying out of the abortion in Gdansk. The imposition of significant delays along the process meant it could have happened that the applicant could have been more than 12 weeks pregnant at the time of the eventual abortion and, so, have been denied her right to an abortion within the permissible legal limit.

51 ibid. at [206].
52 Cabal et al, 'Striking a Balance: Conscientious Objection and Reproductive Health Care from the Colombian Perspective' (2014) 16(2) Health and Human Rights Journal available at: https://www.hhrjournal.org/2014/09/striking-a-balance-conscientious-objection-and-reproductive-health-care-from-the-colombian-perspective/ (accessed 27 January 2017).
53 *P and S v Poland* (Application no 57375/08).
54 ibid. at [59].

The applicants took the case to the ECtHR and alleged that the circumstances of the case provided violations of Articles 3, 5, and 8 of the Convention. In assessing the case, the court gave particular attention to conscientious objection as a right in the Polish legal system. It noted that the existence of a mechanism to ensure that a balance existed between the rights of healthcare professionals and the rights of patients by making it mandatory for reference to be made to the conscientious objection of healthcare professionals in the patient notes and for the patient to be referred to another healthcare professional. The court found in *P and S v Poland* that these mechanisms were not used. In its deliberation, the court held that a breach of Article 8 existed because authorities did not give due regard to their positive obligations to ensure that the applicants were given respect for their private life.[55]

Both Polish cases highlight the way in which the ECtHR has vindicated a right to conscientiously object to abortion. This stance at European level, in practical terms, has an impact on the decisions made in the domestic courts and can provide guidance on how these courts could interpret and apply the relevant Convention rights, including the right to manifest religious belief.

Conscientious objection in the English courts: two seminal cases

This section seeks to establish the fact that English courts give undue attention to semantic interpretation of the Abortion Act 1967 and do not engage comprehensively with human rights arguments when evaluating the right to conscientiously object. The benchmark case in English law on conscientious objection was *Janaway*,[56] an appeal from an employment arbitration wherein a Catholic secretary refused to type a referral letter for a possible abortion and was dismissed. She claimed a right to conscientiously object on the grounds that she would have been an accessory to the abortion. In other words, typing the letter was 'participation' under the Act that constituted counselling or procuring a termination. The Health Authority contended that the clause should only apply to those actually taking part in treatment actions. The Court of Appeal agreed, concluding that typing the referral letter did not assist in the abortion, but merely fulfilled her employment duties, and that it would not be a criminal act in the context of s 1(1) of the Act. On further appeal to the House of Lords, per Lord Keith, dismissed Janaway's appeal, confirming that s 4 only applied to those 'actually taking part in the treatment administered … for the purpose of terminating a pregnancy'.[57] Lord Keith said that the term 'participate' should be given its natural meaning; if Parliament had intended to extend the notion of participation, it could have done so by referring to participation 'in anything authorised by this Act' instead of 'in any treatment [so] authorised'.[58]

55 ibid. at [137].
56 *Janaway* (n 44).
57 ibid. p 570.
58 ibid.

Janaway[59] gave what seemed to be a clear-cut definition of 'participate' and it set out definitive parameters for that participation within the context of abortion. But further legal argument on this topic was to ensue. *Doogan* was recently appealed to the UK SC and provides an analysis of the conscientious objection clause in the 21st century. The case ultimately concerns the scope of conscientious objection under s 4 and further definition of what constitutes or does not constitute 'participation' in an abortion. Due to the fact that the conscientious objection clause was not modified under the 1990 amendments, it has been necessary to wait for judicial clarification.[60] The case was originally taken in the Scottish Outer House of the Court of Session. It was subsequently appealed to the Inner House before finally reaching the SC.

Doogan[61] concerned two Catholic midwives who worked in a Scottish labour ward and claimed that they were entitled to object to participate in abortions. Consequently, they did not take part in the treatment of certain patients. As the number of abortions sought increased, the midwives became dissatisfied with the arrangements made to accommodate their objections, including a refusal to supervise support staff involved in abortions. Their employer, the Greater Glasgow Health Board, contended that the duties of delegation, supervision, and support did not involve 'participating' in the treatment, and so rejected their grievance against so acting. The midwives sought judicial review of this decision.

It was argued by the petitioners in the Outer House that 'participate' referred to everyone involved in the treatment. The Lord Ordinary (Lady Smith) did not accept that the declaratories had a right to a conscientious objection. A very narrow view of s 4(1) was taken. It was held that, due to the fact that the midwives were under no obligation to directly take part in the abortions, they were not being asked to 'participate in any treatment authorised by this Act'. They were seen to have only a supervisory and an administrative role. This decision was then appealed to the Inner House of the Court of Session, where a broader interpretation of 'participate' was accepted.

The Greater Glasgow Health Board appealed this decision to the SC, arguing that interpreting 'participate' as including everyone involved in the treatment team, even those whose role was not hands-on but only supervisory or supportive, would result in an improperly wide right of conscience; one that the health authorities would be unable to manage.[62] The SC has reiterated the fact that conscientious objection is a legitimate and working principle in relevant medical contexts. What is clear is that the SC has put a limiting brake on the scope of conscience by emphasising the perceived intention of Parliament, but also, as will be shown in subsequent analysis, by brushing over the Article 9 ECHR argument.

59 ibid.

60 The Abortion Act 1967 was amended by the Human Fertilisation and Embryology Act 1990. The original limit of 18 weeks for abortion was increased to 24 weeks.

61 *Doogan* (n 1).

62 A point made by Mary Neal, 'The Scope of Conscience-based Exemption in Section 4 (1) of the Abortion Act 1967: *Doogan and Wood v NHS Greater Glasgow Health Board*' (2014) 22 *Medical Law Review*, 409–421, p 412.

I would suggest that there are two critical elements of the case that are important. The first is the meaning of the word 'participate' in the conscientious objection clause of the Abortion Act 1967. This was directly and positively engaged with by the SC; indeed, it was at the centre of the *Doogan* judgment. On this semantic question, the SC took a contextual approach insofar as it drew on the purpose for which the statute was enacted (although it declined to examine the context so far as to consider broader practice consequences for the midwives or the service). Ultimately, the SC endorsed a narrow meaning which limited the right to object to a direct and hands-on involvement in the procedure. Here, the increased number of abortions did not necessitate the midwives actively participating, but rather merely having more administrative and supervisory work (e.g., making calls to arrange medical terminations, or allocating ward staff to support the procedure) none of which were deemed direct enough to be a constituent factor in the performance of the abortion.

In supporting *Janaway* and specifying the meaning of participation, *Doogan* offers some useful clarity to both patients and practitioners around those aspects of professional practice which are direct and so conscience-dependent and those which are indirect and so necessary to undertake in abortions. For some with very deep religious beliefs, however, the decision likely remains unsatisfactory insofar as their conscience may still be offended, and this brings us to the second element of *Doogan*, which is the interaction between the statutory right to object (and therefore to avoid certain healthcare duties) and the protection or strengthening of this right by Article 9 ECHR. On this point, the SC said very little.[63] It held that Article 9 is:

> … a qualified right, which may be subject to 'such limitations as are prescribed by law and necessary in a democratic society in the interests of public safety, for the protection of public order, health or morals, or for the protection of the rights and freedoms of others'. Refusing for religious reasons to perform some of the duties of a job is likely (following … *Eweida v United Kingdom* …) to be held to be a manifestation of a religious belief. There would remain difficult questions of whether the restrictions placed by the employers upon the exercise of that right were a proportionate means of pursuing a legitimate aim. The answers would be context specific and would not necessarily point to either a wide or a narrow reading of section 4 of the 1967 Act.[64]

63 Calling Article 9 ECHR a 'distraction': ibid, at [23].

64 ibid. at [23]. In *Eweida v UK* [2013] ECHR 37, the wearing of religious emblems in an employment context was held to be protected under Article 9 ECHR, but, as a limited right, it was incumbent on employers to strike a fair balance between their wish for a corporate image and the employee's right to manifest her beliefs. The ECtHR confirmed that the freedom to manifest one's belief may be limited under Article 9(2) if necessary in a democratic society, including for the protection of the rights and freedoms of others.

In the result, it deferred the question of the operation of Article 9 and appropriate accommodations to Employment Tribunals, giving no specific indication as to how those tribunals ought to deal with this issue. A Tribunal was deemed by the Court to be a more suitable place for resolution.[65]

Addison argues that *Doogan* improperly emasculated the conscience objection clause without any factual or legal basis to say that the narrow interpretation of 'participate' was in line with Parliamentary intention, and that it is incorrect because it did not allow for (or even discuss) 'reasonable accommodation' as outlined in the Article 9 jurisprudence.[66] This position might be overstated insofar as there is no apparent change of the position of conscientious objection; the case replicates *Janaway* and hardens the narrow construction of participation without erasing the right of healthcare professionals to conscientiously object. Having said that, the GMC Guidance on personal belief and medical practice clearly situates conscientious objection within various ECHR rights (including, of course, the patient's right to be free from discrimination).[67] The scope of the right to object and of the need for the employer to accommodate one's objection may be coloured by whether the right to conscientious objection is viewed as a private or a public issue,[68] or perhaps an amalgam of both.[69] On this view, we have the right to hold personal beliefs, and in many cases to act on them, but with a responsibility to function in a public domain in accordance with the rights expressed therein. And of course, there must be some limits to the degree to which religious beliefs can be used to absolve a licensed practitioner from undertaking social or medical responsibilities. Either way, some instruction from the SC would have been welcome.

A judgment in a court of law, even in the SC, is part of the informing of conscience, but it is not the absolute contributor to the formation of that conscience. The dialogue around the meaning of a word and the intention of a word is important because words have power, not as a consequence of their semantic meaning, but as a consequence of the way in which they are used. The final interpretation of 'participate' as something narrow and confining finally puts to bed attempts to move away from what most reasonable people to be the intention of those who originally drafted the Abortion Act 1967. It is important in our

65 ibid. at [24].

66 Neil Addison, 'Call the midwife I want an abortion', available at: http://religionlaw.blogspot.co.uk/2014/12/call-midwife-i-want-abortion-3.html (accessed 27 January 2017). And in this, he has some support from Neal (n 62).

67 General Medical Council, *Personal Beliefs and Medical Practice*, available at: http://www.gmc-uk.org/guidance/ethical_guidance/21177.asp (accessed 27 January 2017) at [8]–[16].

68 As argued by Jonathan Montgomery, 'Conscientious Objection: Personal and Professional Ethics in the Public Square' (2015) 23 *Medical Law Review*, 200–220.

69 On this issue, there is some scholarly discussion about conscience, its relationship to integrity, internal dialogue, and external—and public—factors like court decisions: see C McLeod, 'Taking a Feminist Relational Perspective on Conscience' in J Downie and J Lewllellyn (eds), *Being Relational: Reflections on Relational Theory and Health Law and Policy* (University of British Columbia Press, 2011) pp 161–181.

exploration of the law that the spirit of the Act is adhered to and not just the words that exemplify the spirit. Within that sense of the spirit of the act is an implicit understanding that the Abortion Act 1967 involved a compromise position.

Is conscientious objection protected by this judgment? There is no real change of any substance to the position of conscientious objection arising from it. The result replicates and strengthens the findings of *Janaway* and sets in stone the narrow construction of participation. It does not detract in any way from the rights of healthcare professionals to conscientiously object. There is no threat to the spirit of s 4 of the Abortion Act 1967. This position is consistent with the GMC's guidance on personal belief and medical practice, which sets out very clearly, and, in an arguably mutually respectful manner, the way in which conscientious objection may result in opting out of providing particular procedures because of the personal beliefs and values of the doctor. This guidance situates freedom to conscientiously object within a context of respecting patients' dignity and views and recognising the need to ensure that conscientious objection 'does not result in direct or indirect discrimination'.[70] The guidance also aims to ensure that doctors are mindful that a patient has the right to discuss options for treatment with another practitioner who does not share the same conscientious objection.[71]

Question 2: Why is this sufficient or insufficient in the context of the PGC?

A right to abortion under the PGC?

To provide an interpretation of the degree to which current law in respect of the right to conscientiously object to abortion is sufficient under the PGC, it is necessary to firstly determine whether the right to abortion itself exists under the PGC. Beyleveld provides a reflective interpretation of his stance on the moral status of the foetus, which need not be replicated here.[72] Some of his more relevant conclusions include the following: Gewirthians must reject the 'pro-life' position—which assumes that human life is the sufficient condition for the granting of full moral status. Agents do need to accord intrinsic moral status to the embryo/foetus and the PGC supports a 'compromise' position on the moral status of the embryo/foetus.[73] He points to the fact that the Catholic position, granting full moral status to the foetus or embryo, is difficult to accept, particularly if such a position is given legislative protection because agents may exist within society who do not accept this position. Indeed, 'no societies exist in which there is absolute consensus'.[74] According to Beyleveld, the PGC adopts a position

70 General Medical Council (n 67).
71 ibid. See section 8.
72 Deryck Beyleveld, 'The Moral Status of the Human Embryo and Fetus' in Deryck Beyeveld and Hille Haker, *The Ethics of Genetics in Human Procreation* (Ashgate, 2000) pp 59–85.
73 ibid. p 59.
74 ibid. p 63.

whereby it is possible to deal with the conflict between the rights of the foetus/embryo (as apparent possible agents) and those who espouse a position supporting those rights and the rights of the mother (as an apparent agent), by adopting the 'method of consent' involved in indirect applications of the PGC 'by which democratic decisions may be imposed on those who do not agree with them'.[75] This compromise position is, however, limited by the fact that the PGC cannot confer such rights on the foetus/embryo that would override the rights of the mother under precautionary reasoning. Thus, under precautionary reasoning, a right to abortion exists under the PGC, as is implied in the assignment of this moral status and in the assignment of the consequential gradation in status to both foetus/embryo and mother. How can this right to abortion be weighed against the right to conscientiously object?

The interaction between the right to abortion and the right to conscientiously object: sufficiency under the PGC

Failure to allow for conscientious objection can, in some circumstances, constitute infliction of basic harm, as such an action affects a generic condition of agency that is required by an agent to act for any purpose at all.[76] The conscientious objection with which I am concerned is to participating in something that, for example, some Catholics believe to be murder and, as such, a sin of the greatest magnitude. The failure to allow a conscientious objection will (sometimes) result in the infliction of such an action-paralysing harm. Thus, when conscientious objection is invoked by someone whose well-being would be dramatically intruded upon, if the conscientious objection were not allowed, then this would constitute basic harm and, thus, the PGC is breached. To disallow the conscientious objection would be, in effect, a 'worse wrong' than allowing the conscientious objection to be invoked. Gewirth himself refers to the conundrum that exists whereby for some people 'the duty to maintain freedom takes priority to maintain life itself' or where, in Gewirth's terms, 'it is better to be a starved Socrates than a starving pig'.[77] The same infliction of basic harm would also be caused if such a Catholic healthcare professional were deprived of the right to conscientiously object to assisting in suicide, where such assistance would involve, for this Catholic, the deliberate taking of life and so contravene the sanctity of life perspective adhered to as a fundamental part of their belief structure (see chapter 3).

This book does not, however, argue for an extension of the right to conscientiously object to areas other than those that have the potential to inflict basic harm in this way.[78] For example, in the case of a Jewish parent's conscientious insistence on ritual

75 ibid.

76 Alan Gewirth, *Reason and Morality* (University of Chicago Press, 1978) p 216. According to Gewirth, 'rights and duties vary in degree of moral urgency according to the degree to with they affect well-being and hence possibilities of purposive action…'

77 ibid. p 346.

78 The recent Royal College of Surgeons/General Medical Council's implicit extension of conscientious objection to areas other than the ambit of s 4 potentially needs to be reconsidered. See Royal College of Surgeons of England, *Caring for Patients who Refuse Blood* (Royal College of Surgeons of England, 2016).

circumcision, the expression of belief being hindered in that case is not as firmly connected to what an adherent will regard as extremely serious sin. Frustrating that belief is, consequently, likely to give rise to only additive harm, whereas frustrating this anti-abortion belief, or indeed, anti-assisted suicide perspective, is likely to give rise to basic harm. Equally, for someone whose conscience is only mildly troubled by an action, the refusal of conscientious objection would not constitute basic harm because the degree to which the consequence of the action impacts upon the agent is not significant here and a 'worse wrong' would be created by allowing the conscientious objection. In situations involving contention over conscientious objection, the courts need to interrogate conscience as it applies at individual level against the values of the PGC, as set out in PGC-compliant mechanisms such as the HRA, and if they find that the right to conscientious objection is breached, then they must act accordingly.

To solve the question of whether conscientious objection should be allowed or disallowed involves, in instances, applying the PGC directly or indirectly (see chapter 2). This constitutes a complex evaluative procedure involving, in some cases, many variables. Those aspects that can be *directly* addressed by the PGC and those that are properly left to an appropriate procedure (i.e., *indirectly* addressed) could include the following:

1 A conscientious objector will generally have a range of options to avoid compromising his conscience and will have chosen his particular profession or specialism within his profession in the light of his ability to act in accordance with his conscience.
2 The breadth of defensible conscience objection will be connected to the breadth of abortion provision, because the narrower the latter, the weaker the case for the former.

A key factor within this debate is that allowing conscientious objection will have costs to patients (i.e. risks to their generic conditions). Other rights are also protected under the PGC, such as the right of the mother to an abortion. All agents have generic rights, not just those who conscientiously object. While not allowing for conscientious objection will violate the PGC, allowing for the conscientious objection could allow for the violation of other rights. The right to conscientiously object to abortion requires consideration of any rights to abortion that could be infringed by the conscientious objection. Thus, another basic harm also exists; precluding a woman from accessing an abortion would be to contravene her generic rights. And so the challenge exists: under the PGC, abortion is a basic right for the mother and conscientious objection is also a basic right for the healthcare professional and the embryo/foetus has some moral status. The fact that there are potentially three beings with potentially different moral statuses here gives rise to more than 'one variable conflict'. Conscientious objection actions could have 'PGC-relevant costs for other agents who possess moral status'.[79] Conflicts can exist between the duties that are owed to the embryo/foetus and duties owed to

79 Gewirth (n 76) p 71.

other agents such as the mother and the person who conscientiously objects.[80] Can a compromise position be reached between the three variables? The quite simple answer is 'yes'. The act of conscientious objection does not preclude the mother from procuring an abortion because under the PGC-compliant s 4 of the Abortion Act 1967, the mother can have access to this procedure via another professional and, if no other person is available to carry out the abortion, then the person who conscientiously objects must carry out the procedure. The costs to patients of the right to conscientiously object can be reduced to those associated with delay if there is an obligation to refer patients to those who do not object.

There is, therefore, no violation to the basic rights of the mother and, given the statistically limited chance and probability of the person who conscientiously objects being required to carry out this procedure, there is therefore no violation of her basic rights. Consequently, the current law provides a good compromise between protecting the basic rights of the mother and of the professional who conscientiously objects. As a consequence, the current position represents a good faith attempt at applying the PGC.

We have seen that the current law protects the right to conscientiously object under section 4 of the Abortion Act 1967. Defensible limits are put on this freedom in this provision. Practical medical guidelines are in place that support the exercise of conscientious objection. Human rights law, equally, provides an adequate mechanism for the exercise of conscientious objection. The right to conscientiously object is considered under the PGC as a basic generic right. There is a difference between saying that something is a *generic right* (which is to say that the object of the right is something needed by all agents act or act successfully) and saying that something is a right derived from a generic right (which is to say that the object of the right is something needed by a particular agent, or a particular group of agents, to act or act successfully).

The answer to the sufficiency of the law is, in this case, quite simple. Section 4 is appropriate and adequate and is reflective of the PGC. The current approach of English law under s 4 does allow for the evaluation and consideration of differing variables and protection of the generic rights. It, thus, constitutes a permissible option for an indirect application of the PGC. Other options, of course, might also exists so no prescriptive requirement is needed to ensure compliance with the PGC.

Human rights law, equally, defends the exercise of conscience under Article 9 ECHR. The European case law dealing with military service is consistent with the PGC. It is also suggested, from a PGC point of view, that the ECtHR were incorrect in *Pichon*[81] to hold that the refusal of the pharmacists did not fall within the remit of Article 9. The decision to refuse the conscientious objection was a breach of the pharmacists' basic rights for the same reasons as articulated above and so breached the PGC. The failure to use Article 9 appropriately to vindicate this right adversely impacted upon the protection of the pharmacists' generic

80 ibid.
81 *Pichon* (n 48).

conditions of agency. Conscience needs to be protected and the Convention right ought to have been used to support the manifestation of such belief. Conscientious objection to abortion involves healthcare professionals who are involved in carrying out an abortion. In such an instance, if participating in the act of abortion goes against his or her conscience, this can impact upon his/her generic conditions of agency. The facilitation of an abortion by a healthcare professional who regards abortion as unconscionable represents basic harm because this would result in him or her having to go carry out an action that would be so injurious to their conscience and would so compromise their freedom and well-being that it would prevent them from acting at all. This differs from the case of circumcision; in this case the procedure impacts to the greatest degree on the generic rights of the child who lacks the ability to waive the benefits to his generic rights and whose bodily integrity is breached, thus constituting basic harm. The parent in this case is not the pivotal actor. In the case of conscientious objection, the healthcare professional is a primary actor whose generic rights would be immediately infringed if he were not allowed to conscientiously object. Conscientious objection is for him a basic right, something that is necessary for him to act at all, something that encompasses actual action that directly challenges his freedom and well-being.

Obviously, limitations need to exist to the exercise of conscience, but the arguments presented by the Court are unsatisfactory as they fail to recognise the direct breach of the pharmacists' generic rights. It could also, however, be argued that there are difficulties in indirectly applying the PGC, due to the fact that in France there are no other alternatives to pharmacies as outlets for the dispensing of contraceptives. Therefore, for practical reasons, the PGC might hold that this is suitable as a good faith attempt at applying the PGC. In the context of this case, therefore, due to reasonable disagreement by Gewirthians and the societal impact of such a decision, the Court's decision could arguably be regarded as appropriate and an indirect application of the PGC. In theory, therefore, the current legal stance is adequate.

The compatibility of the Doogan *SC judgment with the PGC*

A difficulty lies in the fact that the most recent case law, in the form of the *Doogan*[82] judgment, did not sufficiently consider the human rights, under Article 9 ECHR, that are concurrent with a PGC-compliant position. In Gewirthia, *Doogan* was wrongly decided because it didn't recognise will-rights of the midwives and did not support the voluntariness of action on their part: breach of freedom and well-being. Respect for other Gewirthian viewpoints must be respected but, in the end, those nearest to the values of the PGC will trump those that are at a farther remove from such values.

While case law, in the main, is supportive of the right to conscientiously object, the failure of *Doogan* to properly address the human rights implications, particularly those of Article 9, is inappropriate. It is obvious in *Doogan* that enforcing

82 *Doogan* (n 1).

new practices upon the midwives was causing them to act in a way that was contrary to their moral compass. There is a very definite breach here of Article 9. The PGC does not differentiate between direct and indirect involvement. Instead, it considers the breach of a person's conscience, as a basic generic right, as a violation of the PGC and so impermissible. There is a failure on the part of the courts to use the Convention right adequately.

Doogan interrogated the language and the meaning behind the language used in section 4. This replicated, perhaps, a purely positivist dissection of a legal rule. What was required was an interrogation of the degree to which imposing additional duties on the midwives was, in fact, a breach of their human right to conscientiously object. If their right to conscientiously object, as underpinned by Article 9, were breached, then so too were their generic rights under the PGC. From a PGC point of view, the *Doogan* judgment is incompatible with the need to protect individual generic rights, which include the core values that are unique to individuals. The exercise of core values cannot be seen as a homogenous procedure.

Strasbourg jurisprudence and the PGC

It can be seen from the jurisprudence that assessing the sufficiency of the legal approach, in terms of conscientious objection, will always entail an arbitration of the degree to which the conscientious objection is aligned with the values of the PGC and is weighted against other rights and variables. It is clear that judgments in the Polish ECtHR cases would contravene the PGC, due to the insufficient weight given to the will-rights of the mentally competent (pregnant) women in these cases.[83]

Question 3: Is there an alternative approach that will provide greater compliance with the framework?

This third question invites different types of response. The focus of the method is on the options available in English law now and into the future. For that reason, the following will be considered: (a) the solutions available in Gewirthia and (b) alternative approaches to be adopted by the legislature and the judiciary in English law if Parliamentary time and inclination were available. The decisions in current case law will be compare to decisions that might be made in respect of the same cases in the PGC-compliant approach to English law suggested by this framework.

Approach taken in Gewirthia

In respect of conscientious objection, the legislature in Gewirthia recognises both the generic right to conscientious objection and the scope of that right. It celebrates the extent of the positive right to conscientiously object, but also identifies

83 *RR v Poland* (n 49); *P and S v Poland* (n 53).

the validity of competing and conflicting rights where the claims of, for example, John, a person who wants to conscientiously object can only be satisfied when the rights of Mary, who objects to this, are violated.[84] A strategy is needed to bridge the gap between the rights of people to conscientiously object, the boundaries of its limitations, and the rights of others affected by conscientious objection. A dispute resolution strategy is required that would solve the problems of what direct or indirect harm could be caused to those involved in the process of conscientious objection. In Gewirthia, such a strategy looks not only at the rights of affected rights holders, but as articulated by Beyleveld and Brownsword, at the societal and community implications of any actions that are caused which might result in compromising the PGC so that the needs of dispute resolution around conscientious objection are served.[85] Beyleveld and Brownsword called this context the 'resolution of the internal problem of the authority of the law'. In Gewirthia, there are liable to be disputes between citizens about conscientious objection. These will require 'authoritative determination' that goes beyond resolution merely on the basis of commitment to the PGC.[86] It is a society in which everyone accepts that the PGC is supreme will this not mean that conscientious objections arise in much more limited circumstances. There could, for example, be no one who considers the foetus to have full status in a society in which everyone accepts the PGC.

This stance, however, affects the need for conscientious objections to be protected. It is recognised that in Gewirthia value disagreements only arise over matters that are not deductively answered by the PGC. This can involve disagreements about religion and, in particular, disagreement about the value that is placed upon the agent at different stages of his life, as underpinned by particular religious conviction. For example, May, a nurse who routinely immunises against tuberculosis, refuses to immunise against Human Papilloma Virus (HPV) on the basis that she is religiously opposed to promiscuity and considers HPV immunisation to encourage this promiscuity. Upholding May's conscientious objection would be in breach of the PGC because that objection is not linked to a life-altering (for her) central tenet of her faith. While there is some infringement of her freedoms, the level of harm that is inflicted upon her is additive only. The potential level of harm that would be accrued to her patient by refusing to give her the vaccine, would be a basic harm, in line with the understanding of basic harm discussed previously. Consequently, the patient's need to receive this immunisation would be stronger than the harm that would be inflicted on May by refusing her conscientious objection. Equally, the example can be taken of Laura, a doctor who works in the Accident and Emergency Department and refuses to perform a blood transfusion on the basis that it is contrary to her Jehovah's Witness faith. Once again, the harm that is caused to her by breaching her conscientious objection would be less

84 Deryck Beyleveld and Roger Brownsword, 'Principle, Proceduralism, and Precaution in a Community of Rights' (2006) 19(2) *Ratio Juris*, 141–168, p 157.
85 ibid. p 143.
86 ibid. p 144.

grave under the criterion of degrees of needfulness for action than that caused to the patient by allowing for the conscientious objection. Neither of these examples is, however, subject to a legislative conscientious objection clause.

It has previously been shown that the PGC determines the zone of moral permissibility. Conscientious objection to the HPV immunisation would not be validly upheld within that zone. Conscientious objection has to reflect this zone of moral permissibility and, equally, the thing to which the apparent agent is objecting must be, for him, something that is a grave transgression, a 'mortal sin', a grievous undertaking of action that transgresses the most fundamental precepts of his religious beliefs. These beliefs, however, still must reflect the basic values of the PGC and not constitute any violation of the rights to freedom and well-being. This means that it is unlikely that conscientious objection could apply to arguments based upon the most irrational of religious beliefs and those that are not founded on some sort of commonality of purpose shared by most mainstream religions, including, in particular Abrahamic religions.

Thus, where conscientious objection is derived from a most serious and grave personal affiliation to a life-giving and 'mortal sin'-inducing precept of a religious faith, then conscientious objection must be allowed, in accordance with the PGC. The primary instance of such circumstances, as has been previously articulated, occurs in situations that involve decisions around sanctity of life, in particular, at beginning and end-of-life stages, cradle and grave scenarios. The 'threat to life and limb' of either the unborn or the near-dead must be the central area that invokes the conscientious objection. Basic harm must be accrued to the objector in order for conscientious objection to be allowed but, again, situations may also exist where basic harm is caused not only to the objector but also to the objectee. This is where the evaluative process discussed earlier comes into play, where all complex variables are measured and the final decision essentially comes down to the identification of where the greater the level of basic harm is inflicted. In such circumstances, if the basic harm that is accrued to the conscientious objector is greater than that accrued to that of the objectee, then the conscientious objection is allowed and this complies with the PGC. The alternative, obviously, also applies.

Coming to this resolution is, therefore, a two-step process. An overall principle will apply, whereby conscientious objection is allowed if the refusal of it constitutes basic harm and if this basic harm is greater than the harm that might occur if the refusal were upheld. Pragmatically, this is not often an all-or-nothing situation in the context of abortion. The duty of referral under s 4 means that the rights of the objectee are also upheld. Equally, the provision under s 4 for emergency intervention is compliant with the PGC. This brings us to the second and parallel step where the procedural aspect is applied. In English law, s 4 of the 1967 Act is the procedure by which the PGC supports and vindicates the right to conscientiously object, but does not deny the validity of other rights and professional obligations. However, in Gewirthia, in all its myriad forms, different procedures could exist, which could resemble s 4, but all procedures will reflect the values of the PGC and be respectful of the cultural pluralism of the Gewirthias where these values are enacted.

In Gewirthia, when weighing up the merits of conscientious objection, it will be judged procedurally not so much upon the merits of the arguments but on the merits of the interpretation of the arguments.[87] So in this Gewirthia, where the merits of conscientious objection are being discussed, the moral commitments of the community will 'guide both regulators and regulatorees through both the substance of their public disputes and manner and form of their peaceful resolution'.[88] Thus, in Gewirthia, a judgment will be reached that is founded upon the values of the PGC, that recognises the rights of all agents, that communities can respond to differently, but where consensus is reached by weighting arguments in respect in respect of the degree to which they comply with the values of the PGC. The substantive justification for any position around conscientious objection is, therefore, its compliance with the values of the PGC.

Gewirthia promotes the use of conscientious objection to abortion because denying it causes basic harm to the apparent agent. His generic conditions of agency are compromised at a basic level. In addition to this, hierarchically, there is an infringement upon his mental equilibrium. This means that his mental balance is so disrupted that it is not possible for him to undertake voluntary action and, in the third place, his freedom to make choices would be wholly compromised if his freedom to conscientiously object were taken away from him. So, conscientious objection is favoured in Gewirthia because, if conscientious objection is not allowed you would be preventing the apparent agent from being able to act, rather than just impeding the chances of his actions having a successful outcome. It doesn't matter, therefore, what the outcome of the conscientious objection might be (as an additive right). The issue is that failure to allow for conscientious objection means that the values of the PGC are not recognised or acted on and so, Gewirthians would act in accordance with the values the PGC and would find in favour of conscientious objection.

All of this does not, however, indicate that in Gewirthia, the right to conscientiously object would be a limitless one. For example, Gewirth stresses that the PGC requires that the agent adjusts his own rights of freedom and well-being to the rights of his recipients and the right of freedom does not 'include the total absence of any duty on the part of the agent.[89] The right requires, rather, an accommodation to the rights which his recipients also have to freedom and well-being'. He must avoid inflicting basic harm or failing to prevent such harm, as long as he can do so 'at no comparable cost to himself' and this is where the issue of conscience is most relevant. The conscientious objection must be of such a strong facet of individual self-identity that not acting in accordance with it would be at considerable 'cost to himself'.[90]

87 ibid. p 166.
88 ibid. pp 166–167.
89 Gewirth (n 76) p 227.
90 ibid. p 227.

Non-Gewirthian society

In the context of non-Gewirthian society (future England), there will be an acceptance of conscientious objection due to the infliction of basic harm as well as the human rights implications of refusing someone, for whom the issue is connected with self-identity, the opportunity to conscientiously object. Section 4 of the Abortion Act 1967 vindicates that right. However, in this non-Gewirthian jurisdiction, dissension exists that is more difficult to resolve procedurally.

The right to conscientiously object is currently provided for under legislation in an appropriate manner. This right has been vindicated, to a large degree, in case law and the medical guidelines. The position of conscientious objection in the Abortion Act 1967 is supported, but the courts' interpretation of s 4 and their related failure to address Article 9's rights are problematic. Section 4 of the Abortion Act 1967 is appropriate in the context of the PGC. Therefore, no change in the legislation is required.

It may be that using Article 9 as a tool to argue for the right to conscientiously object might bring about a similar conclusion to focusing solely on the issue of participation. Nonetheless, the question of conscientious objection must be broader and deeper than interrogation of semantics and interpretation of language. Using Article 9 in a more comprehensive way would entail looking at the issues of conscience that underpin the right to manifest religious belief in the context of conscientious objection. A new approach to cases such as *Doogan* would, thus, call upon the courts to give additional focus to human rights arguments and interpretations. Other chapters in this book have called for a human rights framework which is PGC-compliant to underpin the actions of the law makers. The issue of conscientious objection falls within that paradigm and so a new approach to conscientious objection in the courts needs to get deeper into what conscience allows for and what conscience prohibits and must acknowledge both the rights of those who conscientiously object and the rights of those on whom this conscientious objection would impact.

Into the future, how might the recommendations put forward in this chapter be developed in the legal system, interpreted by judges, and challenged by those who contest these positions? It has been contended that the current legislation around abortion is adequate, but that Article 9 ECHR needs to be used in a more PGC-compliant manner when judges deal with the concept of conscientious objection to abortion. Article 9 provides strong support for people to exercise their conscience. In particular, it explicitly protects the manifestation of religious belief. However, if conscientious objection is to be used as the grounds of an appeal, then it must be a conscientious objection that is an integral part of self-identity and a person's moral compass and provides a guide to direct their behaviour. This means that conscience, under Article 9, will need to be interpreted and applied differently in order to give greater significance to the generic rights of those healthcare professionals who conscientiously object to abortion. It is suggested that, in the case of conscientious objection to abortion, those who conscientiously object would need to clearly indicate how working in accordance with these changed practices would contravene tenets of their conscience. Examples of this might include evidence of affiliation to the precepts of Catholic faith, which hold a sanctity of life position, to disallow this conscientious objection in such instances would be to infringe rights under Article 9. The limitations under Article 9(2) should be regarded as applicable because there, in situations where professionals conscientiously object, for example, to abortion, as set out in s 4 of the 1967 Act, there is little challenge to the interests of public safety and allowing this type conscientious object does not impact upon the need to protect public order, health or morals. Therefore, Article 9(2) cannot be used by those two disagree with the recommendations above to limit the application of s 4.

Allowing a person to conscientiously object does have some impact upon the rights and freedoms of others but, in this case, the person who conscientiously objects has rights that are proportionately greater than others', in line with precautionary reasoning. In addition to this, other healthcare professionals are available, in practice, to undertake this work instead of those who conscientiously object to actively participating in abortion procedures. In applying future judicial interpretation of s 4, in light of the above arguments in relation to Article 9 of the Convention, healthcare professionals are entitled to conscientiously object.

Allowing for conscientious objection to abortion, through s 4 of the 1967 Act, the values of the PGC to be respected, particularly when judges balance rights appropriately and consider the relevance of conscience, as fuelled by religious belief (or otherwise), representing an intrinsic part of the self-identity of citizens. Into the future, if judges could interpret Article 9 in this manner, as well as engaging at a deeper level with the concept of conscience, rather than with the semantics of the meaning of 'participate' as in *Doogan* and *Janaway*, would allow for an appropriate indirect application of the PGC in non-Gewirthian English law.

The Irish position following the referendum on the Eighth Amendment of the Irish Constitution, alluded to in chapter 1, is an example of where new developments in terms of conscientious objection can be included within a legislative framework. At this early stage, the Irish Medical Organisation (IMO) has recognised the need for the inclusion of conscientious objection in the proposed new legislation:

> The organisation expects that given the deeply held views which exist on this issue, any legislative proposals will create a regime which facilitates access to abortion services by women while also catering for medical professionals who have deeply held conscientious objections on this matter.[91]

91 Josh Payne, 'Abortion legislation should provide for "conscientious objection", doctors say', available at: https://www.independent.ie/irish-news/abortion-referendum/abortion-legislation-should-provide-for-conscientious-objections-doctors-sa y-36954100.html (Irish Independent, 28 May 2018) (accessed 3 June, 2018). See Irish Medical Organisation, 'IMO Statement' available at: http://www.imo.ie/ news-media/news-press-releases/2018/imo-statement-1/index.xml (Irish Medical Organisation, 2018) (accessed 3 June, 2018).

Legislators in Ireland could consider applying the conscientious objection clause in s 4 of the 1967 Act in so far as that has been shown, notwithstanding some problems with the meaning of 'participate', to be a valid instrument. However, following their deliberation on *Janaway* and *Doogan*, the legislators may give even greater consideration to a wider interpretation of 'participate': this could give the drafters an opportunity to endorse an expanded role for Article 9 in the formation of this legislation.

Conclusion

This chapter has argued in favour of the use of the conscientious objection clause (section 4) in the context of abortion. It is important that healthcare professionals' conscience and/or religious beliefs are protected. The limitations present in s 4 of the Abortion Act 1967 are justified as they ensure that the healthcare of patients is also protected. In determining the validity of the use of conscientious objection, one should, however, not become overly distracted by the form of argument that has been followed in the two appellant decisions on s 4 Abortion Act 1967, namely *Janaway* and *Doogan*. In these cases, the courts have placed too much focus on interpretation of and assessment of the semantic nuances of s 4. Instead, a greater consideration should be given to Article 9 and the related human rights arguments.

To summarise, current Strasbourg jurisprudence recognises the validity of the concept of conscience, as an intrinsic element of Article 9. Conscientious objection is vindicated within the Article 9 jurisprudence, particularly in relation to military service cases. However, in *Pichon*, limits were placed on conscientious objection, primarily due to lack of availability of alternative services. This case indicates that the Strasbourg court will only go so far in recognising the legitimacy of conscientious objection and will balance it with other prevailing issues. English law provides strong support for conscientious objection in particular situations, such as abortion under s 4 of the 1967 Act. However, in English case law, undue focus has been placed upon semantic interpretations of language and insufficient consideration has been given to Article 9 ECHR or to the nature of conscience in the particular cases.

In the context of the PGC, it is argued that the approach of the ECtHR and the English courts does not allow for a sufficient consideration of conscience as a basic generic right. The breach of this basic right and the almost automatic focus on statutory construction is inappropriate. Instead, the law needs to give greater weight to human rights arguments in order for healthcare professionals to carry out their work in a manner that allows them to exercise their will-rights and not breach their fundamental generic rights.

References

Addison, Neil, 'Call the midwife I want an abortion', available at: http://religionlaw.blogspot.co.uk/2014/12/call-midwife-i-want-abortion-3.html (accessed 27 January 2017).

Beyleveld, Deryck, 'The Moral Status of the Human Embryo and Fetus' in Deryck Beyeveld and Hille Haker, *The Ethics of Genetics in Human Procreation* (Ashgate, 2000).

Beyleveld, Deryck and Brownsword, Roger, 'Principle, Proceduralism, and Precaution in a Community of Rights' (2006) 19(2) *Ratio Juris*, 141–168.

Broad, CD, 'Conscience and Conscientious Action' in John Donnelly and Leonard Lyons, *Conscience* (Alba House, 1973).

Brownlee, Kimberley, *Conscience and Conviction: The Case for Civil Disobedience* (OUP, 2012).

Butler, Joseph, *Fifteen Sermons Preached at the Rolls Chapel and a Dissertation upon the Nature of Virtue* (Hackett, 1983).

Cabal, L et al, 'Striking a Balance: Conscientious Objection and Reproductive Health Care from the Colombian Perspective' (2014) 16(2) *Health and Human Rights Journal*, available at: https://www.hhrjournal.org/2014/09/striking-a-balance-conscientious-objection-and-reproductive-health-care-from-the-colombian-perspective/ (accessed 27 January 2017).

Campbell, Mark, 'Conscientious objection and the Council of Europe: The right to conscientious objection in lawful medical care. Resolution 1763 (2010). Resolution adopted by the Council of Europe's Parliamentary Assembly' (2011) 19 (3) *Medical Law Review*, 467–475.

Catechism of the Catholic Church, available at: http://www.vatican.va/archive/ENG0015/_INDEX.HTM (accessed 27 January 2017).

Davies, Brian, *Thomas Aquinas's Summa Theologica: A Guide and Commentary* (OUP, 2014).

Downie, J and Lewllellyn, J (eds), *Being Relational: Reflections on Relational Theory and Health Law and Policy* (University of British Columbia Press, 2011).

Emerson, Claudia I and Daar, Abdallah S, 'Defining conscience and acting conscientiously' (2007) 7(12) *The American Journal of Bioethics*, 19–21.

Fletcher, Joseph, *Situational Ethics The New Morality* (Westminster John Know Press, 1966).

Freud, Sigmund, *Civilization and its Discontents*, Joan Riviere (trans) (Hogarth Press, 1930).

General Medical Council, 'Personal Beliefs and Medical Practice', available at: http://www.gmc-uk.org/guidance/ethical_guidance/21177.asp (accessed 27 January 2017).

Gewirth, Alan, *Reason and Morality* (University of Chicago Press, 1978).

Greasley, Kate, *Arguments about Abortion* (OUP, 2017).

Green, Brian Patrick, 'Catholicism and Conscience', available at: https://www.scu.edu/ethics/focus-areas/more/religion-and-ethics/resources/catholicism-and-conscience/ (accessed 27 January 2017).

Herring, Jonathan, *Medical Law and Ethics* (5th ed, OUP, 2014).

Hill, Thomas, *Human Welfare and Moral Worth, Kantian Perspectives* (OUP, 2002).

Irish Medical Organisation, 'IMO Statement', available at: http://www.imo.ie/news-media/news-press-releases/2018/imo-statement-1/index.xml (2018) (accessed 3 June, 2018).

Hurwitz, Brian, 'Swearing to care: the resurgence in medical oaths' (1997) 315*BMJ*, 1671, available at: http://www.bmj.com/content/315/7123/1671.full (accessed 27 January 2017).

Jafri, Masqood, 'Islamic Concept of Conscience', available at: http://www.irfi.org/articles/articles_151_200/islamic_concept_of_conscience.htm (accessed 27 January 2017).

Kant, Immanuel, *The Metaphysics of Morals* (CUP, 1991 (originally published in 1797)).

Kennedy, Ian, *Treat Me Right: Essays in Medical Law and Ethics* (Clarendon Press, 1998).

Kennedy, Ian and Grubb, Andrew, *Medical Law* (3rd ed, Butterworths, 2000).

McGovern, Kevin, 'The Victorian Abortion law-one year on' (2009) 15(2) *Chisholm Health Ethics Bull* as cited in Fiala, Christian and Arthur, Joyce H, '"Dishonourable disobedience" – Why refusal to treat in reproductive healthcare is not conscientious objection', *Woman – Psychosomatic Gynaecology and Obstetrics*, available at: http://www.sciencedirect.com/science/article/pii/S2213560X14000034 (accessed 27 January 2017).

Montgomery, Jonathan, 'Conscientious Objection: Personal and Professional Ethics in the Public Square' (2015) 23 *Medical Law Review*, 200–220.

Morgan, Fred, 'Conscience: a Jewish Perspective', available at: http://www.jcrelations.net/Conscience%3A+A+Jewish+Perspective.3107.0.html?L=3 (accessed 27 January 2017).

Morton, Natasha T and Kirkwood, Kenneth W, 'Conscience and Contentious Objection of Health Care Professionals refocusing the Issue' (2009) 21(4) *HEC Forum*, 351–364.

Neal, Mary, 'The Scope of Conscience-based Exemption in Section 4(1) of the Abortion Act 1967: Doogan and Wood v NHS Greater Glasgow Health Board' (2014) 22 *Medical Law Review*, 409–421.

Nordberg, Eva, Skirbekk, Helg and Magelssen, Morten,'Conscientious objection to referrals for abortion: pragmatic solution or threat to women's rights?' (2014) 15(1) *BMC Med Ethics*, 15.

Ó Néill, Clayton, 'Review: Kimberley Brownlee, Conscience and Conviction: The Case for Civil Disobedience' (2015) 23(2) *Medical Law Review*, 315–319.

Payne, Josh, 'Abortion legislation should provide for "conscientious objection", doctors say', available at: https://www.independent.ie/irish-news/abortion-referendum/abortion-legislation-should-provide-for-conscientious-objections-doctors-say-36954100.html (*Irish Independent*, 28 May 2018) (accessed 3 June, 2018).

Rawls, John, *A Theory of Justice* (HUP, 1971).

Royal College of Surgeons of England, *Caring for Patients who Refuse Blood* (Royal College of Surgeons of England, 2016).

Sepper, Virginia, 'Taking Conscience Seriously' (2012) 98 *Virginia Law Review*, 1501.

Smith, Adam, *The Theory of Moral Sentiments* (Gutenberg Publishers, 2011 (originally published in 1759)).

Wood, Allen, *Kantian Ethics* (CUP, 2008).

World Medical Association, *Declaration of Geneva* (WMA, 1995).

9 Conclusion

Introduction

This book assessed the adequacy of the legal protection that is afforded to the manifestation of religious belief in difficult and contentious medical law cases. The pathway to the resolution of that particular question was not a linear one. The issues encountered in these contentious cases were morally ambiguous in the sense that competing arguments all had some plausibility. Addressing the idea of the adequacy of legal protection meant manoeuvring away from addressing the uniquely legal aspects of medical law to addressing the moral or principled basis for the decision-making process. This required the determination of a mode of inquiry that would help judges to deliberate in an apparent objective and rational way about issues that are fought on moral, religious, philosophical, and legal grounds.

This research has taken place within a context in which the political and religious ideologies that have traditionally defined human geography are resulting in the reshaping of Europe, geographically, religiously, and politically. Democracy and traditional democratic institutions are themselves also being reshaped as fear and political/religious intransigence impel people increasingly towards partisan political positions. The ghettoising of religious belief and non-religious belief into divided and dividing factions is increasing apace.

Towards a theory of decision-making: the role of the framework, the legislature, the judiciary and its impact on citizens

What would the implementation of the framework mean in practice? The use of double effect would be outlawed and replaced by the defence of necessity or, ideally, explicit recognition of a right to pain relief. There could be some softening in right-to-die situations, the right to conscientiously object would be upheld, the rights of adults who have legal capacity to refuse medical treatment would also be upheld, but the emphasis would shift from the age of the person to the mental competence of the person to make medical decisions based upon religious belief. The framework would determine that circumcision means impairing a child and, as a consequence, no legally incapacitated child can be circumcised; Female

Genital Mutilation (FGM) would continue to be outlawed. The strict application of the framework, in the instance of circumcision, might be very difficult to apply in practice because it is an ingrained facet of historical religious (Jewish and Islamic) practice. But, if the framework is accepted as a legitimate construct, then, more than anything, it prohibits basic harm being inflicted upon people who are not mentally competent to make the specific decisions and it finds no justification for the infliction of basic harm in this instance.

A realisation of the intent of the principled stance of the PGC might, consequently, result in changes to the law or, at the very least, to fulfil the purposes of this book, might result in the judge casting a colder eye on some accepted practice. Applying the PGC will require judges to look at the manifestation of religious belief from a principled stance that transcends both religious belief and non-religious belief. Acceptance of the framework could lead to changes in the law which could, of course, then impact upon people and on the enaction of their rights.

The potential impact of this book

This book has established that English medical law should be grounded on a rights and principled-based mechanism. While proponents of the PGC have considered issues pertaining to religion in some depth,[1] this book takes religious belief, medical law, and the PGC into a new conceptual cauldron and mixes them in a manner not previously encountered, and so provides new perspectives on existing legal conundrums. The framework offers a new way of approaching difficult and contentious issues surrounding the manifestation of religious belief and the law. Religious belief and its expression are supported, but they don't have paramountcy. The framework sets important limits and parameters and boundaries to the expression of that belief.

There is now a mechanism in place to gauge the weight that is given to differing and competing rights. This is of both practical and theoretical value and contributes to the knowledge that currently exists in respect of how judges can weigh the rights that are ascribed to varying positions. Gaps were identified in respect of the adequacy of legal protection afforded to the expression of religious belief: these identified lacunae are worthy of consideration. This book still vindicates and affirms the right to express religious belief, notwithstanding the fact that some aspects are queried, such as the use of double effect as a principle in medical law.

The individual chapters also produce a contribution to the field of medical law and ethics. The case studies involve unique and insightful analysis of the relevant case law, legislation and commentary. The chapters are supported by and build upon the academic commentary dealing with the particular case studies. This allows for engagement with the literature, through the lens of the particular

1 e.g. Deryck Beyleveld, *The Dialectical Necessity of Morality: An Analysis and Defence of Alan Gewirth's Argument to the Principle of Generic Consistency* (The University of Chicago Press, 1991).

framework proposed. Further to this, the book provides a principled and pragmatic PGC-compliant rationale for suggested amendments to English law.

The use of the three-question approach allowed for a consistent and determinant way of establishing the key finding of this book. This resulted in a new way of looking at the intersection between medical law and religious manifestation: principled pragmatism. The adoption of principled pragmatism pushes the reader to consider how the PGC could operate both at principled-led level and, alternatively, in a pragmatic procedural manner in English medical law. The latter builds upon arguments, at times, that have been made by others, while the former includes suggestions for legislative change that push the boundaries of what has been conceived of by others in this particular context. The concepts of societal competence, cultural pluralism and self-fulfilment have been used to expand Gewirthian theory into areas not previously considered by other commentators to any significant degree.

Principal findings of this book

This book dealt with the interface between Abrahamic religious belief and English medical law in the context of contentious cases. Case law was examined, literature was reviewed, in-depth research into religious expression, context, and belief structures was conducted. Human rights law and English medical law were aligned with the legal/philosophical principles that underpinned a proposed methodological framework. The use of the framework would support judges by providing greater clarification to them in the balancing and weighting of conflicting rights. This framework was subsequently applied to the related case studies.

The initial problem posed by this book was how to weigh arguments that seemed, on the face of it, to have unequal moral weight. It is relatively easy to balance arguments that are unequally weighed morally. The difficulty applies when competing arguments appear to be justified by strong moral conviction which, in relation to the case studies reviewed here, was founded upon deeply-held religious belief. The book proposed that a solution to this problem could be found in Gewirth's PGC. This principle assigns parity of esteem to rights that are held by agents but, crucially, it provides a hierarchy that measures the degree to which one right is stronger than another. It applies a precautionary theory to provide appropriate solutions pertaining to the moral status of agents. When the PGC was applied to the case studies, it was found that by assigning a particular status to beings in proportion to their agential status, it was possible to accord will-rights or interest-rights in line with ascribed moral status. This led to the resolution of vexed and difficult questions. This points to a principal finding of the book that the PGC provides a mechanism that can be used by judges in English law when faced with morally-challenging questions. The book has explored how the law might pertain in Gewirthia and how it actually does, and prospectively might, apply in (future) English law. It concludes that there are circumstances in which the societal context of England is such that the PGC idyll may not be replicable in English law. The challenge remains for English law to align itself as closely as possible with the PGC and, so, most appropriately protect the autonomy of mentally competent agents/assign appropriate rights to mentally incompetent agents.

It was found that religious belief is given protection under human rights law. Article 9 of the European Convention on Human Rights (ECHR) provides the most pertinent protection to the manifestation of religious belief. It is recognised as a qualified right, subject to certain limitations. The limitations under Article 9(2) and the fundamental principles of the ECHR/Human Rights Act 1998 (HRA) are aligned with the framework. Religious expression is also supported by Article 10 of the Convention i.e. freedom of expression. The ECHR, in itself, and its core principles, is, for the most part, compliant with the PGC. The Convention respects rights and it views rights from the point of view of the will conception and interest-rights. It vindicates the right to manifest religious belief and also is shown to sensibly balance this with other rights. However, there is insufficient consideration of human rights implications in current English law as it applies to the case studies. In some circumstances, judges are too quick to focus on semantic interpretation of statute, instead of interrogating the issues. When new cases that deal with contention find their way to the courts, it will be important to ensure that these cases are viewed firmly and unambiguously under the interrogative lens of human rights law.

This book concludes, in the main, that Articles 8 and 9 ECHR give effective protection to the manifestation of religious belief, notwithstanding some reservations previously outlined. At a deeper level, it is now opportune to consider the degree to which these Articles give effect to the proposed framework that is founded on Gewirthian principles. Giving effect to the framework requires these Articles to be rights-based. Broadly speaking, Articles 8 and 9 are protective of rights, they are overarching in nature and require judicial interpretation that can be individualised to unique contexts. The framework takes into account individual agency and the will-rights of people. Articles 8 and 9 equally recognise the will conception and give effect to it. However, there are some difficulties in relation to interest-rights and infants: the limitations of Article 9 (2) do not go far enough in the protection of these rights, particularly in the context of ritual male circumcision. The fact that the limitations in Article 9(2), in particular, are not sufficiently hard hitting is a source of anxiety. Human rights law should protect the rights of all individuals and this should include those whose voices are not particularly loud, namely infants. In order for Article 9 to give full effect to the framework, then its limitations need to be interpreted to encompass infants and young children in the interpretation of the limitations posed in order to protect 'the rights and freedoms of others', per Article 9 (2). Equally, the protection of health under Article 9's limitations needs to be interpreted as requiring the explicit protection of the health of infants.

The right to manifest religious belief is, thus, vindicated in this book. It is upheld by English law, Strasbourg jurisprudence, and is not contrary to the PGC. The particular practices that are affiliated to religious belief/manifestation that contravene the PGC should, however, be disallowed due to the PGC's moral and legal supremacy. While the right to manifest religious belief is identified as a right under the PGC, this right must be balanced with other rights and if the right to manifest religious belief is hierarchically lower, then the other right must take precedence. The PGC, as the supreme moral principle, supersedes and transcends religious belief and so provides a constraining brake.

The book investigated issues relating to mental competence and legal capacity and found that change and modification in the law are required if current legal procedures in respect to legal capacity are to be more closely aligned with the PGC. This has particular relevance to children and, indeed, to adults who lack legal capacity. The PGC is focused on the concepts of mental competence and agency. Adults who have legal capacity can accept or refuse any medical treatments or procedures, as long as this is permissible under the PGC. Children who possess sufficient mental competence, encompassing societal competence, can also make valid decisions under the PGC. While great care must be taken in affording these decision-making rights to children, the current paternalism-rich approaches adopted by the courts are not in line with the Gewirthian concept of self-fulfilment, which is outlined in the book as a relevant component in both the determination of legal capacity of children under 16 and, more broadly, as an aspirational goal in English law.

What does all this mean for future law? The monograph identified a number of approaches to dealing with morally contentious issues. The first (and preferable) approach was to adopt a principled stance and to instigate legislative change in line with these principles. Acknowledging the difficulty in implementing such radical change in non-Gewirthian society resulted in consideration of a second stance, namely a pragmatic one where current legal procedures are altered in order to provide a good faith attempt at applying the PGC. It is suggested that this approach of principled pragmatism offers a way forward for legislators and/or the judiciary. This approach should involve judges thinking beyond law as a set of rules and, instead, regard statute/legal principles and procedures within the perspective of legal idealism, reflecting the need to ensure that legal approaches comply, as far as possible or practicable, with the goal of the agent to achieve, in this case, Gewirth's capacity-fulfilment.

The book has led to the overall conclusion that rights matter. They matter at the level of individual voice. They matter at the level of Convention jurisprudence and they matter at every level between these two extremities. There is a right to manifest religious belief. This right is upheld by the PGC, but other rights matter too. The challenge for the courts has been and will be the balancing of these rights. The book has provided one solution to how competing rights should be balanced. That solution is the PGC and its indirect application in English law.

This monograph has focused on an arena that is near to the bone of all individuals because, at some stage, the human body is beset by medical problems. Solutions are not always found within medicine itself. Treatment is dependent on the acquiescence of the legally capacitated patient and such acquiescence can be influenced by many factors, including, as in this case, religious belief. The cases articulated were challenging, but it is safe to assume that medical law cases into the future will be even more challenging as to what constitutes legal capacity, mental competence, and agency. They will all be subject to revision, modification, debate, and redefinition. As the scope of medicine to transcend the boundaries of humanity itself is extended, this will lead to an even greater need for a principle upon which healthcare professionals, the judiciary, the legislature and patients can depend to provide morally-sound answers to questions that will become complex. The PGC can provide appropriate answers into this future landscape.

A number of new approaches, under the mantle of principled pragmatism, are recommended and now summarised.

Alternative approaches argued for in the case studies:

The principle of double effect

Because the principle of double effect is non-compliant with the PGC, the chapter suggests that both a principled and a pragmatic approach to English law is in order to provide a good faith attempt at applying the PGC. The principled approach involves the implementation of a new Act of Parliament which incorporates a right to pain relief. As a result of inherent difficulties in implementing this new Act, a pragmatic stance is also advocated. This would involve either adopting Pattinson's suggested reliance on the doctrine of necessity or relying on a wide interpretation of 'intention', in line with Lord Steyn's approach in *R v Woollin*.[2] Thus, the principle of double effect should be replaced and English law's approach should be more reflective of the PGC.

Jehovah's Witnesses and the refusal of blood transfusions (encompassing Chapters 4 and 5)

In relation to adults, the chapter argued that change is required to the Mental Capacity Act 2005 (MCA). The Act ought to give a greater focus to individual autonomy in order to better accord with the generic rights of agents. It is also argued that the approach taken by Strasbourg in relation to adults is to be commended.

In the context of children, it was argued that the courts, to date, have been overly focused on overriding the decisions of children, even if they have legal capacity. A less paternalistic response is required that gives weight to the will-rights of such children, in line with the PGC. This would involve overruling the cases of *Re R*[3] and *Re W*[4] as they disregard the rights of the child to make a decision and are too age-focused. In order to represent an indirect application of the PGC, *Gillick*[5] and the subsequent case law need to be overridden in favour of a new test that encompasses Cave's suggestion that the MCA capacity test in conjunction

2 *R v Woollin* [1999] AC 82.
3 *Re R (a minor) (wardship: consent to medical treatment)* [1991] 4 All ER 177.
4 *Re W (a minor) (medical treatment: court's jurisdiction)* [1992] 4 All ER 627.
5 *Gillick v West Norfolk and Wisbech Area Health Authority* [1985] 3 All ER 402.

with common law development should apply to children under 16. This would allow for a more mental competence based mechanism that promotes the autonomous decision-making of patients, without being overly focused on age limits, which should not be considered in the determination of legal capacity. Societal competence needs also to be a constituent in the determination of this legal capacity. The examination of legal capacity should extend beyond determining the level of legal capacity in a decision-making process to consider why a child makes a particular decision and the degree to which that decision accords with their capacity-fulfilment. The chapter also contends that the current focus on best interests is inappropriate as it gives undue consideration to what the courts deem to be in the best interests of the patient rather than providing support for the exercise of the will-rights of the mentally competent patient. The best interests test should, therefore, be aligned with other variables identified in the chapter in the context of the decision-making process.

Thus, the law on legal capacity needs to be changed to reflect both adults and children whereby the law is less paternalistic and greater clarity and precision are given to the working of legal capacity in refusal of treatment cases (and English medical law in general).

Ritual male circumcision

It has been argued that ritual male circumcision, in situations where the child does not have the legal capacity to consent to or refuse the treatment, breaches the PGC. As such, a principled approach is advocated: this involves implementing legislation where legally incapacitated children cannot be ritually circumcised until they have the ability to make the relevant decision. Obviously, it is accepted that this approach will be met with opposition. Therefore, a pragmatic approach is also suggested, where change is suggested to the current law's approach, including change to the MCA and the best interests test.

Thus, the ritual circumcision of children who lack legal capacity violates the PGC and ought to be regarded as a violation of their human rights under Article 3 of the European Convention. It is unfortunate that ritual male circumcision has been more or less ignored by the ECtHR and the law needs to reflect the fact that children should not be inflicted with basic harm until they have the ability to waive the benefits to their generic rights.

Female Genital Mutilation

The chapter explains the difference between the approach in Gewirthia and England. The chapter argues that in situations where the child lacks legal capacity, that FGM infringes their generic rights and causes basic harm. However, unlike in the case of ritual male circumcision, FGM is not advocated on a legal capacity-focused basis. The current ban on FGM in the Female Genital Mutilation Act 2003 is supported. This is due to the clear societal and cultural difficulties/dangers in permitting FGM on a legal capacity-basis.

Conscientious objection to abortion

The position of conscientious objection under s 4 of the Abortion Act 1967 is supported, but the courts' interpretation of s 4 (in *Doogan*[6] and *Janaway*[7]) and their related failure to address Article 9 ECHR's rights are problematic. As such, the courts need to develop an alternative approach which puts a greater focus on human rights, in particular Article 9 of the Convention. This would also involve interpreting Article 9 in a manner that is more PGC-compliant. In addition to this, the chapter also suggests that ECtHR's case law needs to interpret Article 9 in a more PGC-compliant manner, in the particular context of the role of 'conscience'. Potentially, there also needs to be a deeper judicial understanding of what constitutes it. This should include a PGC-compliant interpretation of conscience. Thus, conscientious objection ought to be further assessed by judges by reference to the ECHR in a manner that represents a good faith attempt at applying the PGC.

Therefore, conscientious objection is, indeed, a permissible and legitimate position. However, recognition must be given to the conflict that exists between the right to conscientious objection and rights to have access to particular treatments. There has been insufficient direction given by the courts on this subject. The chapter ultimately argued that instead of simply focusing on statutory interpretation and the nuances of language, greater attention must be given to arguments based on human rights, such as Article 9.

Widening the context and broadening the horizon: applying the framework to non-Abrahamic religious beliefs in medical law

In order to ensure that this monograph had manageable parameters, it confined its focus to Abrahamic religions. Coming within the mantle of Christianity, but to a large degree outside the preferred ecclesiastical view of this religious tradition, come other forms of religious belief and expression that do not fit snugly within the confines of the boundaries of this book. There remain many people whose views on, for example, healing have a quasi-Christian, but mainly spiritually-based view of the healing process. Under this umbrella can come ways of thinking and reasoning, such as divine healing, where orthodox medicine is spurned in favour of reliance on divine intervention. Crystal healing and reiki are other examples of tangentially spiritually-inspired reasoning that form the basis for possible alternative approaches to medical treatment. Future research could potentially examine these divergent forms of left-of-centre religious beliefs that can be deeply held and deeply felt, but that sometimes seem to result in irrational and evidentially unsupported reasoning when it comes to medical decisions. Such an analysis is likely to conclude that the wishes of mentally competent patients should be accepted because they are reflective of their autonomous thought, even if such

6 *Greater Glasgow Health Board v Doogan and Another* [2014] UKSC 68.
7 *Janaway v Salford Area Health Authority* [1989] AC 537.

autonomous thought seems based upon the most flaky of religious reasoning and the most irrational of belief structure. A scoping-out of this area does not, however, fall within the sphere of this book, but does offer potential for future analysis.

Other world religions and minor religions, of course, are impacted by medical law and ethics and have their own perspective on areas of debate and contention in this field. For example, Buddhism opposes euthanasia due to the fact that it intentionally involves the taking of life.[8] Monks were forbidden from committing suicide or helping others to commit suicide. Buddha forbade Monks to take their own lives or take direct/indirect role in assisting or inciting others to commit suicide. These acts are regarded as wrong even if they have compassion as a motivating factor. Therefore, suicide goes against the ethics of Buddhism. For Buddhists, death is a process of rebirth and there is no obligation to keep patients alive as long as possible. Life is considered to be sacred, but life does not need to be preserved at all costs.[9] In a similar way to the Catholic principle of double effect, Buddhist ethics permit a doctor to administer palliative care drugs if his or her aim is to kill pain and not the patient. According to Damien Keown, administrating such drugs is acceptable when he or she wills 'the enhancement of life through the elimination of pain, while accepting that his or her efforts may hasten death, but death is not intended as a means or an end'.[10]

Hinduism offers a somewhat different perspective to these and similar issues. Hinduism does not possess an autoreactive text and this results in varied beliefs.[11] It centres upon a belief in reincarnation. For Hindus, there are few difficulties with new reproductive technologies. The spiritual texts of Hinduism disagree with abortion. However, in practice, it is obtainable virtually on demand in modern-day India. What is important in Hinduism in relation to the concept of assisted suicide is whether the individual considers his or her action to be a crime or a courageous act.

Although the focus of the research has been on Abrahamic religions, for practical reasons, the analytical framework has been developed in such a way that its application is not restricted to Abrahamic religious belief. While many of the case studies address questions arising from the adherence of particular patients to beliefs connected to one or more of the Abrahamic religions, the underlying issues often seem to be wider and concern the role of the state and legal system when dealing with matters of faith. For example, in the context of conscientious objection to lawful healthcare practices, the conscientious objection clauses in the Abortion Act 1967 is undoubtedly provoked by recognition of the objections of many of those with Catholic faith. But there are wider questions as to the role of conscientious objection and the procedure for dealing with such objections that

8 Damien Keown, *Buddhism and Medical Ethics: Principles and Practice*, available at: https://www.buddhismuskunde.uni-hamburg.de/pdf/4-publikationen/buddhismus-in-geschichte-und-gegenwart/bd7-k03keown.pdf (accessed 27 January 2017) p 61.

9 ibid.

10 ibid. p 63.

11 See Arvind Sharma, 'Religious Beliefs and Healthcare Decisions' (2002) *The Hindu Tradition*, 1–20.

go well beyond those particular examples and, thus, that particular Abrahamic religion.

Future research in this area has the potential to deal with how the framework might be utilised to interrogate and interpret potential stances by non-Abrahamic religions to ethically sensitive medical procedures. The concept of agency, which underpins the PGC, and which sets agency as being fundamentally more important than either territorial rights or national rights, is likely, for example, to be at variance with the way Buddhism deals with end-of-life issues, but it may accord to the way Hinduism views assisted suicide. The extension of research to non-Abrahamic religions may, thus, provide even more windows into a less explored world.

Further examination of non-Abrahamic religions is likely to find that the apparent universality of the framework can be applicable to all these religious/spiritual contexts, those founded on theistic or spiritual principles and practices or those that are part of organised self-proclaimed religions and those that have significant traction in society. Therefore, the findings of the book and the application of its framework have the potential to evolve into an analysis of the defensibility of the approach of English law to religious belief in general.

A brave new world: religious belief, technology, and medical law into the future

The book has set out the current pervading context in which law and religion operate. Two parallel extremes exist. At one level, it is likely that English law will, into the future, have to deal with the issues that emerge from a population whose religious ethnicity is resulting in a change in the religious demography as migrants and refugees, most of whom are Muslims, continue to populate the State. In parallel to this, current English society and, indeed, English law adopt, broadly speaking, a secular and non-religious stance. It neither heralds nor repudiates religious expression, but accepts it. This perspective is in line with the PGC and human rights law. A new context is also emerging, however. Anti-religious activism propelled, at one level, by the intellectualism of such theorists as Dawkins, who contend that religion has a scientific base whose hypotheses can be tested and, ultimately falsified, is growing.[12] This anti-religious movement is not, at present, fuelled by this somewhat benign intellectual discourse, but by the fear that grows within a population that is threatened by outsiders, by those who fear that the new migrants are, in some way, covert terrorists who bring with them the arms of terrorism under the cloak of religion. Anti-religious activism historically has, for example, been linked to nefarious action, such as the destruction of religious buildings in the Stalinist regime and the purging of thousands of monks in Cambodia by the Khymer Rouge.[13] Anti-religion activism, in the English State, may not, of course, result in such draconian practices, but it has potential to foster

12 Richard Dawkins, *The God Delusion* (Transworld Publishers, 2006).

13 See Henri Locard, 'State Violence in Democratic Kampuchea (1975–1979) and Retribution (1979–200)' (2005) 12(1) *European Review of History*, 121–143.

disagreement, injustice, vilification of religious adherents, and unreasonable behaviour. It is at variance with the PGC, which holds that agents have will-rights and the generic features of agency allow for the manifestation of religious belief. It is at variance with human rights law which protects and balances the rights of people to express their beliefs. An anti-religious State which overly or covertly supports anti-religious activism could potentially be injurious to human rights and the manifestation of religious belief, as protected and confirmed by both human rights law and the framework.

And what of the challenges posed by advancements in reproductive medicine? Medical law is not immune to changing political or ideological landscapes. There is a brave new world out there where advances in technology, particularly in the realm of reproductive technologies will keep changing the goal posts. Macintosh's book on cloning has laid bare some of the fears humanity has about the concepts of creating a *mini me* culture, but she has suggested that these are false and erroneous interpretations on what could be a liberating practice.[14] The issue of surrogacy and the potential moral demands that this can place upon individuals in society is something that is currently happening, but has the potential to occur even more widely as the prospect of creating babies from the genetic makeup of three parents becomes a feasible possibility.[15]

Assisted reproductive technologies (ART) have expanding potential to achieve what would previously have been unachievable. These technologies range from artificial insemination to pre-implantation genetic diagnosis. Even more new technologies will surely evolve. ART in its present and future format has the potential to change the way in which the female body, the status of the foetus and embryo, the status of the father as sperm donor (alive or dead), and the definition of parenthood are conceived of and translated into medical or legal practice.

Posthumous ART potentially shifts the understanding of the finality of death. Multi-foetal pregnancy reduction and stem cell research, the construction of the saviour child, embryo wastage, and gamete intra fallopian transfer all impact upon the definition of the moral status of the embryo. Pre-implantation genetic diagnosis, including that of late-onset diseases, oocyte donation, egg donation, sperm donation all provide ethical challenges before pregnancy. Issues concerning pregnancy in peri-menopausal and beyond women have the potential to conflict with issues concerning the welfare of the child. It is assumed that many conservative people of religious belief or those with a particular moral code will certainly regard aspects of these technologies as morally questionable. In order to protect their rights to conscientiously object, it is, thus, necessary that the current protections

14 See Kerry Lynn Macintosh, *Human Cloning: Four Fallacies and their Legal Consequences* (CUP, 2014). Also see Clayton Ó Néill, 'Review: Kerry Lynn Macintosh, *Human Cloning: Four Fallacies and their Legal Consequences*' (2015) 24(1) *Medical Law Review*, 135–140.

15 See Feuillet-Liger et al, *The Female Body A Journey through Law, Culture and Medicine* (Bruylant, 2013). Also see: Clayton Ó Néill, 'Review: Feuillet-Liger et al, *The Female Body A Journey through Law, Culture and Medicine*' (2014) 14 *Medical Law International*, 172–178.

afforded to healthcare professionals be safeguarded, continued and future proofed. The current legislation balances the rights of the healthcare professional with those of patients. As this brave new world expands, the opinions of those who conscientiously object based upon religious grounds cannot simply be ignored. Moral issues also exist in respect of equity in access to fertility treatments. For example, issues around sexual orientation and the use of ART, the provision of fertility treatments to HIV patients all involve some ethical issue that may result in moral compromise. Thus, reproductive genetics and reproduction itself all herald both hope for infertile people and challenges for legal and moral decision-making.

The Abrahamic religions under primary consideration in this book have specific responses to many of the above dilemmas. In relation to Judaism, notwithstanding some restrictions, the basic principles of Jewish law (*Halakha*) support the use of ART, given an understanding of the request of the Torah: 'be fruitful and multiply.' Judaism permits the use of all techniques of ART, as long as the sperm originates from the husband. The perspective of Islam differs slightly in respect of Islam's two main denominations. According to the guidelines (fatwa) for Sunni Muslims, ART, when necessary for a married couple, is permitted only within the validity of a marriage contract, as long as there is no mixing of genes. It is not permissible after the marriage contract has dissolved. Shia Muslims guidelines, via fatwa, adopt an even more open-minded approach where third-party donation, including egg, sperm and embryo donation and surrogacy itself are all permitted. These positions are seen to affirm the importance of marriage, family formation and procreation that are stated in several verses of the Holy Quran.[16]

Catholic dogma asserts that ART is not accepted and the Vatican issued a statement indicating that IVF clearly disregards human life and separates human procreation from sexual intercourse. Joseph Cardinal Rattzinger (subsequently Pope Benedict XVI) and Alberto Bovane have given explicit guidance to Catholics on new technologies: '[t]o use human embryos or foetuses as the object or instrument of experimentation constitutes a crime against their dignity as human beings'.[17]

This rigidity of stance is contrasted with a more flexible position adopted by the Church of England in respect of its attitudes to emerging technologies. Revd Dr Brendan McCarthy, for example, is open to considering the creation of

16 Joseph Schenker (ed), *Ethical dilemmas in Assisted Reproductive Technologies* (1st ed, De Gruyter, 2011).

17 Joseph Card. Rattzinger and Alberto Bovane, Instruction on respect for human life in its origin and on the dignity of procreation Replies to certain questions of the day' (congregation for the Doctrine of Faith) available at: http://www.vatican.va/roman_curia/congregations/cfaith/documents/rc_con_cfaith_doc_19870222_respect-for-human-life_en.html (accessed 27 January 2017). Also see Article 4 (b), *Charter of the Rights of the Family* (22 October, 1983) available at: http://www.vatican.va/roman_curia/pontifical_councils/family/documents/rc_pc_family_doc_19831022_family-rights_en.html (accessed 15 January 2015).

'three-parent babies' or the process of mitochondrial replacement.[18] The Church of England leaders seek time to consider the ethical dimensions of the process, not in a manner which denies the positive aspects of ARTs in terms of future developments, but one which seeks to 'ensure that as a nation we get such a significant treatment and its regulation right'.[19]

These challenges are not of concern only, of course, to religious adherents. Society in general responds to medical innovation that challenges perceptions of personhood. While this chapter focuses upon the response of religion to emerging ethically sensitive procedures, these issues are of interest to the broader population. It is also likely that many of the concerns and worries that society has about emerging technologies may be based upon false and wrongly held interpretations of these medical procedures that shift the boundaries of reproductive practice.[20]

Religious leaders are not immune to these changes and some accountability is borne by them in terms of how they react to the ethical and theological challenges that are nigh. The potential of adhering to the practices promoted by religious leaders to compromise individual autonomy cannot be understated. A responsibility rests on the shoulders of these leaders to ensure that their directives and advice are in line with human rights law and the PGC, particularly those who are setting the interpretation of the texts and leading the religious denominations.

But the social world in which medical law happens is not a stagnant one. Consider Ireland: traditional, Catholic, entrenched religious state and now, the first country in the world to legalise same-sex marriage by public vote. The changes that happen to how people perceive what is morally good ultimately bring about societal change. The prospective legalising of abortion in Ireland, equally, provides a strong indication of how social change can reduce and even negate the adherence to what had traditionally been understood to be the fundamental precepts of religious belief. In this case, the democratic voice of the people, which some would argue, had been muted since the initial insertion of the Amendment into the Constitution in 1983 and in the consequent referenda, resulted in legal change and paradigm shift in previously entrenched moral values. The reality is that, for Ireland, the interplay between religion, medicine, and the law has forever changed as it pertains to women. The 'pro-life' arguments that emphasised sanctity of life, while given, in many cases, a respectful listening ear, were abandoned in favour of arguments that purported to support compassion, autonomy, and care. Catholicism by ethnicity rather than by belief is, for many, the new reality. That societal change has and will have challenges for medical law and for the rights of people to

18 Revd Dr Brendan McCarthy, 'Medical Ethics: A Christian Perspective' available at:: https://www.churchofengland.org/media/1113350/medethics.pdf (accessed 27 January 2017). Also see Revd Dr Lee Rayfield and Revd Dr Brendan McCarthy, 'Instruction on respect for 'Human life in its origin and on the dignity of procreation replies to certain questions of the day' (*The Guardian*, 1 February 2015) available at: http://www.theguardian.com/commentisfree/2015/feb/01/church-of-england-three-parent-family (accessed 27 January 2017).

19 ibid.

20 See, for example, Macintosh (n 14).

manifest religious belief. Prospective changes in English law include a possible new Bill of Rights, Brexit, the potential removal of the HRA, and a significant refocus on common law. A consequence of the implementation of some of these changes might include less focus on human rights and a diminishing and diminished role of the ECtHR. Any such change should be undertaken with caution.

Conclusion: *a road less travelled*

What is very clear from this research is that the manifestation of Abrahamic religious belief is important, it is something that must be respected and given consideration. The adoption of the PGC does not ignore religious argument. In fact, it celebrates it. Rather, indirect applications of the PGC allow for an apparent objective moral barometer to gauge what is permissible and what is not.

It is suggested that the adoption of the framework offers a viable and sophisticated approach to dealing with difficult issues. The conclusions are not based upon intuition. They are based upon a rational, logical, and objective stance. The PGC is the supreme principle of morality. It offers the best and most appropriate way of attacking issues such as circumcision and the refusal of blood transfusions. The research has produced an approach for judges that respects human agency and can be applied generically with apparent objectivity and rationality.

When people have to make serious decisions in life and when these decisions are not made with universal acceptance within family circles, then there are roads to be travelled. These can involve pathways of internal familial negotiation, external mediation, facilitation by professionals, consultation within and beyond the family circle. Some roads, often the saddest ones, lead to the courts and it is ultimately up to the judge to make Solomon-like decisions. There, in this court of law, the anvil strikes upon decisions that are not easily wrought and that can have far-reaching consequences, particularly where these decisions involve children or mentally incompetent adults. The legal road is a circuitous, stony one, beset by legal argument and counter-argument, test and counter-test. The judge's companions upon this road to deliberation consist, in the main, of precedent, case law, statute, and, perhaps, wise judgement. This book proposes that another companion walk with the judge on a lesser travelled road: this companion is the framework proposed within this work. Gewirth and all the proponents of his theories can walk alongside the judge and offer a procedurally sound, principled-based mechanism that would help him or her to 'make all the difference'.[21]

21 Robert Frost, 'The Road Not Taken', available at: https://www.poetryfoundation.org/resources/learning/core-poems/detail/44272 (accessed 27 January 2017).

References

Beyleveld, Deryck, *The Dialectical Necessity of Morality: An Analysis and Defence of Alan Gewirth's Argument to the Principle of Generic Consistency* (The University of Chicago Press, 1991).

Charter of the Rights of the Family (22 October, 1983) available at: http://www.vatican.va/roman_curia/pontifical_councils/family/documents/rc_pc_family_doc_19831022_family-rights_en.html (accessed 15 January 2015).

Dawkins, Richard, *The God Delusion* (Transworld Publishers, 2006).

Feuillet-Liger, B et al, *The Female Body A Journey through Law, Culture and Medicine* (Bruylant, 2013).

Frost, Robert, 'The Road Not Taken', available at: https://www.poetryfoundation.org/resources/learning/core-poems/detail/44272 (accessed 27 January 2017).

Keown, Damien, *Buddhism and Medical Ethics: Principles and Practice*, available at: https://www.buddhismuskunde.uni-hamburg.de/pdf/4-publikationen/buddhismus-in-geschichte-und-gegenwart/bd7-k03keown.pdf (accessed 27 January 2017).

Locard, Henri, 'State Violence in Democratic Kampuchea (1975–1979) and Retribution (1979–1200)' (2005) 12(1) *European Review of History*, 121–143.

McCarthy, Revd Dr Brendan, 'Medical Ethics: A Christian Perspective', available at: https://www.churchofengland.org/media/1113350/medethics.pdf (accessed 27 January 2017).

Macintosh, Kerry Lynn, *Human Cloning: Four Fallacies and their Legal Consequences* (CUP, 2014).

Ó Néill, Clayton, 'Review: Kerry Lynn Macintosh, Human Cloning: Four Fallacies and their Legal Consequences' (2015) 24(1) *Medical Law Review*, 135–140.

Ó Néill, Clayton, 'Review: Feuillet-Liger et al, The Female Body A Journey through Law, Culture and Medicine' (2014) 14 *Medical Law International*, 172–178.

Rattzinger, Joseph Card. and Bovane, Alberto, 'Instruction on respect for human life in its origin and on the dignity of procreation Replies to certain questions of the day' (congregation for the Doctrine of Faith) available at: http://www.vatican.va/roman_curia/congregations/cfaith/documents/rc_con_cfaith_doc_19870222_respect-for-human-life_en.html (accessed 27 January 2017).

Rayfield, Dr Revd, et al, 'Instruction on respect for "Human life in its origin and on the dignity of procreation replies to certain questions of the day"' (*The Guardian*, 1 February 2015) available at: http://www.theguardian.com/commentisfree/2015/feb/01/church-of-england-three-parent-family (accessed 27 January 2017).

Schenker, Joseph (ed), *Ethical dilemmas in Assisted Reproductive Technologies* (1st ed, De Gruyter, 2011).

Sharma, Arvind, 'Religious Beliefs and Healthcare Decisions' (2002) *The Hindu Tradition*, 1–20.

Index

For Product Safety Concerns and Information please contact our EU representative GPSR@taylorandfrancis.com
Taylor & Francis Verlag GmbH, Kaufingerstraße 24, 80331 München, Germany

www.ingramcontent.com/pod-product-compliance
Ingram Content Group UK Ltd.
Pitfield, Milton Keynes, MK11 3LW, UK
UKHW011007180926
475701UK00004B/610

* 9 7 8 0 3 6 7 5 8 2 7 9 1 *